B O U C H O N

It's all about Sharing

Thomas Keller

B O U C H O N

THOMAS KELLER WITH JEFFREY CERCIELLO

along with Susie Heller and Michael Ruhlman
Photographs by Deborah Jones

ARTISAN
NEW YORK

Also by Thomas Keller

The French Laundry Cookbook with Susie Heller and Michael Ruhlman

Under Pressure with Jonathan Benno, Corey Lee, and Sebastian Rouxel,
along with Susie Heller, Michael Ruhlman, and Amy Vogler

Ad Hoc at Home with David Cruz, along with
Susie Heller, Michael Ruhlman, and Amy Vogler

Published by Artisan
A division of Workman Publishing Company, Inc.
225 Varick Street
New York, NY 10014-4381
www.artisanbooks.com

Published simultaneously in Canada by Thomas Allen & Son Limited

Library of Congress Cataloging-in-Publication Data
Keller, Thomas.
Bouchon / Thomas Keller, with Jeff Cerciello, Susie Heller, and Michael Ruhlman;
photographs by Deborah Jones
p. cm.
Includes index.
ISBN-13: 978-1-57965-239-5
1. Cookery, French. 2. Bouchon (Restaurant). I. Cerciello, Jeff. II. Heller, Susie.
III. Ruhlman, Michael, 1963–. IV. Bouchon (Restaurant). V. Title.
TX719.K448 2004

641.5944—dc22   2004051998

Printed in Singapore

11 13 15 17 19 20 18 16 14 12

Book design by Level, Calistoga, CA

I used to joke that I opened Bouchon, styled after the bistros of Paris, so that I'd have a place to eat after cooking all night at the French Laundry. The truth of it is that bistro cooking is my favorite food to eat. Roast chicken

and a salad of fresh lettuces with a simple vinaigrette. Frisée salad with crisp, chewy lardons and a poached egg. A dense steak with lemon-herb butter and frites. Ask chefs what their notion of a perfect meal is and nine out of ten will name dishes such as these. These preparations, almost universally appealing, represent what's true and durable in the expanding field of the culinary arts, and are forever satisfying to eat.

I love foie gras. One of my most favorite things to eat is white truffle. To poach a lobster tail in butter or to place a crisp-skinned rouget against the vivid green of a parsley coulis is galvanizing to me as a craftsman and cook. But in the daily routine of my life, I enjoy a perfectly cooked quiche with bacon and leeks every bit as much. I am thrilled when an onion soup, with the perfect proportions of broth to onions to crouton to cheese that's molten beneath a golden crust, is set before me. The sight and aroma of a perfectly roasted chicken never fail to excite me.

Why is it that we are drawn to bistro food throughout our lives? What qualities make it excellent rather than good? What are the critical techniques in the kitchen that elevate these seemingly "ordinary" dishes? Why do we keep coming back to that bowl of mussels steamed with wine, garlic, and thyme, or to that lemon tart? And more, what is their impact over time as we eat them again and again? In sum, why is bistro cooking one of the

most important kinds of cooking, and what's the source of its power? These are the questions I sought to understand when I opened Bouchon, and the ones we explore in this book.

Whereas *The French Laundry Cookbook* is about using the ideas and techniques of classic cuisine as a springboard for the imagination to create new dishes, *Bouchon* is about *maintaining* classic traditions, renewing our respect for those great dishes, holding them up to the light to understand them, in order to perfect them. To that end, the recipes detail the important qualities to strive for in each dish—whether it's the ratio of ingredients in onion soup, the size you cut your lardons for a beef bourguignon, the texture of a crème caramel—and the techniques you'll need to achieve them.

The recipes in this book fall into a category of food served at what we think of as a bistro, a type of restaurant with origins in nineteenth-century Paris that has become all but universal. Yet in a way, the bistro and its food have become victims of success. The word *bistro* is used so pervasively in so many different ways that it's in danger of losing its meaning altogether. Indeed, I use the name Bouchon, which is a similar type of restaurant that continues to flourish in Lyon, France, because in America, *bistro* doesn't really mean anything more specific than "casual."

Bistro dishes have become somewhat debased as well by overuse and lack of understanding. The quiche, for instance, never had a chance in America because we were told to make a quiche in a pie shell. You can't make a proper quiche in a pie shell; it needs a deep tart crust. Bistro food is not about specialized ingredients, rather it is about precision of technique brought to bear on ordinary ingredients. It's easy to make foie gras and truffles taste good. But how do you combine lettuce, salt, vinegar, and oil in a way that is elegant and exquisite? Indeed, the very fact that these dishes have fewer main ingredients, typically common inexpensive ingredients—chicken and salt, let's say—only raises the bar.

And this in a way renders moot the question why write a bouchon cookbook now, rather than further exploring cutting-edge haute cuisine. I don't distinguish between the two in terms of quality. The success of any kind of cooking is determined by technique, and its ultimate quality is determined by the standards you bring to the execution of that technique. The standards for bistro cooking are no different from the standards of the French Laundry, though the ingredients and presentation are different.

My love of this food didn't begin in France, where I spent a year in starred kitchens, or, for that matter, in Manhattan, where I ate at my first bistro. I really connected with this kind of cooking at a place called La Rive outside Catskill, New York, in the Hudson Valley, where I worked for several years in my early twenties before I ever set foot in France. There René Macary, who owned it with his wife, Paulette, served traditional French comfort food in a country setting.

All kinds of hors d'oeuvres were set out across a vast table in the dining room—beets, radishes with butter, céleri rémoulade, lentil salad, cornichons, pâtés, and bread, ready to be brought straight to the table. On the piano, all the desserts—the custards and chocolate mousse and tarts—were also on view, waiting to be served. This was my first experience not so much with French cooking but rather with the ethics and aesthetics of the French way with food. One of my great memories is of watching René make a salad. He would salt it, then put on the oil, to coat the lettuce and protect it from the acid, and then he would add the acid. He would never combine the two then pour them on; vinegar was the seasoning element. What made watching him exciting was the anticipated joy of eating that salad, the richness of the oil, the sparks of vinegar that would come through.

I'd been taught the basics of this kind of cookery at a big club in Rhode Island under a Frenchman named Roland Henin. There I learned how to turn inexpensive cuts into elegant stews and how to properly cook vegetables. But my three years in upstate New York marked a time when I was learning on my own and cooking by myself, in what was really a kind of idyll in my career. I learned how to let time and cooking work their natural manipulations, to let the food be what it is. I was very happy there and I associate this food with happy times.

And that, ultimately, is what makes us cherish and revere French comfort food—our emotional connection to it, the feeling we get when we see a perfectly roasted chicken or a beautiful steak and a pile of frites or a dozen perfect oysters waiting to be shared. This kind of food makes us feel good just *looking* at it. This food makes people happy.

MY FAVORITE SIMPLE ROAST CHICKEN—MON POULET RÔTI

One 2- to 3-pound farm-raised chicken
Kosher salt and freshly ground black pepper
2 teaspoons minced thyme (optional)

Unsalted butter
Dijon mustard

Preheat the oven to 450°F. Rinse the chicken, then dry it very well with paper towels, inside and out. The less it steams, the drier the heat, the better.

Salt and pepper the cavity, then truss the bird. Trussing is not difficult (see page 192 for an especially easy method), and if you roast chicken often, it's a good technique to feel comfortable with. When you truss a bird, the wings and legs stay close to the body; the ends of the drumsticks cover the top of the breast and keep it from drying out. Trussing helps the chicken to cook evenly, and it also makes for a more beautiful roasted bird.

Now, salt the chicken—I like to rain the salt over the bird so that it has a nice uniform coating that will result in a crisp, salty, flavorful skin (about 1 tablespoon). When it's cooked, you should still be able to make out the salt baked onto the crisp skin. Season to taste with pepper.

Place the chicken in a sauté pan or roasting pan and, when the oven is up to temperature, put the chicken in the oven. I leave it alone—I don't baste it, I don't add butter; you can if you wish, but I feel this creates steam, which I don't want. Roast it until it's done, 50 to 60 minutes. Remove it from the oven and add the thyme, if using, to the pan. Baste the chicken with the juices and thyme and let it rest for 15 minutes on a cutting board.

Remove the twine. Separate the middle wing joint and eat that immediately. Remove the legs and thighs. I like to take off the backbone and eat one of the oysters, the two succulent morsels of meat embedded here, and give the other to the person I'm cooking with. But I take the chicken butt for myself. I could never understand why my brothers always fought over that triangular tip—until one day I got the crispy, juicy fat myself. These are the cook's rewards. Cut the breast down the middle and serve it on the bone, with one wing joint still attached to each. The preparation is not meant to be superelegant. Slather the meat with fresh butter. Serve with mustard on the side and, if you wish, a simple green salad. You'll start using a knife and fork, but finish with your fingers, because it's so good.

MAKES 2 TO 4 SERVINGS

Jeffrey Cerciello, chef at Bouchon, is an elemental part of this book. He and his staff cook this food seven days a week. He executed every one of these recipes with Susie Heller to ensure they translated to the home kitchen without compromising any of the intricacies that make them work so well in the restaurant. Jeff's and Susie's experience and intelligence infuse every page of this book. Here they are in their own words.

JEFFREY CERCIELLO: In 1994, on the advice of a friend, I spent a day off from my first post-culinary-school job at a new restaurant in the Napa Valley called the French Laundry. I knew already that it was a tiny kitchen doing interesting food, but after a single night there it was obvious: This was not like any kitchen I'd known. The environment was so clean, the vocabularies of the cooks so precise, and the food was perfect. For the first time, it seemed, I saw people really cooking. To be a young cook and land there was lucky.

Having worked previously with Ferran Adria at El Bulli, and then with Thomas Keller, two of the world's most forward-thinking chefs, ironically, I find myself responsible for a kitchen that is retrograde by design.

While these two directions may seem diametrically opposed, in fact there's a perfect symmetry to my course. Neither I nor Thomas thinks of the food I do at Bouchon as being different in any fundamental way from the food of the French Laundry or Per Se, because all of our food relies foremost on close attention to basic techniques and excellent products.

At the French Laundry, Thomas taught me how to work with raw ingredients and how to put those ingredients together on a plate. At the French Laundry, the creativity of coming up with new dishes on a daily basis was a way of life. At Bouchon, creativity runs in the opposite direction, though with equal energy: We take ideas and combinations of ingredients that have been around for decades, even centuries, and try to make them better, not so much to rediscover or reinterpret them, but rather to understand what makes them such a durable part of a great culinary tradition.

The French Laundry is all about inspiration, interpretation, and evolution. Bouchon is all about exploring traditional bistro cooking in order to perfect it. These dishes are made and served in home kitchens and restaurants throughout the world, so what distinguishes one onion soup from another, one lemon tart from another, is not a recipe so much as a standard of technique. What is a perfect beef bourguignon, for instance, and how do I achieve that? Such beef stews are often gelatinous; the flavors can be muted. Therefore, some of the critical techniques in making a great beef stew are straining the sauce and finishing it with enough acid to make it bright and exciting. We take as much care at Bouchon to make a sauce clean for a beef stew as the French Laundry does for its braised short rib. The finished dish, the quantity, and presentation are different. The standard is the same.

My biggest challenge as chef at Bouchon, and one of my greatest sources of pleasure, is maintaining those standards perpetuated by the French Laundry. The dishes in this book are a broad representation of that work.

SUSIE HELLER: To record the recipes for the dishes served throughout the year at Bouchon, Thomas Keller and Jeff Cerciello came into my home kitchen and, with *infinite* care, prepared every dish in this book while I weighed and measured ingredients, kept track of cooking times, noted methods and techniques, all the while patiently answering my questions. It was not always easy for them. At the restaurant, they use professional equipment to cook individual orders as they are taken, measuring by sight, cooking intuitively, reacting to the sight, sound, smell, and taste of a dish. In my kitchen, they cooked four portions at once, using equipment available to a home cook, working diligently, never diminishing the integrity of the food.

Watching the two of them is a testament to how proper technique separates the good and the great; I have witnessed how small steps make big differences. Ladling stock from a stockpot rather than dumping it into the strainer results in a clearer stock, therefore a cleaner sauce. When braising, separating the meat from the aromatics with large pieces of cheesecloth is a technique I always use now: The meat absorbs all the flavor of the aromatics but is kept clean; it doesn't get coated with vegetable fragments.

I have learned so many preparations that I now rely on and use with seasonal variations. The quiche, lighter than air—the careful blending of the batter puts it on a level of its own. Parisian-style gnocchi are always in my freezer for unexpected guests (and they are perfect for vegetarians). Sautéing them at the last minute adds a crisp outer layer that I love. I most often serve them with the brown butter sauce, but in summer I toss them with a bit of vinaigrette. I love to make the gratins, and I know the secret of my favorite, the cauliflower gratin: The florets are in a sauce made of cream and cauliflower puree. And I am never without garlic confit, tomato confit, tapenade, or marinated olives. All of these staples are simple to prepare, and it is amazing how many dishes they enhance.

Versatility is part of what defines this food as bistro cooking—food intended for everyday cooking and eating, satisfying a range of appetites. Too, the recipes can most often be partially or fully prepared in advance, with little work left to the last minute. Furthermore, many of the recipes can be used in a variety of ways. A roast served one night can become a tartine, or open-faced sandwich, for lunch the next day. Onion soup makes a first course, lunch, or late-night snack. A *pain perdu* is delicious for brunch or dessert.

The techniques and tips you learn throughout the book are lessons that can be applied to other recipes in your repertoire. Most important is to enjoy the process of cooking. This is not food that should be rushed. Use high-quality ingredients and don't compromise. If you take pleasure in cooking it, the final dish will be more rewarding.

Most ingredients used in these recipes—for example, garlic sausage, boneless short ribs, and high-quality canned snails— can be easily purchased. Take advantage of the Sources on page 330 to find purveyors who can help make your meals exceptional. And if you have good relationships with your fishmonger and butcher, these experts can help you find the right cuts as well as do much of the work for you.

Last, learn the varying sounds and smells of food as it cooks. Pay attention to the way a piece of lamb or sole feels as it cooks. Don't rely just on your eyesight.

To me, the glory of these recipes is that they have withstood time and the vagaries of fashion and become classics. They are an invitation to sit down with friends, open a bottle of wine, tear into a crusty baguette, and share not only the wonderful food but a piece of history and a way of life.

1

{ **PREMIÈRES IMPRESSIONS** }

FIRST IMPRESSIONS

I wonder if I love the communal act of eating so much because throughout my childhood, with four older brothers and a mom who worked in the restaurant business, I spent a lot of time fending for myself, eating alone—and recognizing how eating together made all the difference.

If there's a single underlying thread that explains my love of the dishes in this chapter, it's that they're communal: They are meant to be shared, and the best meals are the ones you eat with the people you care about.

If bistro cooking embodies a culinary ethos of generosity, economy, simplicity, and excellence, it may be that these first-impression dishes best exemplify it.

From a chef's point of view, this is food that's easily prepared and can be made in big batches from inexpensive ingredients. And that, for me, is part of their excitement—that something so easy and economical can produce such pleasure.

THE IMPORTANCE OF
{ H O R S   D ' Œ U V R E S   V A R I É S }

Big terrines filled with pâtés; lentils with shaved onion, a little vinaigrette, and parsley; beets roasted in the oven, peeled, sliced, salted, and then drizzled with some vinaigrette; a traditional *céleri rémoulade*; and radishes with sweet butter—some of my best memories from La Rive are of the hors d'oeuvres we'd prepare. They embodied the generosity of the place, the spirit of sharing, which truly defined the restaurant.

As you entered the dining room, you'd see a table first, packed with platters and bowls of salads and vegetables and dry-cured ham and sausages, as if to say, "This is for you, have as much as you want, and return for more." It was wonderful to behold the bounty of that table.

Bistro food, especially bistro hors d'oeuvres, is not about lengthy, intricate preparation. Most likely a bistro owner buys his dried sausages and hams from a charcuterie. He doesn't have the space to grind, stuff, and hang a variety of sausages, or the time, especially given that the *charcutier,* or pork butcher, down the street probably sells excellent products. The saucisson and *jambon* are quickly sliced and served to guests. Many items are simply brought to the table as a matter of course, with little strain on the kitchen, such as olives and cornichons, with the tart, salty taste that whets the appetite and complements the charcuterie that begins a meal.

A lot of these dishes are not only relatively easy to make in large batches, they're best made in large batches, because they get better with time. A salad of lentils or chickpeas or celeriac made in the morning will only improve throughout the day. Potted foods often don't need to be refrigerated if they're made with such preservation in mind. That they're ready to serve at a moment's notice is key to a bistro and an advantage to the home kitchen as well.

The foods here represent, perhaps more than any other recipes in the book, the quintessential nature of bistro fare: easy food that is perfect for sharing.

OIL: In a bistro kitchen, oil is not thought of as a flavor in itself, but as a vehicle for heat, as well as for flavor and richness. It's used in sautés, it carries the vinegar and herbs and seasonings in a vinaigrette, and it enriches bean and vegetable dishes. In an efficient bistro kitchen, a chef wouldn't have five different oils on the shelf. Since nut oils and other flavored oils tend to be expensive, they wouldn't typically be in the bistro pantry, and, traditionally, olive oil is limited in use. Grapeseed oil is the best in terms of quality because it's completely neutral and has a high smoking point. Because grapeseed oil is expensive, we use canola oil for everyday cooking. Oil is not durable: Remember that freshness is paramount in the quality of an oil.

Photograph on pages 2–3. *Opposite:* Marinated Olives (page 6).

MARINATED OLIVES—OLIVES MARINÉES

1 orange

1 lemon

One 6-inch rosemary sprig

2 to 3 thyme sprigs

2 oregano sprigs

1 pound (about 2½ cups) mixed olives—about ½ cup each Picholine, Luc, Niçoise, Moroccan oil-cured olives, or other varieties

1 bay leaf

⅓ cup extra virgin olive oil

12 cloves Garlic Confit (page 312)

I am fond of many olives, but the Niçoise is my favorite. I love its shape, its size, its deep black color, and its element of sweetness. We blanch Niçoise—as well as Picholine and Luc—olives first so that they can absorb the marinade. Soft oil-cured olives such as Nyons and Moroccan don't need to be blanched; they'd become mushy. Our marination includes garlic confit, which in turn absorbs the flavor of the olives.

Using a vegetable peeler, peel the zest from half the orange and lemon in long strips. Trim off any white pith. Bang the underside of the zest with the back of a knife to release the oils. Lightly crush the sprigs of rosemary, thyme, and oregano with the back of the knife to release their oils. Pull off and discard any olive stems.

Put the zest, herbs, softer olives, bay leaf, olive oil, and garlic confit in a bowl.

Bring a large saucepan of water to a boil. Put the firmer olives in a strainer that will fit into the pan of water, drop the strainer into the boiling water, and boil for 1 minute. Lift out the strainer and drain the olives well, then add them to the bowl. Toss to combine.

Cover the olives and allow them to marinate at room temperature for at least 2 hours to combine the flavors. (The marinated olives can be refrigerated in a sealed container for up to 2 weeks.)

PHOTOGRAPH ON PAGE 4　　　　　　　　**MAKES 2½ CUPS**

ROASTED BEET SALAD—SALADE DE BETTERAVES

1½ pounds (3 to 4 large) red beets

3 tablespoons extra virgin olive oil

Kosher salt and freshly ground black pepper

About 1 tablespoon red wine vinegar

2 tablespoons fresh orange juice

½ red onion, peeled

1 tablespoon chopped tarragon

1 tablespoon minced chives

Beets are about the best vegetable in the world, hot or cold, even as healthy as they are, loaded with iron and vitamins. Roasted, just out of the oven with some salt, a beet gives you ten times the pleasure of a baked potato.

This salad couldn't be simpler: Beets are roasted, sliced, and served with a vinaigrette and fresh herbs. We use fresh-squeezed orange juice for part of the acid component because we want a light citrus flavor, and orange goes well with beets. Make this at least a couple of hours before serving to allow the flavors to develop. Some red onion tossed in with chives and tarragon shortly before serving adds texture, flavor, and visual appeal, but beets with just a little vinaigrette drizzled on top, nothing else, are great too.

Buy beets with their tops still attached, an indication of their freshness. And be patient when roasting them—they should be cooked until tender all the way through.

Preheat the oven to 375°F.

Wash the beets and trim the stems, leaving about ¼ inch attached. Place them on a large piece of aluminum foil and toss with 2 tablespoons of the oil, 2 tablespoons water, ½ teaspoon salt, and ⅛ teaspoon pepper.

Lift up the edges of the foil and squeeze together to form a packet. Place in a small baking pan and roast for about 1½ hours, or until the beets are tender, offering no resistance when pierced with a knife. Carefully unwrap the beets and let stand just until cool enough to handle.

Rub each beet with a paper towel to remove the skin. Cut off and discard the stems. Cut the beets into quarters, then cut the quarters crosswise into ¼-inch-thick slices and place in a bowl. Season with a light sprinkling of salt and pepper. Add red wine vinegar, orange juice, and the remaining 1 tablespoon oil. Toss and season to taste with additional salt and pepper.

Let the beets marinate for at least 30 minutes, or up to a day, in the refrigerator. Bring to room temperature before finishing the salad.

About 30 minutes before serving, cut three or four ⅛-inch-thick slices crosswise from the onion and separate the slices (reserve the remaining onion for another use). Toss the beets with the onion, tarragon, and chives.

Just before serving, check the seasonings and add additional salt, pepper, and/or vinegar to taste.

PHOTOGRAPH ON PAGE 9   **MAKES 4 SERVINGS**

CELERIAC RÉMOULADE—CÉLERI RÉMOULADE

RÉMOULADE

¹/₂ cup mayonnaise

¹/₂ cup crème fraîche

2 tablespoons minced cornichons

2 tablespoons minced drained nonpareil
  capers, preferably Spanish

2 ¹/₄ teaspoons Dijon mustard

About 1 tablespoon cider vinegar

2 teaspoons minced Italian parsley

2 teaspoons minced tarragon

2 teaspoons minced chervil

2 teaspoons minced chives

Kosher salt and freshly ground black pepper

1 pound (1 large) celeriac (celery root)

Fresh lemon juice (optional)

Céleri rémoulade is a traditional winter dish made by mixing the shredded root vegetable with a mayonnaise-based dressing. Shredded celeriac makes a meaty, texturally satisfying salad. We use a creamy dressing here, but a little vinegar, shallot, and chives would be excellent as well. Make the salad two to eight hours before serving it; the flavors develop, and the acid seems to tenderize the celeriac slightly. Don't overdress it—though the salad benefits from marination, the salt in the dressing will pull moisture from it, resulting in more liquid than you want. Taste and add more dressing, if needed, just before serving.

We serve céleri rémoulade on its own as a salad, but it's also an excellent side dish or garnish, as in the roast pork sandwich (page 100). With a piece of cold chicken, it's a delicious light meal.

FOR THE RÉMOULADE: Stir the mayonnaise and crème fraîche together in a small bowl. Squeeze any excess moisture from the cornichons and capers and stir them into the mixture. Add the mustard, vinegar, and herbs. Season to taste with salt and pepper. Refrigerate for at least 1 hour, or up to 3 days, to allow the flavors of the rémoulade to develop.

Cut off and discard the tops and bottoms of the celeriac. Remove the skin with a paring knife or a sharp, sturdy vegetable peeler. Using a mandoline or knife, cut the celeriac into ¹/₈-inch-thick julienne. (You should have about 4 cups.)

Put the celeriac in a bowl and toss with enough rémoulade to coat the pieces; reserve any remaining dressing. Taste and season the salad as necessary. Cover and refrigerate for at least 2 hours, or up to 8 hours.

Just before serving, toss the celeriac with additional dressing, if desired, and adjust the seasonings a final time, adding a squeeze of lemon juice or more vinegar if needed.

MAKES 3 CUPS; 4 TO 6 SERVINGS

Clockwise from left: Chickpea and Carrot Salad (page 11), Celeriac Rémoulade, and Roasted Beet Salad (page 7)

LENTILS VINAIGRETTE—SALADE DE LENTILLES

SACHET

1 head garlic, split crosswise in half

12 black peppercorns

3 bay leaves

3 thyme sprigs

LENTILS

8 ounces (1 cup) Le Puy lentils
   (see Sources, page 330), picked
   over for stones and rinsed

1 medium leek, white and light green
   parts only

$1/2$ medium onion, peeled

1 large carrot, peeled

2 teaspoons kosher salt

2 teaspoons red wine vinegar

1 small red onion, peeled

VINAIGRETTE

$1^1/2$ tablespoons Dijon mustard

1 tablespoon red wine vinegar

$1/4$ cup extra virgin olive oil

Kosher salt and freshly ground black pepper

2 tablespoons minced chives

1 tablespoon chopped Italian parsley

Lentils are a rich, satisfying ingredient that makes an excellent salad, tossed with a mustard vinaigrette. The salad can be prepared before you need to serve it and it keeps for two days. With some good bread, it is an entire meal. I love the tiny dark green lentils from Le Puy, a city and region in south-central France. They're almost like caviar as they pop against your palate, but with a sensation of creaminess.

Lentils don't need presoaking, but it's important to cook them properly. You have to use just the right amount of water (too much and they'll taste washed out) with plenty of aromatics. Simmer them on the stove, stirring gently and testing them often. When they're done, we spread them out on a baking sheet or in a flat container to cool as quickly as possible; they can overcook if you leave them in the pot.

Some vinaigrette, red onion, parsley, and chives are all you need to complete this classic bistro dish.

FOR THE SACHET: Cut a piece of cheesecloth about 7 inches square. Place the sachet ingredients in the center, bring the edges together, and tie with kitchen twine to form a bundle.

FOR THE LENTILS: Put the lentils in a strainer and rinse with cold water, then place in a large saucepan. Cut the leek lengthwise in half, rinse under cold water, and add to the pan, along with the sachet, onion, and carrot. Add cold water to cover the ingredients by 2 inches, place the pan over high heat, and bring to a boil. Reduce the heat and simmer very gently for 20 to 25 minutes, or until tender. Don't boil the lentils or they may fall apart.

Pour the lentils and their liquid into a large shallow container. Season with salt and red wine vinegar and let cool. Once they are cool, remove and discard the sachet and vegetables. (The lentils can be prepared to this point up to a day ahead and refrigerated in their liquid.)

When you are ready to assemble the salad, drain the lentils in a colander and place in a bowl. Cut the red onion lengthwise in half, then cut it crosswise into $1/8$-inch-thick slices and cut the slices into $1/8$-inch dice. Add $1/2$ cup of the red onion to the lentils (reserve any remaining onion for another use).

FOR THE VINAIGRETTE: Combine the mustard and red wine vinegar in a small bowl and whisk to blend. Slowly whisk in the olive oil. Stir the dressing into the lentils and season to taste with salt and pepper. (The salad can be served immediately or refrigerated for up to 2 days.)

Just before serving, check the seasonings and stir in the chives and parsley.

MAKES 2$1/2$ CUPS; 4 SERVINGS

CHICKPEA AND CARROT SALAD—SALADE DE POIS CHICHES ET CAROTTES

½ cup dried chickpeas, soaked in 3 cups
cold water for 12 hours or quick-soaked
(page 257)
1 medium leek, white and light green
parts only
Bouquet Garni (page 325)

½ onion, peeled
1 small carrot, peeled
Kosher salt
2 tablespoons extra virgin olive oil
2 bay leaves
2 garlic cloves, skin left on, smashed

2 thyme sprigs
1 cup finely julienned carrots
Freshly ground black pepper
1 tablespoon chopped Italian parsley
1½ teaspoons fresh lemon juice

This chickpea salad couldn't be easier—cooked chickpeas warmed in a pan with seasoned oil and grated carrot. Lemon juice, more a seasoning device than a component here, is added at the very end, along with some parsley.

Chickpeas are crunchy legumes that never really lose their dense mealy texture even when fully cooked. They remind me a little of macadamia nuts.

Use dried, rather than canned, chickpeas for the best texture and flavor, but soak them overnight (or use the quick-soak method; see page 257). As with all dried legumes, season them late in the cooking process, or even once they are fully cooked—at the start, they're too hard to absorb anything and salt can inhibit the rehydration process.

Drain the chickpeas, put them in a large saucepan, and add about 6 cups water, or enough to cover them by 2 inches. Cut the leek lengthwise in half and rinse under cold water. Add one leek half to the pan, reserving the remaining half for another use. Add the bouquet garni, onion, and whole carrot to the pan and bring to a boil. Reduce the heat and simmer for about 45 minutes, or until the chickpeas are tender.

Pour the chickpeas and their liquid into a large shallow container and let cool. Once they are cool, remove and discard the bouquet garni and vegetables and season with ½ teaspoon salt. (The chickpeas can be covered and refrigerated in their liquid for 2 to 3 days.)

When ready to assemble the salad, drain the chickpeas in a colander.

Combine the olive oil, bay leaves, garlic, and thyme in a large skillet and heat over medium heat until the oil is hot. Add the julienned carrots and toss in the oil for about 1 minute to cook them slightly. Add the chickpeas and season to taste with salt and pepper. Toss the chickpeas for 1 to 2 minutes, then transfer to a bowl and let cool. (The salad can be refrigerated for up to a day.)

Just before serving, remove the bay leaves, garlic, and thyme from the chickpeas and stir in the parsley and lemon juice.

PHOTOGRAPH ON PAGE 9   MAKES 2 CUPS

FRIED ZUCCHINI BLOSSOMS
BEIGNETS DE FLEURS DE COURGETTES

Peanut oil for deep-frying

½ cup all-purpose flour

½ cup cornstarch

Kosher salt and freshly ground black pepper

2 large eggs

¼ cup milk

16 zucchini blossoms, stamens removed

Olivade (opposite)

In summer, beautiful zucchini flowers grow in abundance in our garden, so it would be a shame not to use the male blossoms, which don't bear fruit. They can be stuffed with ratatouille and braised in vegetable stock for a vegetarian dish, or filled with a meat stuffing and braised in veal or beef stock. Their texture is feathery, their flavor sweet, their color bright—so they're excellent added raw to salad, whole or torn like lettuce. And they can be stuffed, then battered and fried. Here, we give them a simple coating of egg wash and flour before frying, then serve them with olivade.

Heat 3 to 4 inches of oil in a deep fryer or a large deep pot to 350°F.

Meanwhile, mix the flour, cornstarch, and a pinch each of salt and pepper in a shallow bowl. Whisk together the eggs, milk, and a pinch each of salt and pepper in another shallow bowl.

Season the zucchini blossoms with salt and pepper. Dip 4 of the blossoms in the egg mixture, lift out, letting excess liquid fall back into the bowl, and toss in the flour mixture. Gently pat off excess flour and place the blossoms in the hot oil. Cook for 3 to 5 minutes, or until the coating is crispy and golden brown. Drain on paper towels and repeat with the remaining blossoms.

Serve immediately with the olivade on the side.

PHOTOGRAPH ON PAGE 15   **MAKES 4 SERVINGS**

OLIVADE—FROMAGE BLANC AUX
OLIVES ET CÂPRES

7 ½ to 8 ounces fromage blanc (see Sources, page 330)

1 tablespoon drained nonpareil capers, preferably Spanish, chopped

2 tablespoons minced red onion

½ cup finely chopped pitted black olives, such as Kalamata or Niçoise

¼ cup extra virgin olive oil, plus extra for drizzling

1 tablespoon minced chives

Kosher salt and freshly ground black pepper

1 teaspoon chopped Italian parsley

This is a simple spread in which mild, rich fromage blanc is stirred together with salty savory seasonings. Especially refreshing in summer, it has many uses. It can be spread on bread, used as a dip for crudités or Fried Zucchini Blossoms (opposite), formed into quenelles for a more formal canapé, or spread on lightly roasted tomatoes and served as a garnish for Roast Chicken with Summer Squash and Tomatoes (page 195).

Put the fromage blanc in a medium bowl and stir in the capers and onion, then stir in the olives and half the olive oil. Stir in the remaining olive oil and chives. Season to taste with salt and pepper and spoon into a serving crock. (The olivade can be refrigerated for up to 4 days.)

Just before serving, sprinkle the olivade with the parsley and drizzle with a little olive oil.

PHOTOGRAPHS OPPOSITE AND ON PAGE 23   **MAKES 1½ CUPS**

HARD-COOKED EGGS IN RUSSIAN DRESSING—ŒUFS À LA RUSSE

SAUCE

1 cup mayonnaise

3 tablespoons bottled chili sauce

1 tablespoon minced shallots

1 tablespoon minced Italian parsley

2 teaspoons minced chives

1 tablespoon minced green olives

Kosher salt and freshly ground black pepper

Fresh lemon juice to taste

6 hard-cooked large eggs (see page 326)

How good eggs are—they're ordinary and surprising at the same time. I serve these eggs as part of an *hors d'œuvres variés,* rather than as an individual dish. For me, part of the pleasure of this preparation is that it's reminiscent of the 1970s' American version of Continental cuisine, for which I have an abiding nostalgia.

FOR THE SAUCE: Combine all the ingredients in a small bowl, mixing well. Cover and refrigerate for a few hours to allow the flavors to develop.

TO SERVE: Cut the hard-cooked eggs lengthwise in half and place them cut side down on a serving platter. Spoon the sauce generously over the eggs.

TAPENADE OLIVES NIÇOISES EN TAPENADE

---

8 ounces (about 1½ cups packed) pitted Niçoise olives

½ teaspoon Dijon mustard

1 boquerones anchovy fillet (see Sources, page 330), cut into 3 pieces (optional)

1 tablespoon drained nonpareil capers, preferably Spanish

1 tablespoon minced Garlic Confit (page 312)

½ cup extra virgin olive oil

1 tablespoon minced Italian parsley

1 tablespoon minced chives

Kosher salt and freshly ground black pepper

Traditionally, tapenade is made of olives, pureed so that their flavor becomes very concentrated—somewhat like pressed caviar, which is caviar that has been crushed and therefore has an intense flavor. It's a great garnish for fish or lamb; excellent on grilled chicken. It can be added to sauces as a seasoning, thinned out with olive oil and turned into a sauce itself (see the skate recipe on page 180), or made into a vinaigrette. This tapenade is seasoned with a white anchovy from Spain that's cured in vinegar before being stored in oil.

Combine the olives, mustard, anchovy, and capers in a food processor, pulse a few times, then scrape down the sides. Pulse a few more times, leaving the mixture a bit chunky. Add the garlic confit and pulse once or twice. Add ¼ cup of the olive oil and pulse, scraping down the sides as necessary, until the mixture is finely chopped. Transfer it to a bowl and stir in the remaining olive oil, the parsley, and chives. Season to taste with salt and pepper. (The tapenade can be stored, refrigerated, in a covered container for up to 1 week.) Serve it at room temperature.

PHOTOGRAPHS ON PAGES 23 AND 113   MAKES 1½ CUPS

VEGETABLES À LA GRECQUE

The basic technique for the preparation called *à la grecque* is simple: Vegetables are gently cooked in a court bouillon enriched with olive oil and aromatics such as coriander, bay leaf, thyme, and garlic—or whatever your preference happens to be. The acid from the lemon juice helps to maintain their crunch. When the vegetables are almost fully done (they should have some bite to them), they are cooled and stored in their cooking liquid. We serve them glazed with a vinaigrette made of the reduced cooking liquid.

We offer recipes for six vegetables, but this technique works with just about any winter vegetable, including turnips, beets, and carrots. The vegetables can be cooked two to three days before you intend to serve them—one of their advantages in a bistro kitchen—and each will serve about four as part of an hors d'oeuvres plate. Refrigerate them submerged in their cooking liquid, then reduce the liquid the day you plan to serve them—but return them to the refrigerator; they should be served cold.

COURT BOUILLON
SACHET

1 Italian parsley sprig

1 thyme sprig

12 black peppercorns

2 bay leaves

2 teaspoons fennel seeds

2 teaspoons celery seeds

2 teaspoons coriander seeds

1 cup water

1 cup dry white wine, such as sauvignon blanc

¼ cup extra virgin olive oil

¼ cup fresh lemon juice

¼ cup minced shallots

FOR THE SACHET: Cut a piece of cheesecloth about 7 inches square. Place all the sachet ingredients in the center, bring the side edges together, and tie with kitchen twine to form a pouch. Place in a small to medium saucepan that will hold the vegetables and keep them submerged in the liquid, then add the remaining ingredients. Proceed as described below for each vegetable.

BABY ARTICHOKES

1 pound (about 9) baby artichokes

1 lemon, halved

1 tablespoon chopped Italian parsley

Hold an artichoke stem end upward. Working your way around the artichoke, bend the lower leaves back until they snap and break naturally and pull them off. Continue removing the tough outer leaves until you reach the tender inner leaves, which are predominantly yellow. Repeat with the remaining artichokes.

As you trim the artichokes, rub the cut surfaces with lemon juice to keep the flesh from discoloring. One at a time, cut the top off each artichoke at the point where the leaves become yellow. Trim off the end of the stem. Holding the artichoke upright, use a paring knife to trim away any tough dark exterior, cutting downward from the base of the leaves to the base of the stem and creating a smooth line from the bottom of the artichoke to the end of the stem. Place the trimmed artichoke in the court bouillon.

When all the artichokes are submerged, bring the court bouillon to a boil. Reduce the heat and simmer for 30 to 40 minutes, or until the artichokes are tender throughout when pierced with a paring knife.

Pour the artichokes and cooking liquid into a container and let cool. Once they are cool, discard the sachet. (At this point, the artichokes can be refrigerated in their liquid for 2 to 3 days.)

TO COMPLETE: Gently stir the artichokes in the court bouillon so that any shallots clinging to them are released into the liquid. Remove the artichokes and set aside. Pour the court bouillon into a saucepan and slowly bring it to a boil, then lower the heat and simmer very gently until it has reduced to about ¼ cup and coats the back of a spoon. Add the artichokes and stir to coat. Refrigerate for at least an hour, or up to a day.

Just before serving, arrange the artichokes on a serving plate and sprinkle with the parsley.

PHOTOGRAPH ON PAGE 20

CAULIFLOWER

About 1¾ pounds (1 head) cauliflower
½ teaspoon curry powder
1 tablespoon chopped Italian parsley

Trim away any leaves from the cauliflower and break the head into large florets. Cut the florets into smaller pieces, about 1 inch in diameter, trimming the stems to about ½ inch long.

Add the curry powder to the court bouillon and bring to a boil. Add the cauliflower, reduce the heat, and simmer for 15 to 20 minutes, or until the florets are tender when pierced with a paring knife.

Pour the cauliflower and cooking liquid into a container and let cool. Once the cauliflower is cool, discard the sachet. (At this point, the cauliflower can be refrigerated in its liquid for 2 to 3 days.)

TO COMPLETE: Gently stir the cauliflower in the court bouillon so that any shallots clinging to it are released into the liquid. Remove the cauliflower and set aside. Pour the court bouillon into a saucepan and slowly bring it to a boil, then reduce the heat and simmer very gently until the liquid has reduced to about ¼ cup and coats the back of a spoon. Add the cauliflower and stir to coat. Refrigerate for at least an hour, or up to a day.

Just before serving, arrange the cauliflower on a serving platter and sprinkle with the parsley.

PHOTOGRAPH ON PAGE 20

CELERIAC

2 pounds (2 large) celeriac (celery root)
1 tablespoon chopped Italian parsley

Cut off and discard the tops and bottoms of the celeriac. Remove the skin with a paring knife or a sharp, sturdy vegetable peeler. Cut the celeriac crosswise into ¾-inch-thick slices, then cut the slices into ¾-inch-wide strips. Trim the ends to square off the strips and cut across the strips into ¾-inch cubes. (You should have 2½ to 3 cups of celeriac.)

Bring the court bouillon to a boil. Add the celeriac, reduce the heat, and simmer for about 15 minutes, or until it is tender when pierced with a paring knife.

Pour the celeriac and cooking liquid into a container and let cool. Once the celeriac has cooled, discard the sachet. (At this point, the celeriac can be refrigerated in its liquid for 2 to 3 days.)

TO COMPLETE: Gently stir the celeriac in the court bouillon so that any shallots clinging to it are released into the liquid. Remove the celeriac and set aside. Pour the court bouillon into a saucepan and slowly bring it to a boil, then reduce the heat and simmer very gently until it has reduced to about ¼ cup and coats the back of a spoon. Add the celeriac and stir to coat. Refrigerate for at least an hour, or up to a day.

Just before serving, arrange the celeriac on a serving plate and sprinkle with the parsley.

BUTTON MUSHROOMS

1 pound small button mushrooms, cleaned (see page 326) and trimmed
1 teaspoon kosher salt
1 tablespoon minced chives

Bring the court bouillon to a boil. Add the mushrooms, stir, and add the salt. Simmer for 5 to 10 minutes, depending on the size of the mushrooms, until they are tender when pierced with a paring knife.

Pour the mushrooms and cooking liquid into a container and let cool. Once the mushrooms are cool, discard the sachet. (At this point, the mushrooms can be refrigerated in their liquid for 2 to 3 days.)

TO COMPLETE: Gently stir the mushrooms in the court bouillon so that any shallots clinging to them are released into the liquid. Remove the mushrooms and set aside. Pour the court bouillon into a saucepan and slowly bring it to a boil, then reduce the heat and simmer very gently until it has reduced to about $1/4$ cup and coats the back of a spoon. Add the mushrooms and stir to coat. Refrigerate for at least an hour, or up to a day.

Just before serving, arrange the mushrooms on a serving plate and sprinkle with the chives.

FENNEL

$1^1/_2$ pounds (2 to 3) fennel bulbs or 1 pound baby fennel bulbs

$1/4$ cup Pernod

1 tablespoon chopped tarragon

If using regular fennel, trim off and discard the tops. Cut away any tough outer layers from each bulb and discard. Stand the bulbs up and cut them in half through the root. Then cut each half into 4 wedges. If using baby fennel, trim them if necessary and leave whole.

Add the Pernod to the court bouillon and bring to a boil. Add the fennel, reduce the heat to a simmer, and cook for 30 to 40 minutes, or until the fennel is tender when pierced with a paring knife.

Pour the fennel and cooking liquid into a container to cool. Once the fennel is cool, discard the sachet. (At this point, the fennel can be refrigerated in its liquid for 2 to 3 days.)

TO COMPLETE: Gently stir the fennel in the court bouillon so that any shallots clinging to it are released into the liquid. Remove the fennel and set aside. Pour the court bouillon into a saucepan and slowly bring it to a boil, then reduce the heat and simmer very

gently until it has reduced to about $1/4$ cup and coats the back of a spoon. Add the fennel and stir to coat. Refrigerate for at least an hour, or up to a day.

Just before serving, arrange the fennel on a serving plate or platter and sprinkle with the tarragon.

PHOTOGRAPH ON PAGE 20

PEARL ONIONS

One 10-ounce bag red pearl onions

1 teaspoon red wine vinegar

1 tablespoon chopped Italian parsley

Trim the root ends and cut a shallow X in the root end of each onion. Put the onions in a large bowl and bring enough water to cover the onions to a boil. Pour the water over the onions and let them sit until the skins soften and are easy to remove. Drain the onions and peel them.

Add the onions to the court bouillon and bring to a boil, then reduce the heat and simmer for about 12 minutes, or until they are tender throughout when pierced with a paring knife.

Pour the onions and cooking liquid into a container and let cool. Once the onions are cool, discard the sachet. (At this point, the onions can be refrigerated in their liquid for 2 to 3 days.)

TO COMPLETE: Gently stir the onions in the court bouillon so that any shallots clinging to them are released into the liquid. Remove the onions and set aside. Pour the court bouillon into a saucepan and slowly bring it to a boil, then reduce the heat and simmer very gently until it has reduced to about $1/4$ cup and coats the back of a spoon. Add the onions and stir to coat. Refrigerate for at least an hour, or up to a day.

Just before serving, arrange the onions on a serving plate and sprinkle with the parsley.

PHOTOGRAPH ON PAGE 20

MUSTARD: In most bouchons and bistros you'll find a little pot of Dijon mustard on the table. It's like the bottle of ketchup in America, but it's a terrifically versatile condiment. Dijon mustard goes with so many bistro dishes—rillettes, roast chicken, lamb, steak frites, pâtés. It works almost like your own personal finishing sauce, the last ingredient to go on a dish, one that you control. Mustards vary widely in quality; indeed, there may be no other condiment with so many variations. The most common problem with mustard is too much vinegar. Find a straightforward Dijon that you like and stick with it. The brand we use at Bouchon is Edmund Fallot (see Sources, page 330), and Maille is a good alternative.

THE IMPORTANCE OF
{ P O T T E D F O O D }

Potted foods are the many dishes composed of meat, fat, and seasonings, stored in, and usually served from, earthenware pots of ceramic or glass containers. A classic example is rillettes, a preparation in which meat is braised until it's falling-apart tender, then mixed or pureed with some of the cooking liquid, some fat, and some seasonings and allowed to cool in a ramekin or small earthenware container, thickening into a spread. In the bistro kitchen, the technique means excellent food that's ready at a moment's notice—the best kind of snack food there is. Rillettes are served with crusty bread and mustard, and perhaps some cornichons.

Various types of meat can be made into rillettes. Pork is traditional because it's both economical and abundant, but we prefer the more interesting flavors of rabbit or duck. Fish, especially salmon, also work well. Potted foods are an excellent start to a meal because they are shared and there's no better spirit with which to begin a meal. They are perfect for entertaining at home—they are easy to make, can be done ahead of time, are typically inexpensive, keep a long time, and can serve a large group. Yet this kind of food is virtually unknown in America, certainly in the American home kitchen.

Often the meat used in potted dishes is confited, or poached in its own fat, until it's meltingly tender, then stored submerged in that fat. That the results of the confit technique can have multiple uses (for both the meat and the fat) made this a valuable technique in a small kitchen that needed to produce a lot of delicious food quickly. Rillettes were one of many uses to which a chef could put a confit. The kitchen could confit a big batch of pork or duck all at once, then store it for days or even longer, no refrigeration necessary.

Originally, the raison d'être for potted foods was preservation. Properly prepared, they would keep for weeks in a cold cellar. Though we no longer need to pot food to preserve it, the tradition is important, and the technique—which easily translates to the home kitchen—produces deep, rich flavors that you cannot get by other methods.

Here again, these flavorful dishes are meant for a group—one dish to share, thus bringing a distinctive social interaction to the meal.

Clockwise from top left: Toasts topped with Olivade (page 14), Tapenade (page 16), Smoked and Steamed Salmon Rillettes (page 26), Rabbit Rillettes with Prunes (page 27), and Fois Gras (page 24)

FOIE GRAS TERRINE—TERRINE DE FOIE GRAS

About 1 1/4 pounds Grade A or Grade B
    moulard foie gras (see Sources, page 330),
    at room temperature
Milk
2 teaspoons kosher salt

1/2 teaspoon pink salt (see Sources, page 330)
1/4 teaspoon freshly ground white pepper
1/4 teaspoon sugar
8 cups Chicken Stock (page 317), Veal Stock
    (page 318), or water

About 1/2 cup rendered duck fat (see Sources,
    page 330) or Clarified Butter (page 316),
    melted and cooled to room temperature
    (if storing the terrine)
1 baguette (3 inches wide and at least
    10 inches long)
Fleur de sel

If you have the right tools—a tamis (drum sieve), cheesecloth, a pastry bag—this is an excellent terrine to make at home. It's an amazing luxury, a rich sensual pleasure, yet very light and spreadable. I love the elegance and richness of foie gras, certainly, and I also admire its versatility. In a way it's just one step up from butter and toast, it's that simple a pleasure—and what an extraordinary pleasure.

This recipe is similar to the torchon we make at the French Laundry—foie gras cured overnight, rolled up in a dish towel *(torchon),* and quickly poached—but it goes through some extra stages that change its texture from dense to light. It's a four-day process. As at the French Laundry, a whole foie gras is soaked in milk to remove the blood and impurities, then given a dry marinade of salt, pepper, sugar, and pink salt (sodium nitrite, which helps to maintain its color). Next the foie gras is rolled up in cheesecloth and poached for only ninety seconds, just long enough to melt the fat and help distribute the seasonings. Then it's cooled, rerolled, and chilled. Finally, it's pressed through a sieve, which lightens the texture and catches any veins remaining in the liver, then piped into small serving containers (we use six-ounce glass crocks; see Sources, page 330). A layer of fat, either duck fat or fat rendered from foie gras trim, is poured over it to seal it.

DAY 1. SOAKING THE FOIE GRAS: Rinse the foie gras under cold water; pat dry with paper towels. Place in an airtight container and cover with milk. Cover tightly and refrigerate overnight, or up to 24 hours, to draw out some of the blood.

DAY 2. CLEANING AND MARINATING THE FOIE GRAS: Remove the foie gras from the milk, rinse it, and pat dry. Cover it with a damp towel and let stand at room temperature for 45 minutes. (It will be easier to work with if the foie gras is not ice-cold.)

Pull apart the two lobes. Keep one covered with the towel while you work on the other. Remove any membranes from the outside of the foie gras.

To butterfly the large lobe, locate the start of the primary vein at one end of the underside of the lobe. Slice through the lobe to the vein, following its path and pulling the foie gras apart so you can see the vein clearly. Turn your knife at a 45-degree angle and make an outward cut at each side of the vein to butterfly the foie gras. Cut far enough to open the folds and expose the interior. Use your fingers and the knife to remove the primary vein and any smaller veins that are easily removed, bruised areas, and blood spots. It is not necessary to remove all the smaller veins, as they will be left behind when the foie gras is passed through the tamis (drum sieve). Do not worry about how much you cut and scrape; think of the liver as a piece of Play-Doh, easily reshaped. Once the foie gras is cleaned, fold the sides over and return it to an approximation of its original shape.

To *butterfly the small lobe,* with your fingers, follow the line of the primary vein on the bottom of the lobe and pull the lobe open. As with the large lobe, use a knife to scrape and remove the large vein, any easily removed smaller veins, as well as bruises and blood spots. Then form it back into its original shape.

Mix the kosher salt, pink salt, pepper, and sugar together. Press the foie gras into a container in an even 3/4- to 1-inch-thick layer. Sprinkle and press half the marinating mixture over and into the liver. Flip the foie gras and repeat on the other side with the remaining marinating mixture. Press a piece of plastic wrap directly against the foie gras and enclose the container completely in more plastic wrap. Refrigerate for 24 hours.

DAY 3. FORMING AND COOKING THE TORCHON: Remove the foie gras from the container, place it on a piece of parchment paper, and break it up as necessary to form a loaf about 6 inches long and 3 1/2 inches wide. Using the parchment, roll the foie gras into a log, twisting and squeezing the ends of the parchment paper to help compact it. Unwrap the foie gras and transfer the log to a piece of cheesecloth about 1 foot wide by 2 feet long, placing it along a short end of the cheesecloth. Rolling away from you, roll up the log in the cheesecloth into a tight log, again twisting the ends as you roll to force the foie gras into a compact log. (If possible, have a second person hold the far end of the cheesecloth flat on the work surface as you roll.)

Loop a length of twine around your index finger. Using the same hand, hold one end of the cheesecloth tightly and wind the twine around the end of the foie gras. Continue wrapping the twine about 1/4 inch into the foie gras; this will help force the foie gras to compress into a tight roll. Tie a knot around the cheesecloth. Repeat the procedure on the other end. If you have rolled and tied the torchon tightly enough, you will see bits of foie gras being forced through the cheesecloth. Tie 3 pieces of twine equally spaced around the width of the torchon. (These will be used as guides to reshape the log into its original shape after it has been poached.)

Bring enough stock or water to cover the foie gras to a simmer in a wide pot. Meanwhile, prepare an ice bath. Place the torchon in the simmering liquid and poach for 90 seconds. Immediately transfer to the ice bath to cool.

The foie gras will have lost volume (it loses fat in the poaching) and must be reformed. Wrap the log (still in the cheesecloth) in a thin cotton dish towel, compressing it as you go. Twist and tie the ends of the towel, returning the liver to its original density and pressing out excess fat. Tie the ends of the towel with twine and hang the liver from a shelf in the refrigerator overnight.

DAY 4. COMPLETING THE TERRINES: Unwrap the foie gras. Scrape off and discard the outside layer, which will have oxidized and turned gray. Cut the foie gras into sections about 2 inches long.

Prepare an ice bath in a large bowl. Use a plastic scraper to force the foie gras through a tamis into a smaller metal bowl. The tamis will catch any veins you may have missed when you cleaned the foie gras. Set the bowl in the ice bath. To lighten the consistency of the foie gras, beat it vigorously with a sturdy spoon for couple of minutes to achieve the texture of a buttercream frosting.

Transfer the mixture to a pastry bag without a tip or with a large plain tip. Pipe about 1/2 cup of the foie gras into each of three 6-ounce glass crocks or other similar containers. Wipe the edges of the crocks clean. If not serving the same day, pour a 1/4-inch-thick layer of duck fat or clarified butter over the top of each terrine. Refrigerate for up to 2 weeks. Once you remove the fat cap, the foie gras should be served the same day, as it will oxidize and darken.

TO SERVE: Preheat the broiler. Cut the ends off the baguette and cut the loaf into two 4-inch-long sections. Cut each section lengthwise in half and cut the halves lengthwise into thirds. Place cut side up on a tray and broil until golden brown.

Serve the foie gras in the crocks, garnished with a sprinkling of fleur de sel and with the toasts on the side.

PHOTOGRAPH ON PAGE 23   MAKES ABOUT 1 1/2 CUPS

SMOKED AND STEAMED SALMON RILLETTES—RILLETTES AUX DEUX SAUMONS

1 pound center-cut salmon fillet, skin and
    pinbones removed
2 tablespoons Pernod
Kosher salt and freshly ground white pepper
8 tablespoons (4 ounces) unsalted butter,
    at room temperature

½ cup minced shallots
1 tablespoon crème fraîche
8 ounces unsliced chilled smoked salmon,
    cut into ¼-inch dice and brought to
    room temperature

2½ tablespoons fresh lemon juice
1 tablespoon extra virgin olive oil
2 large organic egg yolks, lightly beaten
About ½ cup Clarified Butter (page 316),
    melted and cooled to room temperature
Minced chives (optional)

For traditional rillettes, cooked, shredded meat is mixed with its own fat to make it moist, succulent, and flavorful. Fish, of course, don't have that kind of fat, so butter replaces it. Beaten until it is creamy, butter is folded gently into a mixture of two types of salmon: steamed and cold-smoked. To enrich the salmon further, we add raw yolks and a little crème fraîche, the latter lending some acidity. Clarified butter is poured over the top to seal the rillettes. The rillettes can be stored for up to a week, but the recipe can be halved for a smaller yield. The result is a meaty, creamy spread that tastes very fresh and light.

In the Bouchon kitchen, we steam the raw salmon, which gives us consistent, juicy results. If you don't have a steamer, you can gently poach the salmon in a court bouillon (page 38). It's a little trickier to hit that perfect medium-rare this way, but it does allow you to introduce additional flavors via the cooking liquid.

Trim and discard any dark flesh from the salmon fillet. Place the fish in a shallow baking dish and sprinkle each side with 1 tablespoon of the Pernod, 1½ teaspoons salt, and ¼ teaspoon white pepper. Cover with plastic wrap and refrigerate for 30 to 60 minutes, turning the fish over halfway through the marination.

Bring water to a simmer in the bottom of a steamer. Place the salmon fillet in the steamer and cover with the lid. Steam gently for about 8 minutes; if you see steam pouring out the sides of the steamer, lower the heat. Check the salmon by separating the flesh with the tip of a knife and peering at the center: It should be medium-rare. When it is cooked, remove from the steamer.

Meanwhile, melt 1 tablespoon of the butter in a medium sauté pan over medium heat. Add the shallots and cook, stirring occasionally, for 2 minutes. Season the shallots with ¼ teaspoon salt and continue to cook for another 3 to 4 minutes, until they have softened but not browned. Remove from the heat.

Put the remaining 7 tablespoons butter in a small bowl and beat with a rubber spatula until it is smooth and resembles mayonnaise in consistency. Stir in the crème fraîche. Set aside.

Put the cooked salmon in a large bowl and stir to break it into large chunks. Because you will be stirring in the remaining ingredients, you don't want to break up the pieces too much. Stir in the smoked salmon, shallots, lemon juice, olive oil, and egg yolks. Season assertively with salt and white pepper, since this will be served cold. Fold in the butter mixture.

Transfer the rillettes to small glass crocks (see Sources, page 330), leaving at least ½ inch space at the top. Smooth the top of the rillettes and wipe the inside rims clean. Refrigerate for about 1 hour, until cold.

Pour a ¼-inch-thick layer of clarified butter over the top of the rillettes to seal. Cover and store in the refrigerator for up to a week. TO SERVE: Break through the butter layer and remove it. Spread the rillettes on toasts or crackers and sprinkle on chives, if using. (Once the butter is removed, eat the rillettes within 2 days.)

PHOTOGRAPH ON PAGE 23   **MAKES ABOUT 2 CUPS**

SACHET

1 bay leaf

1 star anise

4 cloves

1 thyme sprig

1/2 teaspoon black peppercorns

PRUNES

20 pitted prunes

1 cinnamon stick

1/2 to 3/4 cup dry red wine, such as
  cabernet sauvignon

2 tablespoons cognac

RILLETTES

4 pieces Rabbit Confit (page 134)

1/4 cup Dijon mustard

Freshly ground black pepper

Kosher salt

While pork is the meat most classically associated with rillettes—because slow-cooked trimmings of pork are readily available, and the result is rich and flavorful—we also use rabbit, which has a sweetness to it. Our technique for all our rillettes begins with confiting the meat. Simmered in fat, the tough legs become tender and succulent. (After using the rabbit legs, we strain the remaining cooking fat and store it in the refrigerator or freezer; it can be used for confiting two or three more times before it grows too salty.) The meat is shredded and then stirred together with seasonings and some of the fat. To finish, we simmer prunes in red wine with anise and cinnamon, puree them, and spread the puree on top of the rillettes. Served atop toasts or crackers, these are a great hors d'oeuvre or midafternoon snack.

FOR THE SACHET: Cut a piece of cheesecloth about 6 inches square. Place the bay leaf, star anise, cloves, thyme, and peppercorns in the center and tie into a sachet with kitchen twine.

FOR THE PRUNES: Place the prunes and sachet in a saucepan just large enough to hold the prunes in a single layer. Add the cinnamon stick and just enough red wine to cover the prunes. Bring to a boil over medium-high heat, then reduce the heat and simmer for 2 minutes. Remove the pan from the heat, partially cover, and let the prunes steep in the liquid for at least 30 minutes.

Swirl the cognac into the prunes, then transfer the prunes, with the liquid, sachet, and cinnamon stick, to a covered container and refrigerate until ready to use, or for up to 2 weeks.

FOR THE RILLETTES: Remove the confit from the refrigerator a few hours before using to allow the fat to soften enough to remove the legs without breaking them.

Remove the legs from the fat, reserving 3/4 cup of the fat. Pull the meat from the bones and shred it, discarding the bones. (There are some very small bones that can be overlooked. You should have about 1 1/4 pounds of meat.)

Set aside about one-third of the rabbit meat. Put the remaining pieces in a large bowl and stir vigorously with a sturdy spoon to break up the pieces. Stir in the mustard and season generously with pepper, which complements the rich flavor of the rillettes. Begin adding the reserved fat to the meat 1/4 cup at a time, using the spoon to mash it into the mixture. A creamy emulsification will form as the meat absorbs the fat. The rillettes should not be dry, but be careful to add the fat slowly, particularly at the end: If too much fat is added, the rillettes will be greasy rather than creamy. Stir in the reserved pieces of rabbit and season with salt and additional pepper to taste.

Refrigerate the rillettes for at least 1 hour, or up to 24 hours.

TO COMPLETE: Make the prune puree. Drain the prunes, reserving the liquid, and discard the sachet and cinnamon stick. Finely mince the prunes and combine with the liquid in a small bowl. (You will have about 1 cup.) Use a spoon to pack the rillettes into small glass crocks or other containers, leaving about 1/2 inch space at the top. With a damp paper towel, wipe the edges of the containers clean. Smooth about 1/4-inch-thick layer of the prune puree over the rillettes and refrigerate for up to 2 weeks.

PHOTOGRAPH ON PAGE 23   **MAKES ABOUT 3 CUPS**

RABBIT PÂTÉ—PÂTÉ DE LAPIN

SPICE MIXTURE

2 tablespoons plus 1 teaspoon kosher salt

1/4 teaspoon pink salt (see Sources, page 330)

1 tablespoon plus 1 teaspoon minced thyme

1 tablespoon plus 1 teaspoon freshly grated
    nutmeg

2 teaspoons black peppercorns

3 bay leaves

PÂTÉ

13 ounces rabbit meat (from 1 whole rabbit or
    3 to 4 legs; see Sources, page 330)

1 1/4 pounds chicken livers

9 ounces (8 or 9 slices) white bread

1 1/4 cups milk

Canola oil

5 bay leaves

1 1/4 pounds thinly sliced slab bacon
    (see below)

9 ounces fresh unsalted pork fatback,
    cut into 1-inch cubes

2 large egg yolks

2 tablespoons cognac or other brandy

Dijon mustard

Cornichons

Radishes

Fleur de sel and freshly ground black pepper

Rabbit pâté is a flavorful, more unusual variation on traditional pork pâté, though the methods of making them are pretty much the same. Rabbit makes a very creamy pâté, and the meat has a certain sweetness to it. Rabbits are small, so you almost always have to buy them whole. You might serve the loin, maybe even braise the legs, but you're still left with a lot of rabbit that you don't want to waste. As cooks, we like to challenge ourselves to use all our skills to make something fine from what might otherwise be thrown away. A rabbit pâté, moist, flavorful, and cleverly seasoned, is an excellent application of those skills.

We line this terrine with thinly sliced bacon—ask your deli department to slice slab bacon one-sixteenth inch thick for you—but you could use blanched leek greens as an excellent and striking alternative.

FOR THE SPICE MIXTURE: Grind the salts, thyme, nutmeg, peppercorns, and bay leaves in a coffee or spice grinder. Set aside.

FOR THE PÂTÉ: Cut the rabbit into 1-inch cubes. (You should have about 1 3/4 cups.) Place in a medium bowl. Clean any fat, sinew, or dark spots from the livers. Add to the rabbit, then add the ground spices and toss well, being sure to coat the rabbit and livers evenly. Cover and refrigerate for at least 2 hours, or up to 6 hours.

About 30 minutes before grinding the meat, remove the crusts from the bread and tear the bread into pieces no more than an inch across. Place in a medium bowl, add the milk, and set aside to soak.

Brush a 12 1/2-by-4 1/2-by-3-inch-high lidded terrine (see Sources, page 330) with a light coating of oil. Line the terrine with plastic wrap, leaving about a 6-inch overhang on all four sides. Arrange the 5 bay leaves in a line down the bottom of the terrine (this will be the presentation side of the terrine).

Line the terrine with the bacon slices, beginning with one end of a bacon slice just slightly past center and the opposite end overhanging the side of the terrine. Continue working around the terrine, overlapping the slices by $1/8$ inch; they shouldn't overlap by much more or the bacon will be too thick. The ends of the bacon that overlap in the center of the terrine should overlap by about $1/4$ inch. If necessary, use scissors to trim the bacon so that the overhang is 3 inches. Place the terrine in a deep roasting pan that is at least three-quarters of the height of the terrine.

Preheat the oven to 300°F.

Fit a meat grinder with a large-holed die. (Be sure that it is bolted securely.) Place a stainless steel bowl set in a bowl of ice under the grinder to catch the ground mixture. First grind the marinated meat mixture, then grind the bread and milk mixture into the bowl. Mix the meat and bread together and transfer to another bowl. Return the first bowl to the ice.

Change the grinder die to the smaller one and grind the mixture a second time. Then run the fatback through the grinder into the bowl. To clean any mixture trapped in the grinder, cut a piece of plastic wrap 3 to 4 inches square and run it into the machine. Once it pushes out any remaining mixture, stop the grinder. (You can remove the plastic wrap when you clean the machine.)

Mix the egg yolks and cognac together in a small bowl, then stir into the pâté with a rubber spatula, making certain that the fat is evenly distributed throughout.

Pack the mixture into the terrine, being careful to avoid air pockets, especially in the corners. Fold the bacon over the terrine, beginning at the two short ends. Then use one side of the plastic wrap to lift one long side of the strips of bacon over to the center. Lift up the plastic wrap and repeat with the second side, then cover the top with the plastic wrap and the lid. Place the terrine in a roasting pan.

Add enough warm water to the roasting pan to come about two-thirds of the way up the sides of the terrine. Place in the oven and bake for 1 hour and 45 minutes to 2 hours, or until the center of the terrine registers 160°F on an instant-read thermometer. (The lid of most terrines has a hole through which you can place a thermometer.) Remove the roasting pan from the oven and then the terrine from the pan; place on a cooling rack set over a small baking sheet (to catch the fat later). Let stand at room temperature for about 20 minutes.

Cut a piece of cardboard to fit over the surface of the pâté and wrap the cardboard in aluminum foil. Puncture the plastic wrap at each end of the terrine and tilt the terrine at each end to drain any fat. Place the cardboard on the terrine and top with several heavy weights, such as clean bricks. (If the weights are resting on the sides of the terrine, add an additional layer or more of cardboard so the weights are sitting on the cardboard, not on the rim of the terrine, so they can compress the pâté.)

Refrigerate the weighted pâté for 24 hours.

TO SERVE: Remove the weights and cardboard from the terrine. Lift up the pâté with the overhang of plastic wrap to release it from the mold, then replace it in the terrine. (If the pâté doesn't release, fill the sink or other large container with warm water and dip the terrine in just long enough to soften the fat and release the pâté.) Carefully run a knife around the edges of the pâté and invert it onto a cutting board. Cut into $1/2$-inch-thick slices.

Serve with a pot of Dijon mustard, cornichons, radishes, fleur de sel, and ground pepper.

MAKES 20 SERVINGS

Charcuterie, the name given to a range of sausages both cooked and dry-cured, pâtés and terrines, and cured ham, is a centuries-old craft in France. It has only recently begun to come of age here, with many chefs throughout the country now curing and drying their own sausages. At Bouchon, we serve a traditional *assiette de charcuterie,* which offers a tasting of several dry-cured sausages, ham, and, perhaps, a slice of pâté.

Charcuterie is not only easy to store, it's also easily and quickly served. A few slices of Petit Jesus or other sausages and Bayonne ham or one cured by the *charcutier* himself, some cornichons for an acidic counterpoint and crunch, a pot of Dijon mustard, some bread, and red wine make the perfect starter or late-afternoon lunch, or the perfect late-night bite.

GLORIA'S CORNICHONS

Gloria Pépin makes the best cornichons from her own organically grown tiny cucumbers. Growing your own cucumbers is easy, but catching them before they get too large is another story. They grow so quickly that you have to check their size each day. Every morning Gloria goes into her backyard and picks the ones that are just the right size, no longer than 1½ to 2 inches. Pick early in the morning or after the sun goes down so as not to disturb the bees. Initially you'll find only a few cukes, but after three or four pickings, they'll start coming more often.

Homegrown cucumbers for pickling (picked while still tiny)

Kosher salt

Tarragon sprigs

Black peppercorns

Bottled pickled cocktail onions (in vinegar)

White vinegar

Rub the cucumbers with a clean damp cloth to remove any prickers and dirt. Place the cucumbers in a small stainless steel bowl and toss them with a light coating of salt. Refrigerate covered for a day.

The following day, remove the cucumbers from the bowl and wipe them with a dry cloth to remove any remaining dirt or prickers. Place a sprig of tarragon, several black peppercorns, and a few pickled onions in a lidded jar. (Gloria uses half-pint jars so that she can give away a few jars while still having some left for herself.) Add the cucumbers and enough vinegar to cover them. It is all right for the tarragon to be left exposed. Seal the jar and refrigerate.

The next day, repeat with newly picked and salted cucumbers, continuing to add enough vinegar to cover each batch. When the jar is half full, add another sprig of tarragon, a few more onions, and vinegar to cover.

When the jar is full, top with a final sprig of tarragon. Seal and write the date on the jar. Store in a cool cellar or in the refrigerator and continue filling more jars with your cucumber harvest. They will need to sit for at least 6 weeks for optimum flavor and can be kept for up to a year.

{ THE RAW BAR }

MIGNONETTE SAUCE: An important type of vinaigrette always associated with the raw bar, and oysters in particular, mignonette sauce is interesting in that it's a vinaigrette that doesn't use oil; the liquor from the oyster takes its place. The term *mignonette* once referred to a sachet of peppercorns and cloves used to season various liquids, but it has come to mean cracked black or white pepper. In mignonette sauces, the kind of vinegar may change from recipe to recipe, but shallots and black pepper are common to all versions.

ZINC BAR: The bright and shining zinc bar in a bistro draws you like a magnet. It reflects the energy of a bistro. A traditional bistro bar was treated with zinc to prevent wear and tear resulting from eating and drinking. Zinc was also easy to clean. Today, pewter is typically used; in fact, it wears better than zinc. Both materials have the same beauty and efficiency, and they retain the nicks and gouges that connect you to the history of that bistro.

The raw bar is one of my favorite elements of bistro-style restaurants, though it's probably the least authentic from a historical standpoint. In Paris, oysters were more likely to be sold outside a bistro than in it. In the 1800s, oysters were plentiful, an inexpensive poor-man's food. Oyster criers would carry them in a wooden crate on their backs, shucking and selling them outside a restaurant in order to lure customers in. And, in a way, that still happens today: A raw bar invites, it entices you to come in.

I like the freshness of oysters and mussels, alive until the moment they're shucked, just before you eat them. I like clams at a raw bar too. Raw clams are all about texture; these bivalves are muscular and chewy. The other shellfish on ice are cooked: crab (Dungeness on the West Coast), lobster, shrimp. Sometimes Jeff is able to find less common items that are also exciting to offer—crawfish, spot prawns, bay scallops (served raw), pink shrimp, sea urchins.

Though mussels and clams can be served raw, the raw bar is really named for the oysters. Low in fat, high in protein, minerals, and vitamins, oysters need almost nothing done to them. They're fun to eat, and the varieties of flavors are distinct and delicious. We use oysters from both coasts. East Coast oysters tend to be crisper in flavor and briny; West Coast varieties tend to be plumper, bigger, and creamier.

I like oysters from very, very cold northern waters. They're crisper and livelier than the more succulent variety from warmer waters. Some flat cold-water *fines de claire*, for instance, begin with a strong melon flavor and then, after you've swallowed them, end with the flavor of cucumber. Belons from the Atlantic coast can be very minerally and briny, a fresh ocean flavor that is also one of the great taste sensations of the oyster. These are festive and luxurious foods.

Oysters Many of the oysters and clams served at Bouchon come from a place called Penn Cove Shellfish, a shellfish grower and distributor on Puget Sound in Washington (see Sources, page 330). Its products are unbelievably fresh because they never see the inside of a walk-in cooler. They go straight from the water into the delivery truck so that they arrive at the restaurant before they've missed a complete tidal cycle.

"We take them when they're still feeding and full of water," explains Ian Jefferds, general manager and a co-owner of Penn Cove. "Some distributors treat shellfish like fish, and this is the problem. When you take them out of the water and hold them in a cooler, they're still alive. All the things that make shellfish taste good—fats and sugars—they're living off those in the cooler; they're metabolizing those fats and sugars. So by the time you eat them, everything that makes them taste good is gone.

"A lot of times when you taste a bad shellfish, it's because of a buildup of that waste, not to harmful levels, but enough to affect the taste. When this kind of shellfish is served, it hurts everyone. The customers wonder what's so special about it. They don't buy more.

That hurts the restaurant. The restaurant doesn't buy more. That hurts the farmer and distributor. We get very frustrated.

"When they're in wet storage—we hang them from rafts—they continue to grow until the last minute before shipping, feeding off the nutrients in the water and staying fat and fresh."

All shellfish by law must be tagged with the date and their place of harvesting. Ian recommends that chefs buying oysters check the tag. If, for example, you're buying oysters three times a week, and your farmer or distributor is harvesting only once a week, the oysters you receive on Friday for the weekend may have been harvested the same day as the ones you bought for Wednesday and have just been sitting in a cooler. If the demand for wet-stored oysters goes up, it should increase the supply, and more people will know how a truly fresh oyster tastes.

Oyster farmers, Ian explains, have two principal ways of growing oysters from seed—either in a beach culture (also called a bed or bottom culture), their natural growing environment, or a suspended culture, in which they're suspended on lines or racks. Because the salinity of ocean water increases the farther from shore you go, oysters grown in a beach culture may be less briny, while those

suspended in saltier water, farther from the coast, are often more

briny. For the farmer, beach culture is less expensive, requiring no

rafts, racks, bags, or other such equipment. And, due to the tidal

action and the jostling the oysters receive, their shells tend to be

harder, making them easier to shuck without being fractured. The

shells can get into the oyster liquor, so proper shucking is critical

(see page 39). But oysters in a beach culture spend a lot of time

out of the water when the tide goes down, and thus tend to take

longer to grow than oysters suspended below the water, the other

seed-growing method. The suspended-culture method results in fast-

growing oysters, which are also protected from predators such

as starfish, crabs, and rays, but it requires more equipment and

handling and therefore is more expensive. Also, the shells of oysters

grown this way tend to be more brittle.

The oysters' flavor, however, depends largely on the region in

which they grow, what they eat, the varying phytoplankton in the

water, the salinity of the water, and how fast they grow rather than

the method by which they're grown.

SHELLFISH PLATTER—*PLATEAU DE FRUITS DE MER*

The *plateau de fruits de mer* describes the abundance of the sea. It is pure celebration. These *plateaux* are served throughout Europe, but most compellingly, I find, most exuberantly, in Spain, Portugal, and France. We present ours on a raised *plateau royal* (it is also called a seafood tray and stand; see Sources, page 330), but you can use any platter that has enough depth to hold a layer of shaved ice to keep the shellfish cold. When ordering the shellfish, ask your fishmonger for seaweed to place on top of the ice.

For four people, Bouchon serves the shellfish listed below. You can serve any combination or all of these. The simplest way to assemble the dish is to make one recipe of court bouillon, which can then be used for the crab, lobster, and shrimp. In fact, this recipe is enough to cook a 2½-pound crab, two 1-pound lobsters, or a pound of shrimp.

THE DAY BEFORE OR EARLY ON THE DAY OF SERVING

1 Dungeness crab: Cook in the court bouillon and refrigerate for up to 24 hours; clean once chilled, or on the following day.

One 1-pound lobster: Cook second and refrigerate for up to 24 hours; clean once chilled, or on the following day.

12 shrimp (21 to 25 count): Cook third and refrigerate for up to 24 hours.

THE DAY OF SERVING

1 pound mussels: Cook a couple of hours before serving.

16 oysters: Open within 1 hour of serving.

12 clams: Open within 1 hour of serving.

COURT BOUILLON

4 quarts water

4 leeks, white and light green parts only, split lengthwise, washed, and cut into ½-inch pieces

4 large carrots, peeled and cut into ½-inch-thick rounds

3 cups coarsely chopped onions

2 medium fennel bulbs, trimmed and coarsely chopped

Bouquet Garni (page 325)

12 black peppercorns

2 cups dry white wine, such as sauvignon blanc

1 cup white wine vinegar

2 lemons, cut in half

SHELLFISH

One 2- to 2½-pound Dungeness crab, left at room temperature for 30 minutes

One or two 1-pound lobsters, left at room temperature for 30 minutes

12 shrimp (21 to 25 count)

1 pound mussels

16 oysters

12 clams

Mignonette Sauce (page 40)

Cocktail Sauce (page 40)

Mustard-Mayonnaise Sauce (page 40)

FOR THE COURT BOUILLON: Combine the water, vegetables, bouquet garni, and peppercorns in a large stockpot and bring to a boil. Reduce to a simmer and add the wine and vinegar. Squeeze in the lemon juice and add the lemon halves. Proceed as directed.

FOR THE DUNGENESS CRAB: Cover the stockpot and bring the court bouillon to a rolling boil over medium-high heat. Add the crab, front claws first. Cover the pot and adjust the heat to keep the liquid at a light boil; you should hear the water simmering, but the lid shouldn't be rattling. Cook for 4 minutes, then remove the pot from the heat and allow the crab to stand in the liquid for 30 minutes.

Transfer the crab to a plate to cool for about 15 minutes, then refrigerate until chilled, at least 1 hour, or up to 24 hours.

To clean the crab, hold it and pull off the top shell. Remove and discard the gills on each side of the crab, as well as the mouth section. Scoop out the yellow matter in the body (this can be eaten or discarded). Turn the crab over to reveal the apron (tail). Pull it downward, twist it off, and discard. Cut the crab lengthwise in half, then cut each piece crosswise in half. Refrigerate until ready to serve.

FOR THE LOBSTER(S): Cover the stockpot and bring the court bouillon to a rolling boil over medium-high heat. Add the lobster(s), head first, return the liquid to a gentle boil, and boil for 1 minute. Remove the pot from the heat and let the lobster(s) stand in the liquid for 10 minutes.

Transfer the lobster(s) to a platter and let cool for about 15 minutes, then refrigerate until chilled, at least 1 hour, or up to 24 hours.

To prepare the lobster(s), bend back each claw and pull off the claw and knuckle. Insert a large sharp knife between the eyes of each lobster and cut straight down the length of the lobster to cut it in half. Refrigerate the halves until ready to serve.

FOR THE SHRIMP: *To clean the shrimp,* pull off and discard the small feet. Using a small pair of scissors (such as nail scissors), cut a slit down the back of each shrimp, beginning at the head and stopping before the last tail segment, cutting just slightly into the flesh of the shrimp. Carefully open the shell and flesh of the shrimp just enough to check for the intestinal tract; if it is dark and gritty, remove it with a paring knife and discard.

Cover the stockpot and bring the court bouillon to a rolling boil over medium-high heat. Turn off the heat, add the shrimp, and let stand, stirring occasionally, for 3 minutes. Drain the shrimp in a colander and allow to cool for about 10 minutes, then refrigerate for at least 1 hour, or up to 24 hours.

FOR THE MUSSELS: *To clean the mussels,* just before cooking them, wash them under cold running water; if necessary, scrub them to remove any grit from the shells. If there is a beard protruding from the shell, pull it out and discard. Check to make sure that all the mussels are still alive: If any shells are not completely shut, squeeze them together like a castanet and release them a few times. If the shells do not close tightly, the mussel is dead and should be discarded.

Heat a heavy saucepan or pot that will hold the mussels in a single layer, or no more than two layers, over high heat until very hot. Add ¹/₂ cup water and bring to a boil, then add the mussels. Cover and cook for 1 to 1¹/₂ minutes, or until the mussels have opened.

Transfer the mussels to a bowl to cool for 15 minutes, then refrigerate for at least 30 minutes, or up to a few hours

FOR THE OYSTERS: *To shuck the oysters,* place a dish towel on a cutting board and place an oyster cupped side down at the end of the towel. Fold the towel over the rounded end of the oyster, with the hinged or narrow side exposed. Wiggle an oyster knife into the hinge and lift up the top shell until you hear a pop, then wiggle the knife back and forth to loosen the shell. Keeping the knife directly against the top shell, run the blade along the right side to cut through the adductor muscle and release the top shell; remove and discard it. Slide the knife under the oyster to detach the muscle holding the oyster in place, but leave the oyster in the shell.

Check for sand or any pieces of shell in the oyster liquor or on the shell and wipe any out with your finger. If the oyster liquor is very sandy, it can be discarded; the newly opened oyster will replenish the liquor. Set the oyster on a tray and repeat with the remaining oysters. (If not being served immediately, the oysters can be refrigerated for up to 1 hour.)

FOR THE CLAMS: *To shuck the clams,* hold a clam in a dish towel in your hand. There is an indentation on one side of the hinge: Insert a clam knife into the hinge and work back and forth until the shell pops; be careful not to jab the meat with the knife. Run the knife along the underside of the top shell, cutting through the muscle that attaches the clam to the shell, and remove the top shell. Slide the knife underneath the clam to detach it from the bottom shell, but leave it in the shell. Check the liquid for sand or any pieces of shell and wipe any out with your finger. Set the clam on a tray and repeat with the remaining clams. (The clams can refrigerated for up to 1 hour.)

TO SERVE: Line the platter with shaved ice and cover the ice with a layer of seaweed. Arrange the shellfish attractively over the seaweed. Serve with the sauces.

PHOTOGRAPH ON PAGE 37

continued

MIGNONETTE SAUCE

When the combined shallots, pepper, and vinegar mix with the liquor from an oyster, it really makes the oyster's flavor pop, which is what a vinaigrette is supposed to do—make flavors bright and clean and sharp. (Some oysters, though, are so delicious and flavorful that red wine vinegar and shallot and pepper may be too much.) The acidity of the peppery vinegar balances the saltiness of oysters and clams. The grind of the pepper is critical to the perfection of this sauce—it should not be so big as to be unpleasantly chunky and chewy, nor should it be so fine that it washes away.

If you can, make this sauce at least several days, or even a few weeks, before you will serve it. It gets better with age, and although the red color fades, the flavor and integrity of the sauce improve.

2 teaspoons black peppercorns
1 cup cabernet vinegar
2 tablespoons minced shallots

Grind the peppercorns in a coffee or spice grinder. Sift through a strainer to remove the finer particles and transfer 1 $^1/_2$ teaspoons of the pepper remaining in the strainer to a small bowl. Mix in the vinegar and shallots. Refrigerate for at least a day to allow the flavors to develop. (The mignonette can be refrigerated for up to 1 month.)

MAKES 1 CUP

COCKTAIL SAUCE

Historians feel that, like the raw bar itself, cocktail sauce is most likely an American invention. We asked all our cooks to come up with their most classic version and we chose the tastiest. This is it. It's especially good with clams.

1 cup ketchup
1$^1/_2$ teaspoons prepared horseradish, undrained
1$^1/_4$ teaspoons Dijon mustard
1$^1/_2$ teaspoons Worcestershire sauce
1 tablespoon fresh lemon juice

Mix all the ingredients together in a small bowl. Refrigerate for at least a day to allow the flavors to develop. (The sauce can be refrigerated for up to 2 weeks.)

MAKES 1 CUP

MUSTARD-MAYONNAISE SAUCE

This sauce was created specifically for mussels and other chilled shellfish. Frequently served in France with oysters and with the plateau royal, it's a standard mayonnaise-based sauce with a subtle mustard flavor, not too sharp, very smooth. Some people even like to dip their bread in it.

1$^1/_4$ cups mayonnaise
$^1/_2$ cup Dijon mustard
1 teaspoon dry mustard
1 tablespoon Worcestershire sauce
1 tablespoon fresh lemon juice

Mix all the ingredients together in a small bowl. Refrigerate for at least a day to allow the flavors to develop. (The sauce can be refrigerated for up to 2 weeks.)

MAKES 2 CUPS

2

{ À TOUTE HEURE }

ANYTIME

Some of the quintessential bistro dishes, and some of my favorite dishes to eat, are those that are often best enjoyed outside traditional mealtimes. Maybe I feel this way because, as a lifelong cook, this is when I get to eat, and it's often what's been available.

When I *staged* throughout Paris, we'd finish lunch service and take a break at a restaurant serving food at that hour—which, of course, was a bistro. There I could order something very satisfying but not so heavy that it would make returning to work in the kitchen unpleasant—an onion soup, or a frisée salad with an egg and lardons, or a slice of quiche with wild mushrooms. Or, if it was after dinner service, perhaps a luxurious croque-madame—grilled ham and cheese with a fried egg and creamy Mornay sauce on top—to make me feel nourished after a long day of cooking fine French cuisine.

These *à toute heure* dishes fulfill that any-time-of-day demand by providing a complete meal on one plate. The croque-madame has all the elements of a bacon and eggs platter. A spinach quiche nourishes with a custard and sautéed greens. You don't tend to share these dishes as you do with starters. Anytime dishes are hunger-specific—they fulfill a craving and so are ultimately very individualistic.

THE IMPORTANCE OF
{ ONION SOUP }

Onion soup is one of the preparations that's so simple in terms of ingredients and yet so rich—both nutritionally and metaphorically—that eating it feels almost ritualistic. Few dishes are so complete, and therefore so gratifying, in themselves. All the components of a great meal are here—the rich cheese, the bread, the sweet vegetable, the meat broth; it's soup and sandwich at once. And if you have it on a cold winter day, few things are more soul satisfying. I find that each bowl of onion soup I eat, because I've eaten this soup throughout my life, has a way of recalling all the onion soups I've ever had.

I think it's important that a bistro offer an onion soup gratinée because the dish embodies so much of what we expect from this kind of restaurant—warmth, comfort, and familiarity. At Bouchon, we offer onion soup all year-round because of this expectation, but traditionally, onion soup is cold-weather food. It's more fun to make when the steamy heat of the kitchen fogs icy windows.

That certainly is one of the pleasures of onion soup—making it. Slice the onions evenly—they must be uniform so that they caramelize evenly. You don't want noodles, you don't want a piece dripping down anyone's chin; you want the pieces to fit on a spoon, not too wide and not too long, but not so narrow or short that they disintegrate. A nice julienne is what you want.

Next you must caramelize the onions, and this should take a long time—the process creates the fundamental excellence of an onion soup. You can't grow impatient and hurry them; you'll burn them, and the soup will taste bitter. By cooking the onions very slowly, you caramelize the entire julienne, not just the surface. Once you've cut your onions correctly and caramelized them just right, uniformly to their center, you're 75 percent of the way there—you've done the most critical of the tasks. Cooking onions well requires dedication—you must stand and stir and watch—and your soup will be better if you enjoy what you're doing.

After that, it's broth and seasoning. The broth can be many things. We use a light beef broth, which is classic. But you could use vegetable stock for a vegetarian soup, or chicken

ONIONS: The onion is one of the sweetest vegetables, and its many varieties, used in numerous forms in this style of cooking, make it the most important vegetable in the bistro kitchen. The common yellow onion is so essential at the French Laundry that we plant hundreds of them to harvest in the spring. At Bouchon, members of the onion family are featured in soups or in cold vinaigrettes; sometimes they are a critical garnish, as the glazed pearl onions in a beef bourguignon. The shallot, one of the most common aromatic seasonings in the bistro kitchen, is also a featured ingredient, as on steak heaped with roughly chopped and quickly sautéed shallots. Because of the onion's unusual cell structure and its sulfur and sugar compounds, its transformations depend on the kind of heat put to it. High heat makes crispy onions; low slow heat brings out deep color and sweetness; poaching avoids caramelization and color.

VESSELS: Certain vessels are associated with specific preparations: the raised platter of the *plateau,* the *pot* for mustard, the egg cup, the toast holder, the glass jar with its rubber gasket, *rillette pots,* even the onion soup bowl—with its bellylike bowl and narrower opening, without which you can't have a perfect onion soup, no matter how well you've caramelized your onions or made your broth. The excellence of onion soup is all about the ratio of its four main components—broth, onions, cheese, and croutons—and without the proper bowl, that ratio is inevitably out of sync.

stock, or even water, depending on how rich or light you want your soup and what you have on hand. (Use water before reaching for canned broth—the sweetness of the onions is so fine that it will be lost in salty processed liquids.) Seasoning should be minimal: a little bit of salt, a few drops of vinegar. Nothing should interfere with the sweetness of the onions.

Try to wait a day before serving the soup—it ages beautifully. Then prepare the croutons and cheese. Traditionally, sliced stale bread is used for croutons. To become a crouton, bread has to be cooked all the way through, in a low oven for a long time, until it's crusty at its center. It has to be the right size—it needs to float and be big enough to support the cheese—about a half inch thick. It can't be too big or it will interfere with the soup.

Use a good Comté or Emmentaler in the correct amount—the last thing you want is too much cheese. At Bouchon, we use slices first, with grated cheese on top of them to ensure uniform melting. You've got to leave the dish under the broiler long enough for it to develop that crust on top while the cheese below the surface melts, and the soup has to be really hot to maintain the molten quality in the cheese. There's a lot going on in onion soup. The richness of the fat, the sweetness of the onions, the satisfying broth, the bread soaked through but with enough body that you need to cut it, and the textures—the molten cheese beneath a crispy crust.

Previous page: Jeff at a market in France
Left: Onion Soup

ONION SOUP—SOUPE À L'OIGNON

SACHET

2 bay leaves

12 black peppercorns

6 large thyme sprigs

SOUP

8 pounds (about 8 large) yellow onions

8 tablespoons (4 ounces) unsalted butter

Kosher salt

1 1/2 teaspoons all-purpose flour

Beef Stock (page 319)

Freshly ground black pepper

Sherry wine vinegar

CROUTONS

1 baguette (about 2 1/2 inches in diameter)

Extra virgin olive oil

Kosher salt

6 to 12 slices (1/8 inch thick) aged
　　Comté or Emmentaler cheese
　　(at least 4 inches square)

1 1/2 cups grated aged Comté or
　　Emmentaler cheese, or a combination

The more basic the soup, the more critical the details: Slice the onions uniformly and brown them very slowly and evenly; slice the bread a half inch thick and dry it completely in the oven; and serve the soup in appropriately sized bowls so that the melted cheese extends over the rim. When you hit it right, there's nothing more satisfying to cook or to eat than this soup.

It's worth reiterating the importance of cooking the onions slowly so that the natural sugars caramelize rather than brown through high-heat sautéing. The onions cook for about five hours and need to be stirred often, but they can be made up to two days ahead. The soup is best if refrigerated for a day or two so that the flavors of the onions and beef broth can deepen.

Comté is traditionally the cheese of choice, but Emmentaler works as well. Gruyère is a bit strong. Use an aged cheese; a younger cheese would just melt and wouldn't form a crust.

FOR THE SACHET: Cut a piece of cheesecloth about 7 inches square. Place the bay leaves, peppercorns, and thyme in the center, bring up the edges, and tie with kitchen twine to form a sachet.

FOR THE SOUP: Cut off the tops and bottoms of the onions, then cut the onions lengthwise in half. Remove the peels and tough outer layers. Cut a V wedge in each one to remove the core and pull out any solid, flat pieces of onion running up from the core.

Lay an onion half cut side down on a cutting board with the root end toward you. Note that there are lines on the outside of the onion. Cutting on the lines (with the grain) rather than against them will help the onions soften. Holding the knife on an angle, almost parallel to the board, cut the onion lengthwise into 1/4-inch-thick slices. Once you've cut past the center of the onion, the knife angle will become awkward: Flip the onion onto its side, toward the knife, and finish slicing it, again along the grain. Separate the slices of onion, trimming away any root sections that are still attached and holding the slices together. Repeat with the remaining onions. (You should have about 7 quarts of onions.)

Melt the butter in a large heavy stockpot over medium heat. Add the onions and 1 tablespoon salt, place a diffuser under the pot, and reduce the heat to low. Cook, stirring every 15 minutes and regulating the heat to keep the mixture bubbling gently, for about 1 hour, or until the onions have wilted and released a lot of liquid. At this point, you can turn up the heat slightly to reduce the liquid, but it is important to continue to cook the onions slowly to develop the maximum flavor and keep them from scorching. Continue to stir the onions every 15 minutes, being sure to scrape the bottom and get into the corners of the pot, for about 4 hours more, or until the onions are caramelized throughout and a rich deep brown. Keep a closer eye on the onions toward the end of cooking when the liquid has evaporated. Remove from the heat. (You will need 1 1/2 cups of onions for the soup; reserve any extra for another use. The onions can be made up to 2 days ahead and refrigerated.)

Transfer the caramelized onions to a 5-quart pot (if they've been refrigerated, reheat until hot). Sift in the flour and cook over medium-high heat, stirring, for 2 to 3 minutes. Add the beef stock and sachet, bring to a simmer, and simmer for about 1 hour, or until the liquid is reduced to 2 1/2 quarts. Season to taste with salt, pepper, and a few drops of vinegar. Remove from the heat.

FOR THE CROUTONS: Preheat the broiler. Cut twelve 3/8-inch-thick slices from the baguette (reserve the remainder for another use) and place on a baking sheet. Brush the bread lightly on both sides with olive oil and sprinkle lightly with salt. Place under the broiler and toast the first side until golden brown, then turn and brown the second side. Set aside and leave the broiler on.

TO COMPLETE: Return the soup to a simmer. Place six flameproof soup tureens, with about 1 1/2 cups capacity (see Sources, page 330), on a baking sheet to catch any spills (the soup will bubble up and over the tureens). Add the hot soup to the tureens, filling them to within 1/2 inch of the tops. Top each serving with 2 croutons: Lay them on the surface—do not push them into the soup. Lay the slices of cheese over the croutons so that the cheese overlaps the edges of the tureens by about 1/2 inch. Scatter the grated cheese over the sliced cheese, filling in areas where the sliced cheese is thinner, or it may melt into the soup rather than forming a crust.

Place the tureens under the broiler for a few minutes, until the cheese bubbles, browns, and forms a thick crust. Eat carefully; the soup will be very hot.

PHOTOGRAPH ON PAGE 46   **MAKES 6 SERVINGS**

LENTIL SOUP—SOUPE AUX LENTILLES

SOUP

4 ounces slab bacon

½ cup drained Soffritto (page 314)

⅔ cup Le Puy lentils (see Sources, page 330),
  picked over for stones and rinsed

½ large onion, peeled

1 large carrot, peeled

1 large leek, white and light green parts only,
  cut lengthwise in half and washed

Sachet (page 325), made with 4 garlic cloves

8 cups Basic Chicken Jus (page 321) or
  4 cups Veal Stock (page 318) plus 4 cups
  Chicken Stock (page 317)

GARNISHES

16 baby turnips, peeled, or 4 small turnips,
  peeled and cut into 4 wedges each

2 thyme sprigs

2 bay leaves

12 black peppercorns

Kosher salt

16 baby leeks, small ramps, or spring onions
  or 32 thin scallions

16 red pearl onions, cooked (see page 326)

16 white pearl onions, cooked (see page 326)

¾ cup diced (¼ inch) carrots, blanched in
  boiling salted water until tender

24 small or medium cloves Garlic Confit
  (page 312)

2 tablespoons chopped Italian parsley

2 tablespoons minced chives

Extra virgin olive oil

Legumes almost always benefit from bacon, and here the soffritto, a rich onion preparation, adds a complexity that earthy lentil soup often lacks. This soup is distinguished by lots of garnish—leeks, red and white pearl onions, carrots, garlic confit, and chopped fresh herbs.

FOR THE SOUP: Score the fatty side of the bacon in a crosshatch pattern about ¼ inch deep. Heat a medium saucepan over medium heat. Add the bacon fatty side down and let it render its fat for about 3 minutes. Add the soffritto, stir, then add the lentils and stir to mix well. Add the onion, carrot, leek, sachet, and jus. Bring to a simmer and cook for 25 to 35 minutes, or until the lentils are tender.

Remove the bacon, onion, carrot, and leek from the soup and discard the vegetables. Cut away the layer of fat from the bacon and cut the bacon into lardons about 1½ inches long and ⅜ inch thick. Return the lardons to the pan if serving right away or transfer to a container and refrigerate until ready to serve. (The soup is best made at least a day ahead, and it can be refrigerated for up to 2 days.)

FOR THE GARNISHES: Put the turnips in a small saucepan with just enough cold water to cover. Add the thyme, bay leaves, and peppercorns and season with enough salt so the water tastes like the sea. Bring to a simmer and cook until the turnips are just tender, 4 to 5 minutes; drain. If using baby turnips, cut each one in half. Set aside.

Prepare an ice bath and bring a large pot of salted water to a boil. Meanwhile, trim away just the tough dark green ends of the leeks, ramps, spring onions, or scallions, leaving some dark green leaves. Add to the boiling water and blanch until tender. Transfer to the ice bath to chill, then drain on paper towels. If you are using leeks or spring onions, cut them lengthwise in half.

TO SERVE: Bring the soup to a simmer over medium heat. Add the turnips, leeks, pearl onions, diced carrots, and garlic confit. Simmer for 5 minutes, then stir in the herbs and salt and pepper to taste. Ladle into bowls and serve with a drizzle of olive oil.

MAKES 6 TO 8 SERVINGS

SPRING VEGETABLE SOUP—SOUPE DE LÉGUMES PRINTANIERS

SOUP

1 large carrot (of as uniform thickness
   as possible)

One 2 1/2-inch-thick wedge of savoy cabbage

1 small leek

4 to 6 baby turnips

1 to 2 celery stalks

4 to 6 small fingerling or marble potatoes
   (no wider than 1/2 inch in diameter)

1 tablespoon extra virgin olive oil

1 tablespoon unsalted butter

2 ounces Bayonne ham or prosciutto
   (not sliced)

2 large garlic cloves, peeled and thinly sliced

Kosher salt and freshly ground black pepper

Sachet (page 325)

One 1-ounce piece of Parmigiano-Reggiano
   cheese or piece of Parmigiano rind

8 cups Chicken Stock (page 317) or
   Vegetable Stock (page 320)

GARNISHES

1 pound fava beans in the pod

16 medium asparagus spears

24 small shiitake mushrooms, cleaned
   (see page 326)

8 pieces Tomato Confit (page 313)

2 tablespoons chopped Italian parsley

2 tablespoons minced chives

Shavings of Parmigiano-Reggiano cheese

Extra virgin olive oil

This straightforward soup is so loaded with vegetables that it's almost like a stew. At the same time, it's very light and brothy, and the Parmigiano cheese and Bayonne ham—the French version of prosciutto or dry-cured ham—provide some meaty, salty seasoning.

This soup is best if refrigerated for a day, or you can serve it the day it's made. It is important, however, to prepare the garnishes shortly before serving.

FOR THE SOUP: You will need 1/2 cup of each of the sliced vegetables for the soup.

Peel the carrot and cut away the ends. Cut it lengthwise in half, then cut each half lengthwise again to give you 4 pieces. Cut each piece crosswise into 1/4-inch-thick slices.

Remove any dark green outer leaves from the cabbage and reserve for another use. Place the wedge cut side down on a cutting board and cut crosswise into 1/4-inch-wide slices.

Cut away the dark green leaves and root end of the leek. Cut the leek lengthwise in half and rinse well under cold water. Cut each piece of leek lengthwise in half and then cut crosswise into 1/4-inch-wide slices.

Peel the baby turnips. Cut off the tops, then cut them into small wedges, about 1/2 inch thick.

Wash and trim the celery. Use a paring knife to pull away the strings, then cut the stalks into 1/4-inch-thick slices.

Wash the potatoes. Cut away and discard the ends, then cut the remaining potatoes into 1 1/2-inch-thick slices.

Heat the olive oil and butter in a large saucepan over medium heat. Add the ham skin or fat side down and the garlic and swirl the pan for a few seconds to coat the garlic, then sweat the garlic for a minute or two. Add the 1/2 cup each carrot, cabbage, leek, turnips, and celery, stir, and season to taste with salt and pepper. Cook gently for 2 to 3 minutes. Add the 1/2 cup potatoes, the sachet, Parmigiano, and stock and bring to a simmer. Add salt and pepper to taste and simmer for 20 to 30 minutes, until the potatoes are tender.

Meanwhile, prepare an ice bath. When the potatoes are tender, pour the soup into a bowl or other container and chill in the ice bath until cold, then cover and refrigerate until ready to serve. (The soup is best if it is refrigerated for a day.)

FOR THE GARNISHES: Prepare an ice bath.

Shell the fava beans and peel the skins from the beans (peeling the beans before cooking them prevents gases from being trapped between the beans and their skins that could cause discoloration). Remove the small germ at the side of each bean. (You should have about 1 cup of beans.) Blanch the beans in a large pot of generously salted water for about 5 minutes or until tender. Using a skimmer, immediately transfer to the ice bath to chill.

Cut away the bottom third of each asparagus spear and discard. Cut the remaining spears on a sharp bias into pieces about 1/4 inch thick and 1 1/2 to 2 inches long. Blanch the asparagus in the boiling water until just tender and transfer to the ice bath to chill. When they are cold, drain the favas and asparagus and spread on paper towels to drain.

Cut off and discard the mushroom stems, then cut the mushrooms into 1/4-inch-thick slices.

Cut each piece of tomato confit lengthwise into 4 pieces.

TO COMPLETE: If any fat has solidified on the surface of the soup, remove and discard it. Transfer the soup to a saucepan, and remove and discard the sachet and Parmigiano. Remove the ham, cut away any excess fat, and cut into lardons about 1 1/2 inches long and 1/4 inch thick. Return the lardons to the soup and bring the soup to a boil.

Add the mushrooms to the soup, reduce the heat, and simmer for a minute. Add the fava beans, asparagus, and tomato confit and remove from the heat. Stir in the parsley and chives, taste the soup, and adjust the seasoning.

Ladle the soup into bowls and garnish each bowl with a few shavings of Parmigiano-Reggiano and a drizzle of olive oil.

PHOTOGRAPH ON PAGE 54   **MAKES 6 TO 8 SERVINGS**

2 pounds (about 3 large) leeks

4 tablespoons (2 ounces) unsalted butter

Heaping ½ cup sliced (about ¼ inch thick) shallots

⅓ cup sliced (¼ inch thick) onions

Kosher salt and freshly ground black pepper

½ pound (about 1 large) russet potato, peeled

1 tablespoon minced garlic

Sachet (page 325)

5½ to 6½ cups Chicken Stock (page 317)

¾ cup heavy cream, warmed

½ cup minced chives

Extra virgin olive oil

Freshly ground black pepper

Potato leek soup, popularized in the United States as chilled vichyssoise by Louis Diaz at New York's Ritz-Carlton, is all about simplicity, economy, and deliciousness. Excellent on its own with abundant chopped chives, it can also be used as a base for any number of other soups by incorporating puréed greens, most notably spicy and sour ones such as arugula, watercress, and sorrel.

Cut away and discard the dark green leaves and roots from the leeks, leaving only the white and palest green sections. Cut them lengthwise in half and rinse under cold water to remove any dirt between the layers. Place the leeks cut side down on a cutting board and cut into ¼-inch-thick slices. (You should have 3 cups.)

Melt the butter in a large saucepan over medium-low heat. Add the leeks, shallots, and onions, and season generously with salt and pepper. Increase the heat to medium and sweat the vegetables, stirring often, for 3 to 5 minutes—the vegetables should wilt but not brown.

Meanwhile, cut the potato lengthwise into quarters, then cut crosswise into ¼-inch-thick slices. (You should have about 1¼ cups.)

Add the garlic to the sautéing vegetables and cook for another minute, then add the sachet and potatoes and cook for 2 to 4 minutes longer.

Add 5½ cups chicken stock and adjust the seasonings. Bring to a simmer, then reduce the heat and simmer for 30 minutes, or until the potatoes are tender. Remove from the heat and let the soup cool for about 15 minutes.

Remove the sachet. If you will be refrigerating the soup, prepare an ice bath.

Transfer the soup, in batches, to a blender and puree, starting at low speed (to release the heat remaining in the soup), then slowly increasing the speed until the soup is smooth. Be careful not to overfill the blender, as the hot liquid can spurt out from the top. For a more refined texture, strain the soup through a fine-meshed strainer.

TO COMPLETE: Return the soup to the rinsed-out pan and bring it to a simmer. Add the cream and simmer for 5 minutes. Remove from the heat. If you are serving the soup hot, stir in the chives, reserving about 1 teaspoon per serving for garnish. If you are refrigerating the soup, pour it into a container and place in the ice bath to cool. Reserve about 1 teaspoon of chives per bowl to garnish the soup and stir in the remaining chives. Cover and refrigerate for up to 2 days.

TO SERVE: Sprinkle the soup with the reserved chives, drizzle lightly with olive oil, and top each bowl with a grind of black pepper.

MAKES 6 TO 8 SERVINGS

SORREL SOUP

This is a variation of potato leek soup, using the very flavorful sorrel leaf as a seasoning and for its intense color. The soup and sorrel are blended, the hot soup blanching the leaves in the process. Other variations can be made by blending the potato leek soup with watercress or garden herbs. That's all there is to it.

$^{1}/_{2}$ recipe (3 $^{1}/_{2}$ cups) Potato Leek Soup (opposite), with the cream
    (6 tablespoons) added but without chives
6 ounces (about 2 cups) packed sorrel leaves, large stems removed,
    plus 3 tablespoons fine sorrel chiffonade
Kosher salt and freshly ground black pepper
$^{1}/_{4}$ cup crème fraîche
Extra virgin olive oil

Heat the soup in a saucepan until hot. Transfer to a blender, in batches if necessary, add the sorrel, and blend at high speed to puree. Season to taste with salt and pepper.

Ladle the soup into bowls and garnish each with a dollop of crème fraîche and a few strands of sorrel leaves. Drizzle lightly with olive oil and top each with a grind of black pepper.

MAKES 4 SERVINGS

A bistro is open all day long and serves food until late at night,

but it is most itself—that is, most distinguished from other kinds

of restaurants—during the hours between mealtimes, when you can

drop in for a soup, salad, sandwich, or, one of my favorites, quiche.

Opposite: Butternut Squash Soup with Brown Butter, Sage, and Nutmeg Crème Fraîche

(page 60)

BUTTERNUT SQUASH SOUP
WITH BROWN BUTTER, SAGE, AND NUTMEG CRÈME FRAÎCHE
SOUPE DE COURGE AU BEURRE NOISETTE ET À LA CRÈME FRAÎCHE MUSCADÉE

One 3- to 3½-pound butternut squash

2 tablespoons canola oil

Kosher salt and freshly ground black pepper

2 sage sprigs

1 cup thinly sliced (⅛ inch thick) leeks, white and light green parts only

½ cup thinly sliced (⅛ inch thick) carrots

½ cup thinly sliced (⅛ inch thick) shallots

½ cup thinly sliced (⅛ inch thick) onions

6 garlic cloves, peeled and smashed

2 tablespoons honey

6 cups Vegetable Stock (page 330), plus extra if necessary

Bouquet Garni (page 325)

4 tablespoons (2 ounces) unsalted butter

¼ cup crème fraîche

Freshly grated nutmeg

Canola oil (if using sage leaves)

8 sage leaves or 1 tablespoon minced chives

Kosher salt and freshly ground black pepper

Extra virgin olive oil

Butternut squash, brown butter, and sage are a classic combination in various cuisines, whether as soup, sauce, or pasta. This recipe combines roasted squash with sautéed squash, onions, and carrots, then is finished in vegetable stock and pureed for a soup that's a little thicker and more substantial than a cream soup. We like to make this a day ahead because the butternut squash gets sweeter if it rests. When serving, be careful not to burn the butter—as soon as it hits an aromatic hazelnut brown, add it to the soup, which will stop the butter's cooking as it seasons the soup.

FOR THE SOUP: Preheat the oven to 350°F. Line a small baking sheet with aluminum foil.

Cut the neck off the squash and set it aside. Cut the bulb in half and scoop out and discard the seeds. Brush each half inside and out with about 1½ teaspoons of the canola oil. Sprinkle the cavities with salt and pepper and tuck a sprig of sage into each. Place cut side down on the baking sheet and roast for about 1 hour, or until completely tender.

Remove the squash from the oven and set aside until cool enough to handle, then scoop out and reserve the flesh (discard the sage).

Meanwhile, using a paring knife or sharp vegetable peeler, peel away the skin from the neck of the squash until you reach the bright orange flesh. Cut the flesh into $1/2$-inch pieces (these will be pureed, so don't be concerned if the pieces are irregularly shaped). (You should have approximately 4 cups diced squash.)

Put the remaining 1 tablespoon canola oil in a stockpot over medium-high heat, add the leeks, carrots, shallots, and onions, and cook, stirring often, for about 6 minutes. Add the diced squash, garlic, $1 1/2$ teaspoons salt, and $1/2$ teaspoon pepper and cook gently for 3 minutes, reducing the heat as necessary to keep the garlic and squash from coloring. Stir in the honey and cook, stirring, for 2 to 3 minutes. Add the stock and bouquet garni, bring to a simmer, and cook for 10 to 15 minutes, or until the squash is tender.

Add the roasted squash and simmer gently for about 30 minutes for the flavors to blend. Remove from the heat and discard the bouquet garni.

Transfer the soup to a blender, in batches, and puree. Strain the soup through a fine strainer into a bowl or other container, tapping the side of the strainer so the soup passes through. Taste the soup and adjust the seasoning. Let the soup cool, then refrigerate until ready to serve.

TO COMPLETE: Place the crème fraîche in a chilled small metal bowl and stir in nutmeg to taste. Whisk with a small whisk until the crème fraiche holds a shape. Cover and refrigerate.

Reheat the soup. If it is too thick, add a little more vegetable stock.

Heat a medium skillet over high heat. When it is very hot, add the butter and rotate the skillet over the heat as necessary to brown the butter evenly, scraping up any bits that settle in the bottom. As soon as the foaming has subsided and the butter is a hazelnut brown, pour it into the pot of soup. (Be careful not to leave the butter over the heat too long, as it can change from rich brown to black in seconds.)

Meanwhile, if using the sage leaves, heat $1/8$ inch of canola oil in a small skillet. When the oil is very hot, add the sage and cook for 30 to 45 seconds, turning the leaves to crisp them on both sides. When the bubbling stops, the moisture in the leaves will have evaporated and the leaves will be crisp. Drain the sage on paper towels and sprinkle with salt.

Ladle the soup into four serving bowls. Top each with a dollop of crème fraîche. Grind some black pepper over the top and garnish each with 2 sage leaves or some minced chives. Drizzle a little olive oil over the top.

PHOTOGRAPH ON PAGE 59   **MAKES 6 SERVINGS**

{ THE VINAIGRETTE }

The vinaigrette may be the most versatile sauce in a cook's repertoire. The idea behind it—combining fat and acid—is simple, and the variations are endless.

Something sharp is often eaten at the beginning of the meal, whether it's a salad or marinated olives or some pâté with mustard. When that sharpness is a vinaigrette, on lentils or leeks, for example, it introduces the primary flavor components that ready your palate for the meal ahead: the rich sensuousness of the oil or other fat, the acidic counterpoint that makes other flavors bright without calling too much attention to itself, and the saltiness. Because it combines these three components so vividly, the vinaigrette is exciting in ways that a jus, a reduction, or a butter sauce can never be. The dominance of the acid, which is bright on the palate, the ease with which the fat can transmit flavors such as mustard or herbs or spices, and the variations possible within these spectrums make the vinaigrette an amazing tool for a cook. You might even call it the perfect sauce.

Look at the choices available to you simply by varying the kinds of oil (neutral, olive, walnut) or using an animal fat (an emulsified vinaigrette in which duck fat is served with a duck confit, for instance). You can vary your vinegars (sherry or champagne or balsamic) or use a different kind of acid (a citrus juice or verjus). Each choice determines the outcome: If citrus is the acid, the vinaigrette will be light and tangy; if an animal fat is used, the result will be complex and rich. A vinaigrette can be used for virtually any course in the meal, from a mustard vinaigrette for a charcuterie plate to a verjus vinaigrette in the dessert course.

All bistros have a standard vinaigrette, and a great one will have a great everyday vinaigrette. The house vinaigrette is typically a straightforward emulsified sauce flavored with shallots and mustard, salt and pepper. This can then be easily varied by adding, say, olives, or fines herbes, but the base is what's important. The bistro kitchen will also have,

Bibb Lettuce Salad (page 66)

FINES HERBES: *Fines herbes* are a mixture of fresh Italian parsley, tarragon, chervil, and chives, sometimes whole, sometimes chopped. I first became aware of the elegant combination of soft herbs in the *omelet fines herbes* in my early twenties. The herbs are spectacular with the delicate flavor of eggs, but they also complete many dishes, from meats to fish to vegetables, enhancing their freshness with very little effort. These herbs are easily grown and widely available. Chervil, which like tarragon is an anise-flavored herb, is the only member of the group that's less commonly available to the home cook; if you can't find it, simply omit it. Originally from Asia and now grown throughout the East and West, chervil is probably the most delicate of the herbs in structure, appearance, and taste, and its delicacy is precisely what makes it so appealing. Parsley adds a bitter note, and chives a sweet oniony component. Combined, these flavors not only enhance salad, chicken, fish, sauces, and shellfish, they do so in a way that is more satisfying than any one of these herbs could do by itself.

MIRRORS: A bistro is traditionally run on a very tight budget. In a city such as Paris, where rent is high, the restaurants tend to be small. Mirrors, of course, give a sense of spaciousness to a small room, and they do something else as well: They encourage people watching. They not only create a sense of space, but they reinforce the notion that this is a social place, one of the bistro's defining qualities. It's a restaurant where you often see the same people, because it's a neighborhood place. The interactions among the people in it are important, a fact that mirrors enhance and reinforce.

as we do, a few ancillary vinaigrettes for different salads, for example, a creamy vinaigrette for a Niçoise salad; ours is almost like a mayonnaise, which is an appropriate texture for a tuna salad. And we have a vinaigrette for spinach salad with hot bacon fat, shallots, and hard-cooked eggs. But again, what pushes the vinaigrette beyond other sauces in terms of its usefulness is that it's good for more than just salads.

We use a mignonette for shellfish at the bar; our version is simply red wine vinegar, shallots, and cracked pepper. The flavorful liquor from the oysters takes the place of the fat. We pair rich and succulent pigs' feet with a gribiche, a sharp vinaigrette made with cooked egg yolk, cornichons, and capers. And for the leek salad we use our house vinaigrette as a marinade.

The only hard part of making a great vinaigrette is finding the right ingredients. If one of them is mediocre (if the oil is old or the wrong kind, if the vinegar is cheap), then the resulting vinaigrette will be mediocre. For a standard vinaigrette, you need a good, fresh, neutral oil and a delicious vinegar, and, if you're using it, an excellent mustard. Everything else is formula, a recipe: three parts fat, one part acid. Adhere to the recipe and you'll have a great vinaigrette every time. As with all preparations, there are matters of finesse. Emulsified vinaigrettes are best the day after they've been made, the flavors having had a chance to mature together. Our basic vinaigrette is simple—no shallots, not even salt and pepper—and makes powerful use of fresh herbs, but they must be added at the last minute or the vinegar will turn them brown. With the Bibb salad, we give a little blast of fresh lemon juice at the end to make it really sparkle.

But ultimately the most important step in making a great vinaigrette is the simplest of ideas: Combine great ingredients in the proper proportions.

BIBB LETTUCE SALAD—SALADE DE LAITUE

4 heads Bibb lettuce

Kosher salt and freshly ground black pepper

2 tablespoons minced shallots

2 tablespoons minced chives

¼ cup Italian parsley leaves

¼ cup tarragon leaves

¼ cup chervil leaves

½ cup House Vinaigrette (page 315)

1 tablespoon plus 1 teaspoon fresh
lemon juice

The word *laitue* comes from the Latin word for milk, from the milky juices some lettuces can exude. Hearty, buttery Bibb leaves are a good example of the rich, juicy quality lettuce can have. They're so big and rich, in fact, that this salad almost qualifies as a meal in itself.

This salad is all about freshness. Use plenty of freshly picked fines herbes: parsley, chives, tarragon, and chervil; harder herbs, such as savory, rosemary, and marjoram, would be too strong. Finish it with a squeeze of lemon juice.

Buy nice rounded, mature heads of Bibb lettuce, with good weight; these will have the greatest amount of tender yellow interior leaves. If the leaves have become at all soft and leathery, a rinse in cold water will refresh them.

Carefully cut out the core from each head of lettuce and separate the leaves, but keep each head of lettuce together; discard any tough outer leaves. Because each head of lettuce will be reassembled, the easiest way to work is with one head at a time. First, place the leaves in a bowl of cold water to refresh them and remove any dirt, then lift out and spin-dry in a salad spinner.

Place the leaves from a single head of lettuce in a bowl. Sprinkle with a pinch of salt, a few grinds of pepper, 1½ teaspoons of the shallots and chives, and 1 tablespoon each of the parsley, tarragon, and chervil. Then toss gently with 2 tablespoons of the vinaigrette and 1 teaspoon of lemon juice. Repeat with the remaining heads.

For each serving, arrange the outer lettuce leaves as a base on the plate and rebuild each head of lettuce, ending with the smallest, most tender leaves.

PHOTOGRAPH ON PAGE 62   **MAKES 4 SERVINGS**

ENDIVE SALAD WITH SMOKED TROUT AND LEMON VINAIGRETTE
SALADE D'ENDIVES ET DE TRUITE FUMÉE À LA VINAIGRETTE CITRONNÉE

LEMON VINAIGRETTE

2 large lemons

1 hard-cooked egg yolk (see page 326)

1/2 teaspoon whole-grain mustard

1 1/2 teaspoons Dijon mustard

1/2 cup canola oil

1 tablespoon minced cornichons

1 tablespoon minced drained nonpareil
    capers, preferably Spanish

POTATOES

8 ounces small fingerling potatoes
    (no wider in diameter than a quarter)

1/4 teaspoon black peppercorns

2 thyme sprigs

1 bay leaf

2 garlic cloves, skin left on, smashed

Kosher salt

SALAD

4 small heads Belgian endive

4 small heads red Belgian endive

8 ounces smoked trout fillet, skin and bones
    removed

1/4 cup minced shallots

1/4 cup minced chives

1 tablespoon plus 1 teaspoon drained
    nonpareil capers, preferably Spanish

Kosher salt and freshly ground black pepper

1/4 cup chervil leaves

1/4 cup tarragon leaves

1/4 cup Italian parsley leaves

12 caper berries, drained

This is a traditional smoked fish salad, with a crisp flavorful lettuce, potatoes, and a thick, creamy, lemony vinaigrette. Here again a preserved food, critical to the bistro kitchen, is at the center of the dish. Smoked fish and potatoes always make a great combination because the potatoes carry the smoked flavor so nicely. This salad also works well with watercress or any spicy lettuce. In the fall, you can add some crisp tart apple, finely sliced or julienned.

FOR THE VINAIGRETTE: Remove the zest from the lemons (a Microplane grater does an excellent job). Finely chop the zest. (You should have about 1 tablespoon.) Set aside. Squeeze 2 tablespoons juice from 1 of the lemons; reserve the remaining lemon for another use.

Place the egg yolk in a small deep bowl and crush it with a fork. Add the lemon juice and mustards and combine well with a hand blender or a whisk. With the blender running, or whisking constantly, slowly drizzle in the oil until emulsified. Mix in the lemon zest, cornichons, and capers.

FOR THE POTATOES: Wash the potatoes and slice them into 1/4-inch-thick slices. Put the potatoes, peppercorns, thyme, bay leaf, and garlic in a medium saucepan. Add cold water to cover by 1 inch and season the water with salt until it tastes like the sea. Bring to a boil over high heat, reduce the heat, and simmer for about 10 minutes, or until the potatoes are tender; drain. Discard the seasonings and garlic.

FOR THE SALAD: Remove and discard any bruised outer leaves from the heads of endive and cut each head lengthwise in half. Cut out and discard the cores. Place the endives cut side down on a cutting board and cut on the diagonal into 1/4-inch-thick slices. Combine the endive and potatoes in a bowl.

Break the trout into 1- to 1 1/2-inch chunks and add to the bowl, along with the shallots, chives, and capers. Toss the salad with about 1/2 cup of the dressing, or as needed to coat the ingredients, and season to taste with salt and pepper. Add the chervil, tarragon, and parsley leaves.

TO SERVE: Mound the salad in the center of four serving plates. Top each salad with 3 caper berries.

MAKES 4 SERVINGS

CHILLED ASPARAGUS WITH VINAIGRETTE AND EGGS MIMOSA
ASPERGES EN VINAIGRETTE ET ŒUFS MIMOSA

2 pounds medium asparagus

1 tablespoon plus 2 teaspoons extra virgin
    olive oil, plus extra for drizzling

Kosher salt

10 hard-cooked large eggs (see page 326)

2 large radishes

½ cup House Vinaigrette (page 315)

Freshly ground black pepper

1 tablespoon plus 1 teaspoon minced chives

Freshly cooked asparagus served cold with mimosa and a house vinaigrette is as classic as leeks vinaigrette. The mimosa—grated hard-cooked egg yolk, sieved so that it almost melts in your mouth—goes as well with the cold asparagus as hollandaise, also a yolk-based sauce, goes with hot asparagus. The flavor is boosted by the addition of an asparagus coulis made from the trimmings. We tie our asparagus in bundles, which helps to protect the delicate tips from being damaged in the agitation of the boiling water.

Remove the tough ends of the asparagus by holding the center of each stalk with one hand and bending the bottom end of the stalk until it snaps off naturally; with the other hand discard the ends. Line up the asparagus spears, tips facing the same direction, on a cutting board and trim the ends so that the spears are of equal length, reserving the trimmings. Place the trimmings in a measuring cup. (You will need 2 cups of asparagus pieces to make the coulis; cut enough additional asparagus spears into 1-inch pieces to make 2 cups. There is no need to peel these trimmings; leaving the skin on will make the coulis a vivid green.) Set aside. Peel the asparagus spears, beginning about 1 inch below the base of the tip.

Bring a large pot of generously salted water to a boil and prepare an ice bath.

Divide the asparagus spears into four piles, again with the tips facing the same way. Cut 4 pieces of kitchen twine about 2 feet long and tie the spears into bundles: Leaving a 3-inch end of the twine free, start by wrapping the twine securely around the top of the bundle (just below the tips), then wrap the remaining twine down and around the bottom and tie the ends of the twine together.

When the water is boiling, add the asparagus and blanch for 4 to 6 minutes, or until just tender. Transfer to the ice bath (leave the water boiling).

Add the trimmings to the boiling water and blanch for 4 to 7 minutes, or until very tender; it is important that they be entirely tender, as they will be pureed.

Meanwhile, when the asparagus bundles are cold, transfer to paper towels, remove the twine, and let drain; then refrigerate for at least 15 minutes. (The asparagus can be prepared up to a day ahead.) Replenish the ice in the ice bath if necessary.

When the asparagus trimmings are tender, remove them and reserve about 1/2 cup of the water. Drain the asparagus pieces in a strainer and immediately plunge the strainer into the ice bath. Once the asparagus are cool, remove the strainer and drain them on paper towels.

Add the asparagus pieces to a blender, along with 3 tablespoons of the reserved cooking liquid, or just enough to allow the blade to turn, and pulse to break up the asparagus, then blend to a puree. It may be necessary to stop and scrape down the sides of the blender several times; be patient. Add more of the cooking liquid only if necessary. When the coulis is smooth, blend in the 1 tablespoon oil. Season to taste with salt. Strain the coulis if there are any fibers in it. (You will have about 1/2 cup. Refrigerate the coulis for at least 15 minutes, or up to a day.)

TO COMPLETE: Remove the yolks from the hard-cooked eggs. Reserve the whites for another use, if desired. Push the yolks through the large holes of a grater, then finely chop.

Wash the radishes and cut off and discard the tops and bottoms. Thinly slice the radishes, then cut the slices into fine julienne.

TO SERVE: Arrange the asparagus in four stacks, with all the tips facing the same direction (check your serving plates to be sure the spears will fit and trim the ends of the stalks if necessary). Sprinkle each stack with a pinch of salt.

Spoon about 2 tablespoons of asparagus coulis into a pool in the center of each serving plate. Top with the asparagus spears. Spoon 2 tablespoons of vinaigrette over the center of each mound of spears. Sprinkle the egg yolks over the vinaigrette, then sprinkle the yolks with a pinch each of kosher salt and a few grinds of black pepper.

Toss the radishes with the chives, 2 teaspoons of the olive oil, and salt and pepper to taste. Place the radish mixture on the egg yolks and drizzle lightly with additional oil.

MAKES 4 SERVINGS

CHILLED LEEKS WITH VINAIGRETTE AND EGGS MIMOSA
POIREAUX EN VINAIGRETTE ET ŒUFS MIMOSA

8 medium leeks (about 1 inch in diameter)

Kosher salt and freshly ground black pepper

2 cups House Vinaigrette (page 315)

¼ cup julienned (¼ inch wide) piquillo peppers (see Sources, page 330)

10 hard-cooked large eggs (see page 326)

2 tablespoons plus 2 teaspoons minced chives

Extra virgin olive oil for drizzling

Leeks are a succulent vegetable. When they're cooked correctly, they have a rich, creamy, full texture in the mouth, though in fact they're very lean. I love how they satisfy a craving for richness without fat. They're sweet, but they finish with an acidic effect. Cold leeks served with vinaigrette is a bistro dish I never get tired of eating. The leeks can be boiled or, as at Bouchon, steamed; in either case, they need to be well cooked or they'll be difficult to cut—but not so cooked that they become mushy.

One of the strengths of this recipe is that the cooked leeks are marinated for a day in a vinaigrette that's been diluted by half, so they really absorb that vinaigrette flavor. We serve it with mimosa—a garnish of sieved hard-cooked egg yolks, named after a family of trees and bushes known for its bright yellow flower. The eggs increase the creamy richness of the dish and balance the acidity of the vinaigrette, but if eating eggs is a concern, use fewer than the recipe calls for.

We julienne a special smoked red pepper, a piquillo, from the Basque region of Spain, to top the mimosa. It's got vivid color and a sweet, smoky flavor that's well worth seeking out, but you can substitute roasted red peppers if you wish. Serve with a great baguette to sop up the dressing and egg yolks.

Trim the hairy roots from the leeks, but leave the root end intact. Remove and discard any tough outer leaves. Cut off and discard the dark green tops. To clean the leeks, split each leek lengthwise, beginning about 1 inch up from the root end and, holding the leek open, rinse under warm water.

Fit a large pot with a steamer insert, add water, and bring to a boil. Tie the tops of the leeks together with kitchen twine to hold them together during steaming. Add the leeks to the steamer, cover, and steam for about 10 minutes, or until tender throughout when pierced with a knife. Remove from the steamer and let cool for about 5 minutes. (Because the leeks will turn "olive drab" after marinating, there is no need to shock them in an ice bath.) Discard the twine and cut through the root ends of the leeks to split them completely in half. Place cut side up in a shallow baking dish and sprinkle lightly with salt and pepper.

Whisk 1 cup of the vinaigrette with 1 cup cold water. Pour over the leeks, cover, and refrigerate for at least 6 hours, or up to 2 days.

TO SERVE: Season the piquillo peppers with salt and pepper. Separate the egg whites and egg yolks. Push the yolks through the large holes of a grater, then finely chop. Reserve the whites for another use, if desired.

Remove the leeks from the marinade; discard the marinade. Trim the root ends, leaving only the tender leek. (If the leeks are longer than your serving plates, trim the greens as necessary to fit.)

Sprinkle the leeks with salt and pepper. Stack the leek halves cut side down in piles of two and crisscross two piles on each plate to form an X. Spoon the remaining vinaigrette over the centers of the salads. Sprinkle the egg yolks over the vinaigrette, then sprinkle the yolks with a pinch of salt and a few grinds of pepper. Garnish the center of each salad with a small mound of peppers, sprinkle each salad with 2 teaspoons minced chives, and drizzle with a little olive oil.

MAKES 4 SERVINGS

WATERCRESS-ENDIVE SALAD WITH ROQUEFORT AND WALNUTS
SALADE DE CRESSON ET ENDIVES AU ROQUEFORT ET AUX NOIX

WALNUT VINAIGRETTE

1 tablespoon Dijon mustard

1 tablespoon plus 1 teaspoon champagne
vinegar

1 tablespoon plus 1 teaspoon lemon juice

$\frac{1}{2}$ cup walnut oil

Kosher salt and freshly ground black pepper

SALAD

32 (about 1 cup) walnuts

3 $\frac{1}{2}$ to 4 ounces (1 to 2 bunches) watercress,
preferably hydroponic

4 heads Belgian endive

Kosher salt and freshly ground black pepper

2 tablespoons minced shallots

2 tablespoons minced chives

$\frac{1}{4}$ cup Italian parsley leaves

$\frac{1}{4}$ cup tarragon leaves

$\frac{1}{4}$ cup chervil leaves

4 ounces Roquefort cheese, finely crumbled

Two excellent salads—watercress and endive for spring
and summer, and mâche and roasted beets (page 76)
for fall and winter—combine peppery, bitter, spicy, rich,
and creamy components. Try to find hydroponic watercress,
which is milder (regular cress can be too spicy), for this salad.

FOR THE VINAIGRETTE: I like to emulsify the dressing,
but it can also simply be whisked.

For an emulsified dressing, combine the mustard, vinegar,
and lemon juice in a small container (a pint container works
well for this) and mix together with a hand blender. With the
blender running, slowly drizzle in the walnut oil. Season to
taste with salt and pepper.

For a whisked dressing, combine the mustard, vinegar, and
lemon juice in a small bowl and whisk together. Place the bowl
on a dish towel to keep it from moving and gradually whisk in
the oil. Season to taste with salt and pepper.

(The dressing can be refrigerated for up to a week. If the
emulsified dressing breaks, it can be recombined with an
immersion blender.)

FOR THE SALAD: Preheat the oven to 350°F.

Spread the walnuts on a baking sheet and toast for about
10 minutes, until lightly browned and fragrant. Set aside to cool.

If using hydroponic watercress, cut off and discard the roots
and bottom 3 inches of the stems. If using regular watercress,
remove and discard any tough stems. If necessary, carefully wash
and thoroughly dry the watercress. Place the watercress in a bowl.

Remove and discard any discolored outer leaves from the endive.
Cut off the root ends and remove about 8 outer leaves from each
head of endive; reserve the hearts of the endive for another use.
Trim the bottoms of the leaves as necessary.

Sprinkle the watercress with salt and pepper Add the endive
leaves and toss with the shallots, chives, and herb leaves. Add just
enough of the dressing to coat the greens and toss gently. Toss in
the walnuts. Carefully toss in the Roquefort.

Arrange 3 or 4 dressed endive leaves in the center of each plate.
Stack the salad on top, interspersing it with the remaining endive
leaves.

MAKES 4 SERVINGS

The bouchon of Lyon is similar to the bistro in its comfortable, convivial atmosphere, but, in fact, it's a distinct type of restaurant. In Lyon, a bouchon association actually designates about two dozen *vrai bouchons,* or "true bouchons," in this city in central France that teems with restaurants.

The first bouchons as we know them today appeared toward the end of the nineteenth century, though they have roots extending back into the Middle Ages, according to the Lyonnais food journalist and author Pierre Grison, serving from the outset as refuge for the traveler—a place to rest himself and his horse, and to have some food and wine.

Bouchon means "cork" or "stopper," and some bouchons today have an image of a cork on their shingles, but the more commonly accepted derivation of the name *bouchon* is that the first proprietors put a pine branch or bouquet—called a *bousche*—above their doors, a reference to Bacchus that announced that they served wine. Others note that the traveler could have his horse rubbed down (*bouchonner*) with a bundle of hay (*bouchon*).

Though bouchons range from those that feel very much like restaurants (Brunet on rue Claudia) to those that are ultra-homey (Chez Paul on rue du Major Martin and Hugon on rue Pizay), the food and the wine are similar, as is the generosity of spirit that infuses their ambience.

The food you'll be served in a bouchon Lyonnais is humble—beans, sausage, stews. The wines are those of the neighboring regions, light and young and easy to drink. The room is so small that you may be seated elbow to elbow. The kitchen stove is typically in view, and sometimes the kitchen refrigerator is in the dining room, beside the bar. Curtains hang in windows, coats hang on hooks, and the husband and wife proprietors—the cook and the server—greet most of their customers by name, because one returns to one's neighborhood bouchon as if it were a second home.

Sometimes you will be given a menu, but just as often the food will simply appear: saucissons, including thin slices of a Lyonnais specialty called *rosette,* and some thinly sliced *jambon cru* (cured ham that should be sliced so thinly, the saying goes, it has only one side). A crock filled with *rillettes de porc* will be lifted from another table and set down on yours for you to enjoy. Headcheese, sliced thin, is set down, too. A bowl of white beans with a light dressing and chopped chives will appear. All these are passed around the table. A tray of bread will be replenished continually throughout the meal. Empty *pots* (the bistro version of carafes) of Côtes du Rhône are refilled. A dish of steamed cauliflower arrives with a sharp vinaigrette as thick as mayonnaise to spoon over the vegetable, along with a bowl of lentils also dressed with a vinaigrette. Then a bowl of herring preserved in oil with onions and other aromatics. As the table finishes with each, the proprietress will carry the bowls to the next ready table, then return to tell you the day's main courses.

These courses seem to be all but unvarying and are among the most emblematic descriptions of *le vrai bouchon*: the *tête de veau* (braised veal head) and *pieds de cochon* (braised pigs' feet), the andouillettes, which are chitterlings sausage—sausage casings filled with pork intestines and sometimes other offal, caul fat, perhaps some tripe—served on a mustard cream sauce, nothing else on the plate. Or some hot garlic sausage and a few boiled potatoes, a thick cake of salted butter

for the sauce, or tripe breaded and fried for a dish called *tablier du sapeur* ("fireman's apron") for its leatherlike appearance and texture. And there's always beef bourguignon with noodles and sautéed spinach, or *steak frites*.

These will be followed by some cheeses, invariably the creamy local specialty, St. Marcellin, as well as fresh plain curd cheese, or the crème-fraîche-like *cervelle de canut* (cow's milk curd mixed with shallots and herbs). And then dessert, a simple apple tart, perhaps, and a bowl of prunes stewed in spiced wine. Last, coffee and, depending on your mood, some marc, a spirit made from the grapes of nearby vineyards.

If you've lingered over lunch and are among the last to leave, you'll see the owner starting his *blanquette de veau* for the evening's service, and slicing leftover headcheese to dress it with vinaigrette for a dinner salad: Nothing is wasted.

And that's a typical meal at an authentic bouchon Lyonnais, a style of restaurant I really admire. Prepared with care, the meal is a fine and soul-warming experience.

ROASTED BEET AND MÂCHE SALAD WITH GOAT CHEESE AND TOASTED WALNUTS

SALADE DE BETTERAVES ET MÂCHE AU CHÈVRE FRAIS ET AUX NOIX

16 walnuts (about ½ cup)

8 baby beets (about the size of golf balls)

2 tablespoons plus 1 teaspoon extra virgin olive oil

Kosher salt and freshly ground black pepper

1 teaspoon red wine vinegar

2 ounces mâche

2 teaspoons minced shallots

2 teaspoons minced chives

2 teaspoons chervil leaves

2 teaspoons tarragon leaves

2 teaspoons Italian parsley leaves

2 to 3 tablespoons Walnut Vinaigrette (page 71)

4 ounces fresh goat cheese

Walnut oil

The hardest part of making this recipe is keeping myself from eating the beets straight out of the oven with a little salt and butter. Honestly, it's pure joy to eat a roasted beet the moment it's out of the foil. When I was young, the only kind of beet I knew came from a can. Why do we put beets in cans? When I lived in France, beets were the only vegetable at the open markets that was sold cooked. Sometimes they were still steaming. People would buy them to make a salad like this, with creamy cheese, crunchy nuts, and an excellent green.

For a good variation, add pear and "mountain spinach," or *arroche*.

Preheat the oven to 350°F.

Spread the walnuts on a baking sheet and toast for about 10 minutes, until lightly browned and fragrant. Set aside to cool.

Wash the beets and trim the stems to about 1 inch. Place them in a small baking pan and toss with the 2 tablespoons of olive oil, 2 tablespoons water, ½ teaspoon salt, and ⅛ teaspoon pepper.

Cover the pan with aluminum foil and roast for about 50 minutes, or until there is no resistance when the beets are pierced with a sharp paring knife. Remove the beets from the oven and let cool.

When they are cool enough to handle, place a warm beet on a paper towel and rub gently with the towel to remove the skin. Repeat with the remaining beets. Trim away and discard the stems and any roots. Quarter the beets, place them in a bowl, and toss with a pinch each of salt and pepper, the remaining 1 teaspoon olive oil, and the vinegar. Set aside.

Place the mâche in a small bowl. Toss with the shallots, herbs, and about 1 tablespoon of the vinaigrette, or just enough to lightly coat the greens. Season to taste with salt and pepper.

Place a mound of mâche in the center of each plate. Arrange the beets around the mâche and garnish with the walnuts. Use a spoon to scoop small pieces of the goat cheese and distribute them among the salads. Spoon a little additional dressing around each salad and drizzle the plates with a little walnut oil.

MAKES 4 SERVINGS

MARINATED SQUID SALAD WITH ENGLISH CUCUMBER AND TOMATOES
SALADE D'ENCORNETS AUX TOMATES ET CONCOMBRE

1 pound small squid (2 to 3 inches long)
Canola oil
Kosher salt and freshly ground black pepper
2 tablespoons extra virgin olive oil, plus more
    for garnishing

1 tablespoon red wine vinegar
1 English cucumber
16 thin slices red or yellow heirloom or vine-
    ripened tomatoes
1 tablespoon minced shallots

1 tablespoon plus 1 teaspoon chopped Italian
    parsley, plus whole leaves for garnish
1 tablespoon plus 1 teaspoon minced chives
16 cherry tomatoes, halved
1/4 cup thinly shaved red onion

While squid doesn't play a huge role in traditional bistro cookery, because Bouchon is in northern California, we've got some of the sweetest squid around, so it makes perfect sense in our context. Buy the smallest squids you can; they will be the most tender and yield the most rings.

Here summer vegetables and herbs are the base for the quickly cooked squid. Because squid is so mild, the success of this refreshing salad is dependent upon excellent tomatoes. Since the salad is served cold, all the ingredients can be prepared ahead, then tossed together at the last minute.

One at a time, hold each squid under cold running water, pull off the head, and reserve. Pull away and discard the outer skin from the body. Pull out and discard the piece of cartilage from the body cavity and use your fingers to clean the inside of the cavity. Lay the bodies on a cutting board.

Hold each body down on the board and use the blade of a knife to scrape it from the tapered end toward the head to force out anything left in the body. Cut each body crosswise into 1/2-inch-wide rings. Line a baking sheet with paper towels and spread the squid rings on half the paper towels to dry.

Cut away the squid tentacles below the eyes and discard the heads. Lay the tentacles on the other half of the paper towels.

Film a large nonstick sauté pan with a light coating of canola oil and heat over high heat. Season the squid with salt and pepper. Add the tentacles to the pan and toss for a moment, then add the rings and quickly sauté for 30 to 45 seconds, just until they become opaque; be careful not to overcook or the squid will be tough. Remove from the pan and drain briefly on clean paper towels.

Place the warm squid in a wide shallow bowl and drizzle with the olive oil. Toss, then add the vinegar and toss again. Cover and refrigerate for 2 hours.

Peel the cucumber, halve it lengthwise, and use a small spoon to scrape away and discard the seeds. Sprinkle the cucumber on all sides with about 2 teaspoons salt and let stand on a plate for 30 minutes.

Rinse the cucumber well under cold water and dry on paper towels. Cut the cucumber halves crosswise into 2-inch-long sections. Cut each section lengthwise into 1/4-inch-thick bâtons. Trim the bâtons if necessary into even sticks. Taste a piece; if it is too salty, place the cucumber in a colander, rinse again, and dry on paper towels. Refrigerate for at least 30 minutes.

Place the tomato slices on a large plate and sprinkle with a pinch of salt and pepper. Put the tomatoes in the refrigerator to chill for 15 to 20 minutes before serving.

TO SERVE: Add the cucumber bâtons, cherry tomatoes, shallots, parsley, chives, and red onion to the squid and toss gently.

Arrange 4 slices of tomato in each serving plate. Drizzle the tomatoes with olive oil and season to taste with salt and pepper. Mound the squid salad on the tomatoes and intersperse the parsley leaves in the salad. Serve cold.

PHOTOGRAPH ON PAGE 80   **MAKES 4 SERVINGS**

CHILLED SALAD OF HARICOTS VERTS AND TOMATOES
SALADE FRAÎCHE DE TOMATES ET HARICOTS VERTS

SALAD

12 ounces haricots verts

1 small red onion, peeled

1 small fennel bulb

Kosher salt

2 teaspoons Pernod

2 teaspoons extra virgin olive oil,
    plus more for drizzling

16 thin slices red or yellow heirloom or vine-
    ripened tomatoes

Freshly ground black pepper

3 hard-cooked large eggs (see page 326),
    cut into quarters

20 Niçoise olives

4 boquerones anchovy fillets
    (see Sources, page 330)

DRESSING

¼ cup Basil Puree (page 315)

1 tablespoon plus 1 teaspoon House Vinaigrette
    (page 315)

¼ cup minced shallots

2 teaspoons minced chives

1 teaspoon tarragon leaves

1 teaspoon chervil leaves

1 teaspoon Italian parsley leaves

Kosher salt and freshly ground black pepper

This is a pretty straightforward salad: beans tossed with a vinaigrette, fresh tomatoes, hard-cooked eggs, and an anchovy garnish. The keys to making it great are to cook the beans perfectly (in lots of heavily salted water at a rapid boil), to have an ice bath ready for the beans when they come out, and to use a variety of fresh garden tomatoes (varieties we like include Early Girl, which comes in the spring; Mandarin, which is an orange summer tomato; and the low-acid Green Zebra). Properly cooked eggs with bright yellow yolks are essential. Be sure the vegetables are well chilled before serving.

FOR THE SALAD: Bring a large pot of generously salted water to a boil. Prepare an ice bath.

Cut off and discard the stem ends of the haricots verts and cut each bean in half. Blanch the beans (see page 238) in the boiling water for 3 to 6 minutes, or until they are just cooked but still have a bite to them. Drain the beans and plunge into the ice bath to chill. Drain again, then drain well on paper towels. Refrigerate the beans for at least 30 minutes, or up to a day.

Meanwhile, cut the onion lengthwise in half. Place cut side down on a cutting board and slice crosswise into ⅛-inch-thick slices. Toss to separate the onion pieces. (You need about 1 cup onion slices; reserve any extra for another use.) Refrigerate the onions for at least 30 minutes, or up to a day.

Cut off and discard the root end and stems of the fennel. Cut the bulb lengthwise in half and cut out and discard the core. Lay the halves cut side down on a cutting board and slice crosswise into ⅛-inch-thick slices. (You should have about 1 cup.) Place the fennel slices in a small bowl and toss with a pinch of salt, the Pernod, and 2 teaspoons olive oil. Refrigerate for at least 30 minutes, or up to a few hours.

Place the tomato slices on a large plate and sprinkle with a pinch each of salt and pepper. Drizzle lightly with olive oil. Put the tomatoes in the refrigerator to chill for 15 to 20 minutes before serving.

FOR THE DRESSING: Place the beans in a medium bowl. Add all the dressing ingredients and toss well. Toss in the onion and fennel.

Arrange 4 slices of chilled tomato in a square in the center of each serving plate. Season to taste with salt and pepper.

Mound the bean salad over the tomatoes. Arrange 3 egg quarters and 5 olives around each salad. Garnish the top of each salad with an anchovy fillet.

MAKES 4 SERVINGS

MARKET GREENS WITH WARM GOAT CHEESE AND HAZELNUTS
SALADE MARAÎCHÈRE AU CHÈVRE CHAUD ET AUX NOISETTES

VINAIGRETTE

½ cup Dijon mustard

½ cup red wine vinegar

1½ cups canola oil

CROUTONS

1 baguette (2½ inches wide)

Extra virgin olive oil for drizzling

Kosher salt

SALAD

½ cup skinned (blanched) whole hazelnuts
    (see Note)

Four 2-ounce disks of Cabécou cheese
    in oil or 8 ounces fresh goat cheese
    divided into 4 portions

6 ounces mesclun

2 tablespoons minced shallots

2 tablespoons minced chives

¼ cup Italian parsley leaves

¼ cup tarragon leaves

¼ cup chervil leaves

Kosher salt and freshly ground black pepper

A spring or early summer *salade maraîchère,* or "market salad," is by definition a salad of what's available in the market on any given day. In winter, it could be beets and nuts. In this summer combination, we use mesclun greens with hazelnuts and a basic vinaigrette, served with croutons and chèvre. Cabécou cheeses are small disks marinated in olive oil and herbs. If you can't find them, a fresh goat cheese will work nicely; just be sure whatever cheese you use is soft enough to spread over the croutons once they're warmed. As always, an abundance of fresh chopped herbs elevates the flavors.

FOR THE VINAIGRETTE: Combine the mustard and vinegar in a blender and blend at medium speed for about 15 seconds. With the machine running, drizzle in ½ cup of the canola oil. Transfer the dressing to a medium bowl and add the remaining oil in a slow stream, whisking constantly. (Adding all the oil to the dressing in the blender would make it too thick; the consistency should be very creamy.) (Refrigerate the dressing for up to 2 weeks. Should it separate, use a blender or immersion blender to re-emulsify it.)

FOR THE CROUTONS: Preheat the broiler. Using a serrated knife, cut the baguette on a severe diagonal to make slices that are about 9 inches long; you need 4 slices for the salad. Place the croutons on a baking sheet, drizzle both sides lightly with olive oil, and sprinkle with a pinch of salt. Place under the broiler until lightly browned on the first side, then turn and brown the second side. Set aside on the baking sheet. Turn the oven down to 350°F.

FOR THE SALAD: Place the hazelnuts on a baking sheet and bake for 3 to 4 minutes, or until fragrant and lightly browned. Let cool. Leave the oven on.

Cut half the hazelnuts in half and set aside. Roughly chop the remaining hazelnuts.

Drain the cheese, if using Cabécou. Place one portion in the center of each crouton and top each one with 2 to 3 teaspoons of the chopped hazelnuts. Place in the oven to warm for about 5 minutes, or until the cheese is soft enough to spread.

While the cheese warms, place the greens in a mixing bowl and toss with the shallots, herbs, hazelnut halves, and just enough dressing to coat the greens. Season to taste with salt and pepper.

Arrange a mound of the salad on each serving plate and place a crouton at its side.

MAKES 4 SERVINGS

NOTE: If skinned (blanched) hazelnuts are not available, roast skin-on hazelnuts on a baking sheet at 350°F until they are fragrant and the skins have loosened, 7 to 8 minutes. Rub the warm nuts in a towel to remove as much of the skin as possible. You will not need to toast them again for the salad.

FRISÉE SALAD WITH A JULIENNE OF BACON AND POACHED EGG—SALADE FRISÉE AUX LARDONS ET ŒUF POCHÉ

POACHED EGGS

1 tablespoon white wine vinegar

4 large eggs

8 ounces slab bacon

BACON VINAIGRETTE

2 tablespoons sherry vinegar

1 tablespoon whole-grain mustard

2 teaspoons Dijon mustard

5 tablespoons rendered bacon fat (reserved),
    plus duck fat (see Sources, page 330) or
    canola oil as needed

Kosher salt and freshly ground black pepper

SALAD

4 heads frisée

Four ³/₈-inch-thick slices Brioche
    (page 324) or other egg bread

1 heaping tablespoon minced shallots

2 tablespoons minced chives

1 heaping tablespoon parsley leaves

1 heaping tablespoon tarragon leaves

1 heaping tablespoon chervil leaves

Kosher salt and freshly ground black pepper

This is a great version of bacon and eggs that can be eaten, really, at any time of the day, as part of a meal or as an entire meal. After lunch service in Paris, some of us cooks would head out for a bite at a local bistro, where we'd order a croque-monsieur or this salad. It's a common bistro dish, because all the components are simple ingredients always on hand, that can be prepared ahead of time and warmed on request. The egg and bacon make it very rich and satisfying, and the bitter frisée and the sharp bacon vinaigrette help to balance that richness. An extraordinary variation on this classic is to use poached duck eggs, if they're available to you, and duck fat in place of the canola oil.

FOR THE POACHED EGGS: Bring at least 4 inches of water to a boil in a large deep saucepan. Prepare an ice bath. Add the vinegar to the boiling water and reduce the heat to a simmer. Crack 2 of the eggs into small cups or ramekins. Using a wooden spoon, stir the water around the edges of the pan twice in a circular motion to get the water moving, add 1 egg to the center of the pan and then quickly add the other. Simmer gently for about 1¹/₂ minutes, or until the whites are set but the yolks are still runny. With a slotted spoon, carefully remove the eggs and place in the ice bath. Repeat with the remaining eggs. (The eggs can be poached several hours ahead and stored in the ice water in the refrigerator.)

Cut the slab bacon into 3/8-inch-thick slices and then cut the slices crosswise into lardons that are about 1 1/2 inches long and 3/8 inch thick. Spread them in a single layer in a 9- to 10-inch nonstick skillet and place the skillet over high heat just until the bacon begins to sizzle. Reduce the heat to medium and sauté, stirring occasionally, for about 10 minutes, or until the lardons are cooked about halfway through and are a light golden brown. Drain the lardons in a strainer set over a bowl, reserving the fat, and return them to the skillet. Set aside.

FOR THE VINAIGRETTE: Whisk together the vinegar and mustards in a small bowl. If the bacon fat has solidified, reheat it to a liquid state. Measure the bacon fat; if you do not have 5 tablespoons, make up the difference with duck fat or canola oil. Whisking constantly, drizzle the fat into the vinegar mixture. Season to taste with salt and pepper.

FOR THE SALAD: Remove the dark green outer leaves from the heads of frisée and reserve for another use. Cut off the root ends and discard. Separate the leaves. Wash if necessary, spin-dry, and place in a bowl.

Toast the slices of brioche. Trim away the crusts and cut each piece into 2 triangles.

Bring about 4 inches of water to a gentle simmer in a medium saucepan. Remove the eggs from the ice bath and trim off any ragged edges.

Meanwhile, cook the lardons over medium heat until hot and crispy.

Toss the frisée with the shallots, about 1 heaping tablespoon of the chives, the remaining herbs, the warm lardons, and just enough of the vinaigrette to lightly coat the greens. Season to taste with salt and pepper.

Mound the salad in the center of four shallow serving bowls. Flatten the centers slightly so the eggs won't slide off.

Gently place the eggs in the simmering water and reheat for about 1 minute, just to warm them but keep the yolks runny. Remove each egg with a slotted spoon, blot on a paper towel, and place atop the salads. Sprinkle the eggs with the remaining chives and salt and pepper to taste. Place 2 brioche triangles on the side of each salad.

MAKES 4 SERVINGS

THE IMPORTANCE OF
{ CUSTARD }

Custard is one of the great transformations of the egg. No other preparation, certainly none made from such a common or inexpensive ingredient, achieves such elegant voluptuousness through cooking. Custard is universally appealing because of our emotional response to a texture that in one bite combines both childhood comfort and adult luxury.

Custard is as equally at home in a country inn as it is in a Michelin three-star restaurant, but in a bistro its customary forms—the quiche (pages 88 to 95) and dessert custards (pages 264 to 269)—are especially appropriate because they are so efficient from both a cost and a service standpoint.

As the quiche reminds us, custard shouldn't be relegated solely to the dessert category. When you take a custard into the savory realm, it's much more versatile, happily taking on any number of flavor profiles. Bone marrow is an exquisite flavoring for a savory custard, one that would make a great garnish for a grilled filet mignon. As oils can be infused with herbs, so too can custards: a basil custard in tomato soup, for instance; a tarragon custard with diced orange as a refreshing opening course. Some of the cream in the custard can be replaced by a vegetable juice to lighten it and intensify the flavor.

Texture is the key to the custard's power. It should be smooth and creamy, holding its shape but giving no resistance on the palate. When you take a spoonful of a perfectly cooked custard, you notice a sheen on its surface: It draws you to it. If there is too much egg, the custard will be heavy, too solid. If it has been cooked too long or has gotten too hot, it will be curdled.

While there are all kinds of variations on the custard, a basic ratio is one and a half eggs for each cup of liquid, which typically includes cream (fat content is also a key part of texture). It's best if the custard base is hot to begin with and gets cooked in a water bath to maintain a continuous gentle heat. The water, a shield against the heat, should come as high as the level of the custard. The ramekins should be set on parchment paper in the pan, and the pan should be covered so that the custard cooks in a steamy environment, doesn't lose too much moisture, and maintains a soft surface. Then cook your custards until the jiggle becomes uniform. That's the basic technique.

LARDONS: Lardons are small bâtons of bacon—about one-quarter inch thick and an inch to an inch and a half long when cooked. The name comes from the French term for cured smoked pork belly, known here as bacon. Lardons are the classic garnish for a *salade frisée;* they distinguish quiche Lorraine and they add a rich, smoky, salty flavor to many traditional stews and soups, such as coq au vin and beef bourguignon. They also add a great crunchy, chewy textural contrast to an otherwise soft stew or salad. I find much of the bacon in the United States to be too smoky— think about it when you are choosing bacon. Slab bacon, from which we cut lardons, isn't a common grocery item here, so it is not common in the home cook's repertoire. I hope that changes.

Quiche It's almost sexual, a great quiche. It's "the seductive pie." And it's hard to say adequately what an important part of cooking it represents for me. It's the essence of luxury, a great delicacy, again using the most common ingredients.

A great quiche has a rich, flaky crust and a custard about two inches deep. When it is sliced, the edges should be clean, and the exposed custard should have a smooth, almost liquid sheen. When it arrives hot, it should tremble as if it were on the verge of collapse. It maintains its form—just—but you can see what's going to happen when you take a bite. It collapses on the palate, molten, spreading out luxuriously.

Why didn't the French quiche ever really translate to America? American culinary culture embraced it, then trashed it without ever knowing what it was. And now it's all but gone. I think it was a mechanical problem, not having the right tool—a ring mold about two inches high. When the modern quiche took off here in the 1970s, that wasn't widely available. Instead, a pie pan was commonly substituted for the two-inch ring mold. And then came the premade pie shell. Who would want to eat quiche made in that?

Like foie gras, a quiche has to have a specific thickness (or depth) or you cannot cook it properly: It must be two inches high, in a crust thick enough to remain crisp, and not become soggy, during cooking. You need this depth for two other reasons. First, a quiche that deep takes a long time to cook, which allows the flavors of the ingredients to develop and distribute themselves throughout the custard. Second, because the custard is in such a hostile environment—heat unmitigated by a water bath—it needs that volume to cook slowly and therefore evenly. Custard in a pie shell invariably overcooks (if you cooked it slowly enough, the crust would become soggy).

What are the craft elements of preparing quiche? The right tools are a ring mold and parchment paper. Pâte brisée is the standard pastry, a short pastry—very, very important. Good pâte brisée, the next best thing to puff pastry, is harder to make well because it requires some touch, some finesse. I make it pasta style: I put flour on a board and form a well, combine water and butter in the well, squeezing the butter into half-inch chunks in the water so the butter and water become even in temperature, then gradually stir in the flour as if I were making a pasta dough. I'm old-fashioned and always make it by hand, but a heavy-duty mixer with a paddle attachment works well too. Do not mix the dough too much or overwork it. If you do, you'll overdevelop the gluten, the protein in the flour; the dough will become elastic rather than "shortened," and the crust will take on a dense, doughy quality rather than a light, flaky one.

To maintain the proper shape without cracks, you have to let the dough rest before you roll it out. It must be rolled out to the right thickness, about three-sixteenths of an inch, or it will be soggy rather than crisp. After you line the mold, you should let the dough rest again. It's best to put it in the freezer for a couple of hours and blind-bake it still frozen.

When you're ready to fill the quiche, it's important that all the ingredients be warm: The custard needs to start cooking as soon as it's in the oven. The milk and cream should be scalded. The custard has to be mixed vigorously so that it's frothy, both to help achieve a light finished texture and because the froth helps to suspend the garnish ingredients within the quiche.

Then the quiche must go into an oven heated to the right temperature, no higher than three hundred and twenty-five degrees. If the custard gets too hot, it can curdle. If the oven is not hot enough, or if the custard isn't warm when it's poured into the mold, it can saturate the crust and make it soggy. Finally, the quiche must be cooked for the right amount of time, something learned through experience. Sticking a paring knife into the center is a helpful check; be aware, though, that if the blade comes out clean, the quiche may end up overcooked, since it continues to cook after it's out of the oven. With experience, you'll recognize the right jiggle and know when it's done. At first, the jiggle is quicker in the center than at the edges. When the custard is done, the jiggle will be more uniform throughout. Really, the only way to learn is to pay attention each time you make a quiche. And since quiche is something that's good to make regularly, learning doneness by sight shouldn't take too long. Leftovers keep well; it's also excellent cold. At Bouchon, we chill it overnight before slicing it, then reheat slices to order.

Garnish is purely a matter of personal taste and seasonal availability: Whatever goes well with eggs works. I prefer the traditional flavors represented by the variations here: mushrooms when they're in season, or spinach, bacon, and onion for the classic Lorraine, or even a blue cheese with leeks.

I'm sorry America has lost the quiche—or, really, has never had it. I'd like to see it return to its proper form, and for more people to know about it and appreciate it.

BASIC QUICHE SHELL

In this pâte brisée dough, it's crucial that the butter be completely incorporated, with no visible specks remaining. Although pieces of butter will make a dough flaky, they would leave holes in the quiche crust and the batter would leak out. Save the dough trimmings to repair any cracks. This crust is a little thicker than some: You want the custard to set before it soaks all the way through. Also, as the quiche chills, moisture from the custard will weep into the crust. If the crust is too thin, it will become soggy rather than crisp.

2 cups (about 12 ounces) all-purpose flour, sifted,
    plus additional flour for rolling
1 teaspoon kosher salt
8 ounces chilled unsalted butter, cut into ¼-inch pieces
¼ cup ice water
Canola oil

Place 1 cup of the flour and the salt in the bowl of a heavy-duty mixer fitted with the paddle attachment. Turn the mixer to low speed and add the butter a small handful at a time. When all the butter has been added, increase the speed to medium and mix until the butter is completely blended with the flour. Reduce the speed, add the remaining flour, and mix just to combine. Add the water and mix until incorporated. The dough will come around the paddle and should feel smooth, not sticky, to the touch.

Remove the dough from the mixer and check to be certain that there are no visible pieces of butter remaining; if necessary, return the dough to the mixer and mix briefly again. Pat the dough into a 7- to 8-inch disk and wrap in plastic wrap. Refrigerate for at least 1 hour, or up to a day. (If the dough does not rest, it will shrink as it bakes.)

Lightly brush the inside of a 9-by-2-inch-high ring mold with canola oil and place it on a parchment-lined baking sheet.

Place the dough on a floured work surface and rub on all sides with flour. Flatten it into a larger circle using a rolling pin or the heel of your hand. Roll the rolling pin back and forth across the dough a few times, then turn it 90 degrees and roll again. Continue to turn and roll until the dough is ³⁄₁₆ inch thick and about 14 inches in diameter. (If the kitchen is hot and the dough has become very soft, move it to a baking sheet and refrigerate for a few minutes.)

To lift the dough into the ring, place the rolling pin across the dough about one-quarter of the way up from the bottom edge, fold the bottom edge of dough up and over the pin, and roll the dough up on the rolling pin. Lift the dough on the pin, hold it over the top edge of the ring and unroll the dough over the mold, centering it. Carefully lower the dough into the ring, pressing it gently against the sides and into the bottom corners of the ring. Trim any dough that extends more than an inch over the sides of the mold and reserve the scraps. Fold the excess dough over against the outside of the ring. (Preparing the quiche shell this way will prevent it from shrinking down the sides as it bakes. The excess dough will be removed after the quiche is baked.) Carefully check for any cracks or holes in the dough, and patch with the reserved dough as necessary. Place in the refrigerator or freezer for at least 20 minutes to resolidify the butter. Reserve the remaining dough scraps.

Put a rack set in the middle of the oven and preheat the oven to 375°F.

Line the quiche shell with a 16-inch round of parchment. Fill the shell with pie weights or dried beans, gently guiding the weights into the corners of the shell and filling the shell completely.

Bake the shell for 35 to 45 minutes, or until the edges of the dough are lightly browned but the bottom is still light in color.

Carefully remove the parchment and weights. Check the dough for any new cracks or holes and patch with the thin pieces of the reserved dough if necessary. Return the shell to the oven for another 15 to 20 minutes, or until the bottom is a rich golden brown. Remove from the oven and allow the shell to cool completely on the baking sheet. Once again, check the dough for any cracks or holes, and patch if necessary before filling with the quiche batter.

MAKES ENOUGH FOR ONE 9-INCH QUICHE

BASIC QUICHE BATTER

Using a blender aerates the batter and makes a very light quiche. The directions here are for a standard-size blender. However, the ingredients can be combined in one batch if you use an immersion blender or a large-capacity professional blender. Be sure to reblend the batter for a few seconds before pouring each layer of the quiche.

There may be a little excess batter, depending on how much air is incorporated into the batter as it is blended. The quiche may sink slightly as it bakes, so check it after about twenty minutes and, if there is room, you can add a bit more of the batter to the top. Any remaining batter can be baked in custard cups.

The quiche needs to be thoroughly chilled before it's cut, so make your quiche at least a day, or up to three days, before serving it.

2 cups milk
2 cups heavy cream
6 large eggs
1 tablespoon kosher salt
$^1/_4$ teaspoon freshly ground white pepper
6 gratings fresh nutmeg

Combine the milk and cream in a large saucepan and heat over medium heat until scalded (meaning a skin begins to form on the surface). Remove from the heat and let cool for 15 minutes before continuing.

Put 3 eggs, half the milk and cream mixture, 1$^1/_2$ teaspoons salt, $^1/_8$ teaspoon white pepper, and 3 gratings of nutmeg in a blender and blend on low speed for a few seconds to combine the ingredients. Increase the speed to high and blend for 30 seconds to a minute, or until the batter is light and foamy.

This is the first layer of the quiche. Once you have assembled it, add the remaining ingredients to the blender and repeat the process to complete the quiche.

MAKES ENOUGH FOR ONE 9-INCH QUICHE; 8 SERVINGS

3 pounds (4 large) leeks

6 ounces Roquefort cheese, crumbled
(about 1⅓ cups)

Basic Quiche Shell (page 88), cooled
Basic Quiche Batter (page 89)

FOR THE LEEKS: Cut off the dark green leaves and discard. Cut off and discard the root end and bottom 1 inch of each leek. Cut the leeks lengthwise in half and wash well under cold running water. Place cut side down on a cutting board and slice crosswise into ¼-inch-thick slices. (You should have 4 to 5 cups packed leeks.)

Bring a large pot of salted water to a boil. Add the leeks and cook for about 5 minutes, or until tender throughout. Drain the leeks and spread them on a baking sheet to cool.

Put a rack in the center of the oven and preheat the oven to 325°F.

Squeeze the cooled leeks to remove excess water and dry on paper towels. Scatter half the chopped leeks and half the Roquefort evenly into the cooled quiche shell (still on the baking sheet).

Blend the quiche batter again to aerate it, then pour in enough of the batter to cover the ingredients and fill the quiche shell approximately halfway. Top the batter with the remaining leeks and cheese. Blend the remaining batter and fill the quiche shell all the way to the top. (If you don't have a very steady hand, you might spill some of the batter on the way to the oven; fill the shell most of the way, then pour the final amount of batter on top once the quiche is on the oven rack.)

Bake for 1½ to 1¾ hours, or until the top of the quiche is browned and the custard is set when the pan is jiggled. Remove the quiche from the oven and let cool to room temperature on a rack. Refrigerate until chilled, at least 1 day, or up to 3 days.

Once the quiche is thoroughly chilled, using a metal bench scraper or a sharp knife, scrape away the excess crust from the top edge. Tilt the ring on its side, with the bottom of the quiche facing you, and run a small paring knife between the crust and the ring to release the quiche. Set the quiche down and carefully lift off the ring. Return to the refrigerator until ready to serve.

TO SERVE: Preheat the oven to 375°F. Line a baking sheet with parchment paper and lightly oil the paper.

Using a long serrated knife, and supporting the sides of the crust, carefully cut through the edge of the crust in a sawing motion. Switch to a long slicing knife and cut through the custard and bottom crust. Repeat, cutting the quiche into 8 pieces. Place the pieces on the baking sheet and reheat for 15 minutes, or until hot throughout. To check, insert a metal skewer into the quiche for several seconds and then touch the skewer to your lip to test the temperature of the quiche.

MAKES 8 SERVINGS

BACON AND ONION QUICHE—QUICHE LORRAINE

1 pound slab bacon, cut into lardons about
    1½ inches long and ⅜ inch thick
2 cups Onion Confit (page 312)
¾ teaspoon kosher salt

¼ teaspoon freshly ground black pepper
2 teaspoons chopped thyme
½ cup grated Comté or Emmentaler cheese

Basic Quiche Shell (page 88), cooled
Basic Quiche Batter (page 89)
Canola oil

Put a rack in the center of the oven and preheat the oven to 375°F.

Spread the bacon on a baking sheet and bake for 20 to 25 minutes, or until it has rendered its fat; the bacon will not be crisp at this point. Transfer the bacon to paper towels to drain. Reduce the oven temperature to 325°F.

Combine the onion confit and bacon in a large sauté pan over medium heat. Sprinkle with the salt, pepper, and thyme, then stir together until warm, 3 to 4 minutes. Drain on paper towels.

Scatter ¼ cup of the cheese and half the onion mixture evenly into the cooled quiche shell (still on the baking sheet). Blend the quiche batter again to aerate it, then pour in enough of the batter to cover the ingredients and fill the quiche shell approximately halfway. Top the batter with the remaining ¼ cup cheese and the remaining onion mixture. Blend the remaining batter and fill the quiche shell all the way to the top. (If you don't have a very steady hand, you might spill some of the batter on the way to the oven; fill the shell most of the way, then pour the final amount of batter on top once the quiche is on the oven rack.)

Bake for 1½ to 1¾ hours, or until the top of the quiche is browned and the custard is set when the pan is jiggled. Remove the quiche from the oven and let cool to room temperature on a rack. Refrigerate until thoroughly chilled, at least 1 day, or up to 3 days.

Once the quiche is thoroughly chilled, using a metal bench scraper or a sharp knife, scrape away the excess crust from the top edge. Tilt the ring on its side, with the bottom of the quiche facing you, and run a small paring knife between the crust and the ring to release the quiche. Set the quiche down and carefully lift off the ring. Return to the refrigerator until ready to serve.

TO SERVE: Preheat the oven to 375°F. Line a baking sheet with parchment paper and lightly oil the paper.

Using a long serrated knife and supporting the sides of the crust, carefully cut through the edge of the crust in a sawing motion. Switch to a long slicing knife and cut through the custard and bottom crust. Repeat, cutting the quiche into 8 pieces. Place the pieces on the baking sheet and reheat for 15 minutes, or until hot throughout. To check, insert a metal skewer into the quiche for several seconds and then touch the skewer to your lip to test the temperature of the quiche.

MAKES 8 SERVINGS

SPINACH QUICHE—QUICHE FLORENTINE

2 tablespoons unsalted butter

¼ cup minced shallots

1 pound spinach, large stems removed
    and washed

2 teaspoons kosher salt

1 teaspoon freshly ground black pepper

¾ cup grated Comté or Emmentaler cheese

Basic Quiche Shell (page 88), cooled

Basic Quiche Batter (page 89)

Canola oil

Melt the butter in a large pot or sauté pan over medium heat. Add the shallots and cook gently for about 2 minutes, until they have softened but not colored. Add half the spinach, 1 teaspoon of the salt, and ½ teaspoon of the pepper. (To season the spinach evenly, it is best to sprinkle the leaves with salt and pepper before they wilt.) Stir for a minute to wilt, then add the remaining spinach, 1 teaspoon salt, and ½ teaspoon pepper. Cook for 1 to 2 minutes, stirring until all the spinach has wilted. Drain the spinach on paper towels and let cool.

Put a rack in the center of the oven and preheat the oven to 325°F.

Squeeze the cooled spinach to remove excess liquid and chop coarsely to make cutting the quiche easier. Scatter ¼ cup of the cheese and half the spinach evenly into the cooled quiche shell (still on the baking sheet). Blend the quiche batter again to aerate it, then pour in enough of the batter to cover the ingredients and fill the quiche shell approximately halfway. Top the batter with another ¼ cup of the cheese and the remaining spinach. Blend the remaining batter and fill the quiche all the way to the top. Sprinkle the remaining ¼ cup cheese on the top of the quiche. (If you don't have a very steady hand, you might spill some of the batter on the way to the oven; fill the quiche most of the way, then pour the final amount of batter on top once the quiche is on the oven rack. Then top it with the remaining cheese.)

Bake for 1½ to 1¾ hours, or until the top of the quiche is browned and the custard is set when the pan is jiggled. Remove the quiche from the oven and let cool on a rack to room temperature. Refrigerate until thoroughly chilled, at least 1 day, or up to 3 days.

Once the quiche is thoroughly chilled, using a metal bench scraper or a sharp knife, scrape away the excess crust from the top. Tilt the ring on its side, with the bottom of the quiche facing you, and run a small paring knife between the crust and the ring to release the quiche. Set the quiche down and carefully lift off the ring. Return to the refrigerator until ready to serve.

TO SERVE: Preheat the oven to 375°F. Line a baking sheet with parchment paper and lightly oil the paper.

Using a long serrated knife and supporting the sides of the crust, carefully cut through the edge of the crust in a sawing motion. Switch to a long slicing knife and cut through the custard and bottom crust. Repeat, cutting the quiche into 8 pieces. Place the pieces on the baking sheet and reheat for 15 minutes, or until hot throughout. To check, insert a metal skewer into the quiche for several seconds and then touch the skewer to your lip to test the temperature of the quiche.

MAKES 8 SERVINGS

2 pounds mixed mushrooms, such as oyster,
    king trumpet, clamshell, cremini, porcini,
    and chanterelle, cleaned (see page 326)
Canola oil

$1\frac{1}{2}$ teaspoons kosher salt
$\frac{3}{4}$ teaspoon freshly ground black pepper
1 tablespoon unsalted butter
3 tablespoons minced shallots

1 tablespoon thyme leaves
$\frac{3}{4}$ cup grated Comté or Emmentaler cheese
Basic Quiche Shell (page 88), cooled
Basic Quiche Batter (page 89)

The amount of mushrooms may seem like a great deal, but the mushrooms will reduce by half when cooked. Pat the mushrooms dry if necessary, then trim away any tough stems and tear larger mushrooms into smaller pieces. It is important to cook each type of mushroom separately, as cooking times will vary. Divide the salt, pepper, butter, shallots, and thyme proportionally according to how much of each type of mushroom you are using.

Coat a large sauté pan with a thin film of canola oil and heat over high heat until the oil begins to smoke. Add the first batch of mushrooms, season with salt and pepper, and sauté for about a minute. The mushrooms will absorb the oil and should not be weeping any liquid at this point. Add the butter, shallots, and thyme, toss, and sauté until they are cooked thoroughly, 3 to 4 minutes. Drain the mushrooms on paper towels and cook the remaining mushrooms, wiping the pan with a paper towel between batches.

Put a rack in the center of the oven and preheat the oven to 325°F.

Scatter $\frac{1}{4}$ cup of the cheese and half the mushrooms evenly into the cooled quiche shell (still on the baking sheet). Blend the quiche batter again to aerate it, then pour enough of the batter to cover the ingredients and fill the quiche shell approximately halfway. Top the batter with another $\frac{1}{4}$ cup of the cheese and the remaining mushrooms. Blend the remaining batter and fill the quiche all the way to the top. Push down any mushrooms that float up. Sprinkle the remaining $\frac{1}{4}$ cup cheese on the top of the quiche. (If you don't

have a very steady hand, you might spill some of the batter on the way to the oven; fill the quiche most of the way, then pour the final amount of batter on top once the quiche is on the oven rack. Then top it with the remaining cheese.)

Bake for $1\frac{1}{2}$ to $1\frac{3}{4}$ hours, or until the top of the quiche is browned and the custard is set when the pan is jiggled. Remove the quiche from the oven and let cool to room temperature on a rack. Refrigerate until thoroughly chilled, at least a day, or up to 3 days.

Once the quiche is thoroughly chilled, using a metal bench scraper or a sharp knife, scrape away the excess crust from the top edge. Tilt the ring on its side, with the bottom of the quiche facing you, and run a small paring knife between the crust and the ring to release the quiche. Set the quiche down and carefully lift off the ring. Return to the refrigerator until ready to serve.

TO SERVE: Preheat the oven to 375°F. Line a baking sheet with the parchment paper and lightly oil the paper.

Using a long serrated knife and supporting the sides of the crust, carefully cut through the edge of the crust in a sawing motion. Switch to a long slicing knife and cut through the custard and bottom crust. Repeat, cutting the quiche into 8 pieces. Place the pieces on the baking sheet and reheat for 15 minutes, or until hot throughout. To check, insert a metal skewer into the quiche for several seconds and then touch the skewer to your lip to test the temperature of the quiche.

MAKES 8 SERVINGS

Tuna Niçoise Tartine (page 98)

Tartine The word *tartine* literally means a slice of bread, typically a baguette, and butter, but its meaning has broadened to indicate an open-faced sandwich. An open-faced sandwich is a great lunch item, and in the life of a bistro kitchen, the tartine is an excellent way to serve leftovers. Yesterday's leg of lamb or pork roast sliced cold becomes a special meal in itself, on delicious bread, heaped with a garnish, such as a celeriac rémoulade. (A rich acidic garnish is a necessary pairing for cold meat.) With most tartines, we serve additional greens as well as *pommes frites*. Following are some of the tartines we serve at Bouchon, but you can make a tartine out of many things, from fish to rillettes to vegetables. The tartine is an idea, a vehicle.

TUNA NIÇOISE TARTINE—TARTINE DE THON À LA NIÇOISE

SALAD

1½ pounds good-quality canned tuna
   packed in olive oil

1 tablespoon plus 1 teaspoon minced shallots

1 tablespoon plus 1 teaspoon minced
   cornichons

1 tablespoon plus 1 teaspoon minced drained
   nonpareil capers, preferably Spanish

1 tablespoon minced chives

2 teaspoons minced Italian parsley

2 teaspoons minced tarragon

2 teaspoons minced chervil

1 tablespoon fresh lemon juice

¾ cup mayonnaise

Kosher salt and freshly ground black pepper

1 baguette (about 2½ inches wide)

Extra virgin olive oil

Kosher salt

¼ cup Aïoli (page 315)

12 to 16 small young Bibb lettuce leaves

Freshly ground black pepper

4 hard-cooked large eggs (see page 326)

12 large radish slices

12 Niçoise olives, pitted and halved

¼ cup minced chives

12 cornichons

4 small bunches mâche or watercress,
   cleaned, or Pommes Frites (page 249)
   (optional)

Just as it's important to use perfectly cooked lamb or pork when making tartines featuring those ingredients, a good-quality canned tuna will make the difference between a good tuna salad and an excellent one. The salt content can vary from brand to brand, so taste as you season. At Bouchon, we use an Italian brand packed in oil (see Sources, page 330). Even very fancy bistros sell a tuna Niçoise.

Put the tuna in a strainer set over a bowl to allow excess oil to drain off but do not squeeze dry. Transfer the drained tuna to a large bowl and break it apart with a fork. Add the shallots, cornichons, capers, chives, parsley, tarragon, and chervil and toss together. Gently stir in the lemon juice and mayonnaise; do not let the mixture become a paste. Season to taste with salt and pepper.

Preheat the broiler. Lay the baguette on its side and cut it on a severe bias to get 4 slices approximately 10 inches long and ½ inch thick. Drizzle both sides of each slice lightly with olive oil and sprinkle with salt. Place under the broiler until golden brown on the first side, then turn to brown the second side.

Spread one side of each toast with 1 tablespoon of aïoli. Arrange the Bibb lettuce over the aïoli and sprinkle with a pinch each of salt and pepper. Mound the tuna salad down the length of each baguette slice.

Cut 4 slices from each egg and arrange the slices over the tuna. Season the egg with a pinch of salt.

Arrange 3 radish slices over the egg slices on each baguette.

Press 3 olive halves into the tuna mixture on either side of each baguette. Sprinkle 1 tablespoon of chives over the top of each sandwich. Grind black pepper over the top of the sandwiches and drizzle with some olive oil.

Serve the tartines with cornichons, garnished with a small bunch of mâche or watercress, if desired, or frites.

PHOTOGRAPH ON PAGE 97   **MAKES 4 SERVINGS**

TARTINE OF LAMB WITH PICKLED RED ONIONS
TARTINE DE GIGOT D'AGNEAU ET OIGNONS ROUGES AU VINAIGRE

1 baguette (about 2¹/₂ inches wide)
Extra virgin olive oil
Kosher salt
¹/₂ cup Aïoli (page 315)

1 large bunch watercress, coarse stems
  removed
1 pound rare roasted leg of lamb, thinly sliced
Freshly ground black pepper

1 cup Pickled Red Onions (below), drained
1 tablespoon plus 1 teaspoon minced chives
12 cornichons
Pommes Frites (page 249) (optional)

An opened-faced sandwich featuring leg of lamb from the previous night (page 220), garnished with generously pickled red onions and watercress, and served with pommes frites. Cold meats can easily become dry, so fat and acidity are very important additions when using leftovers. Here the acidity comes from pickled red onions; the fat from the aïoli.

Preheat the broiler. Lay the baguette on its side and cut it on a severe bias to get 4 slices approximately 10 inches long and ¹/₂ inch thick. Drizzle each side lightly with olive oil and sprinkle with salt. Place under the broiler until golden brown on the first side, then turn to brown the second side.

Spread one side of each slice with 2 tablespoons aïoli. Cover the aïoli with about half of the watercress. Cover the watercress with overlapping slices of lamb. Sprinkle the lamb with salt and pepper to taste. Arrange ¹/₄ cup of the pickled onions over each sandwich and sprinkle the onions with the chives.

Garnish each plate with a small bundle of watercress and 3 cornichons. Serve with frites, if desired.

MAKES 4 SERVINGS

PICKLED RED ONIONS

For this very simple pickle, vinegar and sugar are brought to a boil and, once the sugar has dissolved, poured over sliced onions and refrigerated for a day. You could add pickling spices, if you wish, but we like the flavor clean and simple. In addition to being an excellent lamb garnish, these onions are delicious in salads or with cheese.

About 1¹/₄ pounds (2 large) red onions
1¹/₂ cups red wine vinegar
³/₄ cup sugar

Trim any roots from the onions and cut them lengthwise in half. Remove and discard the outer layer of peel. Cut a V in the bottoms and remove the roots. Place the onions cut side down on a cutting board and slice lengthwise into ¹/₈-inch-thick slices, following the natural lines on the outside of the onion. Cutting with the lines, or grain, rather than against them will help the onions soften more quickly. Pack the onions into a 1-quart canning jar; reserve any slices that don't fit.

Combine the vinegar and sugar in a small saucepan and bring to a boil, stirring to dissolve the sugar. Pour the hot vinegar mixture over the onions. Once the onions begin to wilt, you can add any remaining onions to the jar. Let cool.

Refrigerate for at least 24 hours, or up to several weeks.

MAKES ABOUT 4 CUPS

TARTINE OF PORK WITH CELERIAC RÉMOULADE
TARTINE DE RÔTI DE PORC AU CÉLERI RÉMOULADE

1 baguette (about 2 ¹/₂ inches wide)

Extra virgin olive oil

Kosher salt

¹/₂ cup Aïoli (page 315)

1 large bunch watercress,
    coarse stems removed

1 pound cold cooked pork, thinly sliced

Freshly ground black pepper

1 tart apple, such as Granny Smith,
    cored, quartered, and sliced into
    thin wedges

2 cups Celeriac Rémoulade (page 8)

1 tablespoon plus 1 teaspoon minced
    chives

12 cornichons

Pommes Frites (page 249) (optional)

A tart celeriac salad and tart apple accompany this open-faced sandwich of leftover Rack of Pork (page 224). Again, an acidic garnish is a critical component in a dish featuring cold meats—as is fat, here aïoli.

Preheat the broiler. Lay the baguette on its side and cut it on a severe bias to get 4 slices approximately 10 inches long and ¹/₂ inch thick. Drizzle each side lightly with olive oil and sprinkle with salt. Place under the broiler until golden brown on the first side, then turn to brown the second side.

Spread one side of each slice with 2 tablespoons aïoli. Cover the aïoli with the watercress. Cover the watercress with overlapping slices of pork. Sprinkle the pork with salt and pepper to taste. Arrange one-quarter of the apple slices in an overlapping layer over each sandwich. Top each sandwich with ¹/₂ cup celeriac rémoulade and sprinkle with 1 teaspoon of the chives.

Serve with the cornichons and, if desired, frites.

MAKES 4 SERVINGS

GRILLED HAM AND CHEESE SANDWICH
WITH A FRIED EGG AND MORNAY SAUCE
CROQUE-MADAME, SAUCE MORNAY

Eight ½-inch-thick slices Brioche (page 324), other egg bread, or pan de mie (about 4 inches square)

8 ounces thinly sliced boiled ham

8 slices (about ½ ounce each) Swiss cheese

3 tablespoons unsalted butter

4 large eggs

1 cup Mornay Sauce (page 316), warmed

Freshly ground black pepper

2 teaspoons chopped Italian parsley

Pommes Frites (page 249) (optional)

Croque-monsieur, or grilled ham and cheese, is a classic sandwich, but the croque-madame—grilled ham and cheese topped with a fried egg and covered with a creamy Mornay sauce—is a meal. After working in a restaurant all night, eating a croque-madame really restores me; it's nourishing, rich, and hearty.

Preheat the oven to 375°F.

Lay out the bread slices. Divide the ham among them, making sure it doesn't extend over the edges of the bread. Place the cheese over the ham. If the cheese is larger than the bread, bend it over to fit.

Heat two large ovenproof nonstick pans or griddles over medium heat. (If you have only one large pan, make 2 sandwiches and keep them warm in the oven while you make the second batch.) Add 1 tablespoon of the butter to each pan. When it has melted, add half the bread cheese side up to each pan and cook for 1 to 2 minutes, or until the bottoms are golden brown. Transfer the pans to the oven for 2 to 3 minutes to melt the cheese.

Meanwhile, melt the remaining 1 tablespoon of butter in a large ovenproof skillet and fry the eggs. Cook the eggs until the bottoms are set, then place the skillet in the oven for a minute to set the top of the whites. (We cook the eggs in 4- to 5-inch individual skillets; see Sources, page 330.)

When the cheese is melted, remove the sandwiches from the oven. Place 2 slices together to make each sandwich and put each sandwich on a serving plate. Place an egg on top of each sandwich. Pour about ¼ cup of the sauce over the white of each egg, leaving the yolk uncovered. Grind black pepper over each egg and garnish the eggs with a diagonal sprinkling of chopped parsley. Serve with frites, if desired.

PHOTOGRAPH ON PAGE 43   **MAKES 4 SERVINGS**

3

{ **ENTRÉES** }

FIRST COURSES

In France, first courses—or *entrées,* "entrances into the meal"—

are distinguished largely by size. They're smaller courses. But

that doesn't mean lighter. The clever bistro chef often will make

them very rich so that they are small but very satisfying. You

might have a brandade, at Bouchon one that is deep-fried and

crispy, or a duck confit, duck leg poached in fat, or trotters,

meat from the shank of the pig, braised then sautéed until crispy

and served with a chunky vinaigrette called *gribiche.*

Or escargot, one of my favorites. I'm a fan of what I think of

as interactive foods, foods that you must work a little bit to eat—

a *grand plateau,* or rillettes that you spread yourself and season

with mustard from the pot on the table. Escargots are fun to eat

because of their interactive nature—levering the dense chewy

muscle out of the shell, then sopping up the butter that's rich

with garlic and parsley.

This course offers salads, too, though these tend to feature

meat—smoked trout or lamb's tongue, for instance. And it offers

a wide range of seafood, shellfish, and meat very specific to the

bistro style of cooking.

First courses are a fine way to begin a larger meal, or alone

may comprise a smaller simpler meal.

SALMON TARTARE—TARTARE DE SAUMON

12 ounces center-cut salmon fillet, skin and
   any pinbones removed

1 teaspoon kosher salt, or to taste

2 teaspoons minced shallots

4 teaspoons minced chives

2 teaspoons extra virgin olive oil

4 hard-cooked large eggs (see page 326),
   peeled

Two ⅛-inch-thick rounds red onion

2 tablespoons drained nonpareil capers

4 teaspoons crème fraîche

½ lemon

4 chervil sprigs

Toasts or baguette slices

Tartare requires the best-quality salmon. Try to use wild Atlantic salmon in season if at all possible; its fat content—higher than that of Pacific salmon—makes it great for this dish. It has a pleasing oily flavor when served raw. In this preparation, which uses customary salmon pairings, it's important to arrange each in the manner described below. There should be plenty of chopped egg white and yolk, minced red onion, chives, and capers.

Using a sharp knife, trim away and discard any dark portions (blood lines) from the salmon and mince the trimmed salmon. (The minced salmon can be wrapped tightly and refrigerated over ice for 2 to 3 hours.)

Transfer the salmon to a small bowl. Stir in the salt, shallots, 2 teaspoons of the chives, and the olive oil. Taste and adjust the seasonings if necessary.

Separate the whites and yolks of the eggs. Push each separately through the large holes of a grater, then chop, keeping them separate. (Using a grater first allows for more uniform pieces when chopped.)

Stack the onion slices and cut them in half. Remove the few small rings from the center, leaving the outer rings. Cut the rings into ⅛-inch squares.

Put a 4- to 4½-inch ring mold in the center of a large serving plate. Place one-quarter of the salmon mixture in the ring and use the back of a spoon to spread the mixture into a thin layer. Remove the ring and repeat with the remaining salmon on three more plates. Sprinkle the egg yolks in a 2-inch-wide band around the salmon. Sprinkle one-quarter of the onions over each band of yolk. Sprinkle the egg whites over the onions. Finish with the capers and the remaining 2 teaspoons chives.

If the crème fraîche is too loose to hold a shape, place it in a small bowl and whisk until thickened. Place a teaspoon in the center of each serving of tartare. Squeeze a few drops of lemon juice over the salmon and garnish each small mound of crème fraîche with a sprig of chervil. Serve with toasts or thin slices of baguette.

MAKES 4 SERVINGS

Left and right: Salmon Tartare; Smoked Salmon with a Frisée Salad with Oranges and Radishes (page 108)

SMOKED SALMON WITH A FRISÉE SALAD
WITH ORANGES AND RADISHES
SAUMON FUMÉ ET SALADE FRISÉE AUX ORANGES ET RADIS

CITRUS VINAIGRETTE

³/₄ cup fresh orange juice, simmered until
    reduced to 3 tablespoons

1 tablespoon sherry vinegar

1 tablespoon extra virgin olive oil

Kosher salt and freshly ground black pepper

2 Cara Cara (red or pink navel) oranges or
    blood oranges

1 to 2 heads frisée lettuce

40 tarragon leaves

40 Italian parsley leaves

40 chervil leaves

1 heaping tablespoon minced chives

12 slices (about 8 ounces) smoked salmon

2 large breakfast or Icicle radishes, trimmed
    and thinly sliced (to get 24 rounds)

Extra virgin olive oil

Here smoked salmon is paired with bitter greens, citrus vinaigrette, and peppery radishes. Fresh herbs are meant to be one of the dominant flavors, and they go well with all the elements here, so don't be shy about using them. And notice how light the vinaigrette is—just three tablespoons of reduced orange juice, one tablespoon of vinegar, and one of olive oil.

FOR THE VINAIGRETTE: Whisk together the reduced orange juice, sherry vinegar, and olive oil in a small bowl. Season to taste with salt and pepper.

Cut off the top and bottom of 1 orange. Stand the orange up and use a serrated knife to cut away the peel and pith in wide strips, working from top to bottom of the orange. Cut between the membranes to release the segments, letting them fall into a bowl. Squeeze any juice from the membranes over the segments. Repeat with the second orange. Set aside.

Remove the dark green outer leaves from the frisée and reserve for another use. Cut off and discard the core from the inner yellow leaves. Separate the leaves, trimming the bottoms as necessary to separate them. Wash the leaves and spin-dry. Place 1 ¹/₂ cups greens (reserve any extra for another use) in a medium bowl and add the herbs.

TO SERVE: Arrange 3 slices of salmon in the center of each of four serving plates, overlapping them, their edges following the perimeter of the plate, to make a large circle.

Toss the frisée salad with enough vinaigrette to lightly coat the leaves. Season to taste with salt and pepper. Toss in the radish slices.

Drizzle the salmon with olive oil and some of the juice from the oranges. Mound the salad in the center of the salmon and distribute the orange segments among the salads.

PHOTOGRAPH ON PAGE 107   **MAKES 4 SERVINGS**

DUNGENESS CRAB SALAD WITH CAVAILLON MELON
SALADE DE CRABE AU MELON DE CAVAILLON

CITRUS VINAIGRETTE

³/₄ cup fresh orange juice, simmered until
  reduced to 3 tablespoons
1 tablespoon sherry vinegar
1 tablespoon extra virgin olive oil
Kosher salt and freshly ground black pepper

CRAB SALAD

12 ounces Dungeness crabmeat
¼ cup crème fraîche
½ teaspoon finely grated lemon zest
1 teaspoon minced chives
1 teaspoon minced tarragon
1 teaspoon minced Italian parsley
1 teaspoon minced chervil
A squeeze of lemon juice
Kosher salt and freshly ground white pepper

1 small Cavaillon or other ripe melon
Kosher salt and freshly ground black pepper
About 2 ounces mâche
4 slices Brioche (page 324), crusts removed,
  cut into 2 triangles each and toasted

Dungeness crabs live in the Pacific Ocean and don't travel well, which is why people who have eaten the crab on the East Coast aren't always that impressed. For me, as someone who grew up eating and cooking exclusively on the East Coast, they took on a mythic quality. Still I didn't understand what all the fuss was about. When I got to California, I found out. When they're full grown, in the fall, they are big and plump and meaty; they still take some cleaning, but not nearly so much as, for example, the East Coast peekytoe.

This salad pairs the sweet crab—simply dressed with crème fraîche, herbs, and lemon—with sweet fragrant melon, salt, and pepper. We love the Cavaillon melon from France, which we grow ourselves. But any ripe sweet melon, say, a really good cantaloupe, will work.

FOR THE VINAIGRETTE: Whisk together the reduced orange juice, sherry vinegar, and olive oil in a small bowl. Season to taste with salt and pepper.

FOR THE CRAB SALAD: Drain the crabmeat well and place in a medium bowl. Pick through the meat to be certain that there are no pieces of shell or cartilage remaining. Stir in the remaining salad ingredients, seasoning to taste. (The crab can be refrigerated for up to 2 hours before serving.)

Cut the melon in half and scoop out and discard the seeds and fibers. Cut 4 melon wedges, 1 to 1½ inches thick (reserve the remaining melon for another use). Cut the melon away from the rind, then slice each wedge crosswise into bite-sized pieces, leaving the pieces on the rind for presentation.

TO SERVE: Arrange a sliced wedge of melon on one side of each serving plate and sprinkle lightly with salt and pepper. Form the crab mixture into quenelles (oval shapes). Scoop up one-eighth of the crab mixture with a soupspoon, then use a second soupspoon to scoop the crab from the first spoon, pressing the crab gently against the bowl of the spoon to shape it, and repeat, scooping the crab from spoon to spoon until you have an oval shape, and place it on a plate. Repeat to make 7 more quenelles, arranging 2 on each plate.

In a small bowl, toss the mâche with a light coating of the vinaigrette and season with salt and pepper to taste. Place a mound on each plate alongside the crab and melon. Drizzle some of the remaining dressing around the plates and arrange 2 triangles of toasted brioche on each plate.

MAKES 4 SERVINGS

COD BRANDADE WITH TOMATO CONFIT AND FRIED SAGE
BEIGNETS DE BRANDADE DE MORUE AU CONFIT DE TOMATES ET SAUGE FRITE

1 pound Atlantic cod fillet (of even thickness;
    about 1 inch), skin and bones removed
Kosher salt

BRANDADE
1½ pounds (2 large) russet potatoes
Milk
5 large cloves Garlic Confit (page 312),
    chopped to a paste
Pinch of sweet paprika

About 1 cup extra virgin olive oil
Freshly ground white pepper

BATTER
1 cup cake flour
¼ cup plus 2 tablespoons cornstarch
1 tablespoon baking powder
1½ teaspoons kosher salt
About 1 cup beer

3 to 4 cups peanut oil for deep-frying
18 pieces Tomato Confit (page 313)
18 sage leaves
Kosher salt

This is Bouchon's version of the dish called *brandade,* which dates to the early nineteenth century. It's poached salt cod mixed to a virtual paste with olive oil and milk (and sometimes potato), then served as a spread or sautéed as a fish cake. Here the cod mixture is coated in a fritter batter and deep-fried—our version of Mrs. Paul's fish sticks—served on some tomato confit and garnished with fried sage leaves. But it can also be put in a baking dish, sprinkled with panko (Japanese bread crumbs), and baked until hot, then spread on a baguette. A quintessential bistro dish. Bouchon salts its own cod; the entire process can take up to six days, but it can be made well ahead (we like to salt it two months ahead to give it added character). It's easy to do and ensures an excellent result, but salt cod can be found in many specialty markets as well; you will need eight ounces of prepared salt cod for this recipe.

FOR THE COD: Measure the thickness of the cod fillet: A 1-inch-thick piece will cure in 4 days, a ¾-inch-thick piece in about 3, so calculate the curing time based on the fillet you have. Line a container that just holds the cod and is at least 3 inches deep with about an inch of kosher salt. Nestle the cod in the salt and cover with another layer of salt. Cover and place in the refrigerator to cure. When ready, the salted cod will be very stiff.

Rinse the salt off the fish and dry the fish with paper towels. Place on a rack set over a plate and refrigerate uncovered for 24 hours to allow all the moisture to evaporate.

(At this point, the cod can be wrapped well in plastic wrap and refrigerated for several days or frozen for up to 2 months. You will need an 8-ounce piece of cod for this recipe; extra cod can be frozen for another use.)

To rehydrate the cod, place the fish in a large deep container and cover with 4 quarts of cold water. Soak the cod in the refrigerator for 12 to 24 hours, depending on the thickness; a 1-inch-thick piece will take the full 24 hours. Change the water every 8 hours or so. The cod is ready when it feels like fresh cod fillet again.

FOR THE BRANDADE: Preheat the oven to 350°F.

Prick the potatoes with a fork, place them on an oven rack, and bake until tender, about 1 hour.

Meanwhile, organize the remaining ingredients and equipment—it is important to work with the cod and potatoes while they are still warm. Rinse the cod and place it in a small saucepan with milk to cover. As soon as the potatoes are baked, place the saucepan over medium-low heat, heat the milk to just below a simmer, and poach the fish gently for 3 to 5 minutes. The poached fish should be tender and flaky. Remove from the heat.

As soon as the potatoes are done, halve them, scoop out the flesh, and press it through the finest disk of a food mill or a ricer. At the restaurant, we then put it through a tamis (drum sieve) for an even finer texture, but that is optional. Cover the potatoes with plastic wrap to keep them warm.

Drain the poached cod, discarding the milk; place the cod in a food processor and pulse a few times to break it up. Keep the pulsing brief: If the cod is overprocessed, it will become mushy. Add the garlic and paprika and pulse a few times. Add ¼ cup of the olive oil and pulse a few times, then add another ¼ cup and pulse. Add another ¼ cup and pulse a few times. Then transfer to a large bowl.

With a rubber spatula, fold half of the warm potatoes into the cod mixture. Taste the mixture and begin to add the remaining potatoes, tasting often: Brandade is generally made with equal parts of potatoes and cod, but the amount of potato added depends on the saltiness of the cod—you should still be able to taste the salt cod.

Add 3 to 4 tablespoons more olive oil: You want a good balance of potato, cod, and the fruitiness of the olive oil. Season to taste with salt and white pepper.

FOR THE BATTER: Mix the cake flour, cornstarch, baking powder, and salt in a medium bowl. Add the beer and stir with a spoon; the batter should remain slightly lumpy and be thick. Let the batter sit for about 10 minutes, or up to 2 hours.

Preheat the oven to 300°F.

TO COMPLETE: Roll the brandade into 18 balls of about 2 tablespoons each. Heat at least 3 inches of peanut oil to 350°F in a deep fryer or large deep saucepan. You will need to cook the brandade in several batches: The first ones can be kept warm on a platter in the oven until all are completed. Add about half the balls of brandade to the batter and spoon batter over them to cover on all sides, then carefully place in the hot oil, without crowding. Turn the balls as necessary to brown all sides evenly; total cooking time will be 4 to 5 minutes per batch. To test for doneness, insert a metal skewer into the center of a ball. Remove it after a few seconds and touch your lip with the skewer: It should be warm.

Meanwhile, when the last batch goes into the oil, put the tomato confit in a pan and warm in the oven for about 5 minutes.

When all the brandade is cooked, throw the sage leaves into the hot oil and cook for a few seconds, until crisp, then drain on paper towels.

TO SERVE: Place 3 pieces of tomato confit in the center of each plate. Place a ball of brandade on top of each piece and garnish the plates with the sage leaves and a sprinkling of salt.

PHOTOGRAPH ON PAGE 112   **MAKES 6 SERVINGS**

CLAMS MARINIÈRES WITH SOFFRITTO
PALOURDES MARINIÈRES AU SOFFRITTO

CROUTONS

1 baguette (about 2 ½ inches wide)

Extra virgin olive oil

Kosher salt

CLAMS

2 ½ pounds Manila clams

¼ cup olive oil

⅓ cup minced shallots

2 teaspoons minced thyme

24 cloves Garlic Confit (page 312)

¼ cup Soffritto (page 314)

Kosher salt and freshly ground white pepper

4 tablespoons (2 ounces) unsalted butter

1 cup dry white wine, such as sauvignon blanc

¼ cup Aïoli (page 315) or Tapenade
   (page 16)

2 tablespoons chopped Italian parsley

Cracked black pepper

This recipe combines a standard steaming technique for the clams—they're quickly steamed with wine until they open, a minute or so—with very intense, aromatic, sweet preparations of onion and garlic. The term *marinière* traditionally indicates fish or shellfish cooked with white wine and onions; here the onions are in a soffritto, cooked long and slow in oil until they are deeply caramelized. The soffritto gives the dish real depth, especially with the garlic confit.

This also works well with cockles or similar mollusks.

FOR THE CROUTONS: Preheat the broiler. Using a serrated knife, cut the baguette on a severe diagonal to make 4 slices that are about 9 inches long and ¼ inch thick. Place the croutons on a baking sheet, brush both sides lightly with olive oil, and season with a pinch of salt. Place under the broiler and toast until lightly browned on the first side, then turn each crouton over and brown the second side. Set aside.

FOR THE CLAMS: Wash the clams under cold running water; if they are very dirty, scrub with a clean scouring pad.

The clams cook very quickly: Have all the ingredients and the serving bowls ready before you begin to cook. Heat a pot (one with a tight-fitting lid) large enough to hold the clams no more than two deep over medium-high heat. (If you don't have a large enough pot, use two smaller saucepans and split the ingredients between them.) When the pot is hot, add the oil and reduce the heat to medium. Add the shallots and sweat them for a minute, then add the thyme, garlic confit, soffritto, and salt and pepper to taste. Stir the mixture for a minute to bring out the flavor of the soffritto.

Increase the heat to high, add the butter and clams, and toss the clams in the soffritto mixture. Cook for 30 seconds, then add the wine. Cover with the pot lid and let the clams steam until they open, 30 seconds to a few minutes, depending on the pot. If the clams have not opened after a minute, stir them and cover the pot again.

Meanwhile, spread each crouton with a tablespoon of aïoli or tapenade.

When all the clams have opened, stir in the parsley and a large pinch of cracked black pepper. Divide the clams and broth among four serving bowls, place a crouton alongside each, and serve immediately.

PHOTOGRAPH ON PAGE 113   **MAKES 4 SERVINGS**

CLAMS MARINIÈRES WITH TOMATO CONFIT
Substitute ¼ cup minced Tomato Confit (page 313) for the soffritto. (The tomato confit is a little easier to make and it's delicious, too.)

COQUILLES ST. JACQUES

MUSHROOM DUXELLES

6 ounces chanterelles, morels, or other
    seasonal mushrooms

2 tablespoons unsalted butter

¼ cup minced shallots

Kosher salt and freshly ground black pepper

3 tablespoons chopped Italian parsley

1 tablespoon chopped tarragon

VELOUTÉ

3 cups Fish Fumet (page 320)

3 tablespoons Roux (page 316),
    at room temperature or cold

½ cup heavy cream

Kosher salt and freshly ground white pepper.

2 tarragon sprigs

Eight 1-ounce sea scallops, muscle removed

¼ cup panko (Japanese bread crumbs)
    or dried bread crumbs

1 teaspoon chopped thyme

Seaweed or rock salt (optional)

I cooked this dish at the very first French restaurant I worked in, Le Seine, in Florida, and it's a measure of the integrity of the combination of ingredients that we cook it almost the same way at Bouchon, a quarter of a century later. Now as then, meaty scallops and mushroom duxelles are combined with a creamy wine sauce—made with a fumet, thickened with roux—and gratinéed to serve. It's so good to eat and is very easy to do because it's all put together ahead of time.

Coquilles St. Jacques is traditionally served in scallop shells (see Sources, page 330), but you can also use individual gratin dishes or any small ovenproof dishes.

FOR THE DUXELLES: Clean the mushrooms and trim away the bottom of the stems (see page 326). Finely chop with a knife or in a food processor. (You should have about 1½ cups chopped mushrooms.)

Melt the butter in a large nonstick skillet over medium-high heat. Add the shallots and sauté for a minute, stirring constantly, then add the mushrooms, reduce the heat to medium, and season with salt and pepper to taste. Cook for about 3 minutes, stirring often, or until the mushrooms are almost dry. Stir in the parsley and tarragon and spread on a plate to cool. (You will have about 1 cup.)

FOR THE VELOUTÉ: Bring the fish fumet to a gentle boil in a saucepan and boil until reduced to 2 cups. Reduce the heat to a simmer and whisk in the roux. Simmer for about 20 minutes, until thickened and reduced slightly. Add the cream and simmer for 10 minutes, skimming any foam—move the pan to the edge of the burner so the foam accumulates all to one side of the pan, making it easy to skim. Add salt and pepper to taste.

Strain the sauce into a bowl. Add the tarragon and let cool to room temperature. Once it has cooled, remove and discard the tarragon.

Divide the duxelles among four scallop shells or individual gratin dishes. Cover each portion with 2 to 3 tablespoons of the sauce. Cut the scallops horizontally in half and nestle them in the mushrooms. Cover the scallops in each shell with another 2 to 3 tablespoons of the sauce. (At this point, the scallops can be covered and refrigerated for a few hours. Remove from the refrigerator 20 to 30 minutes before baking.)

TO COMPLETE: Preheat the oven to 375°F.

Combine the panko and thyme and sprinkle over the scallops. Bake the scallops for 5 to 10 minutes, or until the sauce is bubbly. If desired, brown the tops under the broiler.

Meanwhile, line each serving plate with a bed of seaweed or rock salt, if desired. Place the hot shells or dishes on the plates and serve.

MAKES 4 SERVINGS

The bistro The first time I set foot in a bistro—it was in Manhattan, but that's neither here nor there—an amazing thing happened. I felt as if I'd been there already, knew the place in my bones, as if the bistro were already a part of me before I was conscious of it, and that by stepping into one, I simply engaged a part of myself that had always been there but until that moment was dormant. The restaurant was a classically designed bistro, dark and smoky, big dark wood banquettes, a great bar. It was sexy. It was an example of one of the few restaurant designs that almost universally seduce people.

Regardless of where it is, the bistro is a familiar place, a restaurant in which you feel immediately comfortable. The way onion soup and roast chicken are perfect bistro dishes and feed us bodily and spiritually, the bistro itself has that same impact. I feel an almost mystical connection to it; it's a place that evokes both a nostalgia and a sense of timelessness. The bistro somehow taps into a universal notion of food and comfort. It's an archetype of the public eating place.

The word *bistro* first appeared in the early nineteenth century. Some sources argue that the name derives from the Russian word for "quick," which the Cossacks would shout when calling for food during their occupation of Paris in 1815. More likely, says *Larousse Gastronomique*, the name derives from *bistrouille*, a mixture of coffee and brandy. Regardless, the idea of a bistro seems now to be so universal that restaurants all over the world have adopted the name and its associations with simple food and a place where you are always welcome. Bistros are boisterous and energetic and jostling, servers squeezing between tables, the smells of sizzling steak and fried potatoes in the air. You enter a bistro and you feel almost as if you've walked onto a stage and are part of a drama.

Bistro food is utilitarian by necessity—the bistro owner had to be frugal because costs were high and the space was small. Ingenious use of leftovers was the norm. An owner bought less-expensive, therefore tougher, cuts of meat, so braises and stews were abundant—blanquette de veau, lamb shanks, trotters. Roasts that could be

TILE FLOOR: Wood floors are a pleasure in old bistros because you can often see the path the wait staff has worn over decades of service, and this connection to the history of a bistro is part of the fun of eating there. But tile floors are really the quintessential bistro floor. Like mirrors, they were a matter of economy—inexpensive, durable, easy to clean—yet they too enhanced the environs by reflecting sound—the shuffling chairs, clicking heels, and conversation. And when tiles cracked, they tended to be left cracked rather than being replaced, making them another part of the aged feeling that is so appealing about a bistro. The bistro floors I like most are those made from broken tile fragments.

cooked ahead of time would serve many people. Dried beans, inexpensive and easily stored, could always be found in the pantry.

Because a bistro served all day long, the staff relied on dishes that were easily put together—soup that could be kept warm or an array of charcuterie items such as dry-cured sausages and hams ready to slice, and potted meats that could be sent as is to the table. Eggs, amazing in their versatility, inexpensive and abundant, could be transformed into all kinds of wonderful food from savory to sweet dishes and were one of the menu's linchpins.

But what I love so much about this food is not that it's efficient and practical from a chef's point of view, but rather the way it tastes and the feeling I get in this particular type of restaurant. The food and the place together, the energy, the smells, and the people—they make for a unique experience.

With luck, the bistro you find yourself in will be old, the walls scuffed, the central aisle worn from decades of traffic. That is its own pleasure—to be in an old place, eating the great old dishes. To place your foot on a step that is concave from countless footsteps before yours, to lean against a banquette that was new in 1924 and eat a bowl of onion soup—you feel so good, so satisfied, so connected. When you eat like this, in this kind of place, you are, in a way, immortal. You become a part of the continuum of the bistro's history.

SNAILS WITH HERB BUTTER—ESCARGOTS DE BOURGOGNE

HERB BUTTER

4 to 5 garlic cloves, peeled and
  finely minced

2 teaspoons kosher salt

8 ounces unsalted butter,
  at room temperature

½ cup finely minced Italian parsley

¼ cup finely minced chives

2 tablespoons minced shallots

Pinch of freshly grated black pepper

1 tablespoon fresh lemon juice

1 tablespoon Pernod

24 "very large" top-quality canned snails
  (see Sources, page 330), drained

Sheet puff pastry, homemade or store-bought

Here are two different ways to serve snails: in their shells (see Sources, page 330), with piping-hot garlicky butter and plenty of herbs and shallots, or out of their shells, with puff pastry tops.

This is a perfect dish for entertaining because it can be prepared ahead of time, refrigerated, then finished in a hot oven for less than ten minutes. The Pernod is an important flavoring and helps to keep the butter from separating as it cooks. If you don't care for its anise flavor, use white wine instead.

FOR THE HERB BUTTER: Mince the garlic and salt together and crush with the blade of a knife to make a paste. Put the butter in a large bowl (or the bowl of a mixer fitted with the paddle attachment), add the garlic paste, and cream together. Add the parsley, chives, shallots, pepper, lemon juice, and Pernod and mix well. Remove the bowl from the mixer and use a spatula to make certain the ingredients are distributed throughout the butter. The butter can be piped or spooned over the snails—if desired, transfer it to a pastry bag without a tip or with a large plain tip.

FOR THE SNAILS: If using snail dishes instead of snail shells, place a snail in each indentation and pipe or spoon about 2 teaspoons of butter over each. If using snail shells, place a snail in each shell and pipe in about 2 teaspoons of butter. Refrigerate for at least an hour, or up to 12 hours. (Any extra herb butter is wonderful melted over meats or fish.)

Meanwhile, if using snail dishes, preheat the oven to 450°F. With a round cutter that is about ¼ inch larger in diameter than the indentations in the snail dishes, cut 24 rounds from the puff pastry. Line a baking sheet with a Silpat or sheet of parchment. Arrange the puff pastry rounds on the baking sheet and top with a second Silpat or cover with another sheet of parchment and then a second baking sheet.

Bake for 15 to 20 minutes, or until the pastry is golden brown. Remove from the oven and let cool.

TO SERVE: Preheat the oven to 450°F.

If using snail dishes, bake the snails for 5 to 8 minutes, or until the butter is bubbling. Top each snail with a round of puff pastry and heat for about 30 seconds.

If using snail shells, arrange the shells in snail dishes or other ovenproof serving dishes. Bake for 5 to 8 minutes, or until the butter is bubbly.

PHOTOGRAPH ON PAGE 103   **MAKES 4 SERVINGS**

FROGS' LEGS PROVENÇAL—CUISSES DE GRENOUILLE À LA PROVENÇALE

MARINADE

1 cup tightly packed basil leaves,
    coarsely chopped

1 garlic clove, peeled and smashed

1 tablespoon chopped thyme

1 piquillo pepper (see Sources, page 330)
    (optional)

1 cup extra virgin olive oil

8 pairs (about 3 ounces per pair) frogs' legs
    (see Sources, page 330)

30 Niçoise olives

Kosher salt and freshly ground black pepper

All-purpose flour

Canola oil

2 tablespoons extra virgin olive oil

2 tablespoons minced shallots

Heaping ¼ cup Tomato Confit (page 313),
    cut into small dice

2 teaspoons minced thyme

1 cup dry white wine, such as
    sauvignon blanc

12 cloves Garlic Confit (page 312)

2 tablespoons unsalted butter

½ cup Fish Fumet (page 320) or
    Chicken Stock (page 317)

2 tablespoons roughly chopped
    Italian parsley

T he best frogs' legs are so meaty and fatty and sweet that I've always thought a butcher rather than a fishmonger should sell them. Choose your source carefully so you don't wind up with dry and flavorless ones. Here they're joined with an infallible pairing—garlic and parsley. The frogs' legs are first marinated (wrapping them in cheesecloth allows all the flavor of the marinade to permeate the legs but keeps the herbs from clinging to the meat), then seared. A quick pan sauce is made with shallots and thyme, both tomato and garlic confit, and white wine and butter, and the frogs' legs are returned to the pan and finished in the oven.

FOR THE MARINADE: Combine all the ingredients in a food processor and puree.

FOR THE FROGS' LEGS: If the backbones or belly flaps are still attached, cut them off and discard. If the feet are still on, pinch each foot to extend the toes, then cut them off and discard.

Choose a square or rectangular baking dish that will hold the frogs' legs in a single layer. Cut a piece of cheesecloth long enough to line the dish twice, wet the cheesecloth, and wring it dry. Coat the bottom of the dish with half the marinade. Cover the marinade

with a single layer of cheesecloth, letting what remains hang over one end of the dish, and arrange the frogs' legs on the cheesecloth. Fold the remaining cheesecloth over the legs and pour the remaining marinade over the cheesecloth. Press a piece of plastic wrap against the cheesecloth. Refrigerate for at least 3 hours, or up to 6 hours.

TO COMPLETE: Preheat the oven to 350°F.

Cut the Niçoise olives away from the pits; discard the pits. Set aside the pieces of olive. Line a plate with paper towels.

Remove the frogs' legs from the marinade (discard the cheesecloth and marinade) and dry well with paper towels. If the legs are joined in pairs, cross them, poking one of the legs through the space between the calf muscle and bone of the other leg so the calf muscle is on top; this will keep them from splitting apart as they cook. Season both sides of the legs with salt and pepper.

Heat an ovenproof sauté pan large enough to hold the legs in one layer over high heat (or use two pans if necessary). Meanwhile, dredge the legs in flour and pat away any excess. Add a thin film of canola oil to the pan. Reduce the heat to medium and add the legs calf side up—stand back, because the oil may "pop" when the legs are added. Sauté for about 1 minute, or until the legs are a light golden brown, then turn and cook for another minute. Drain on paper towels.

Drain off any oil and set the pan over medium-low heat. Add the olive oil and then the shallots to the pan and cook for 1 to 2 minutes to sweat and soften the shallots. Add the tomato confit and cook for another minute, then stir in the thyme. Add the wine and cook for 2 to 3 minutes, or until the liquid is reduced by about one-third. Add the garlic confit, olives, and butter,

season to taste with salt and pepper, and stir to combine. Add the fish fumet, then add the frogs' legs and bring to a simmer.

Place the pan in the oven for 3 to 5 minutes, or until the frogs' legs are thoroughly cooked. Remove the pan from the oven and swirl in the parsley.

Crisscross 2 sets of frogs' legs on each serving plate and pour the sauce over them, evenly distributing the garlic cloves and olives.

MAKES 4 SERVINGS

Left and right: Marinating frogs' legs; Crispy Frogs' Legs (page 124)

CRISPY FROGS' LEGS—CUISSES DE GRENOUILLE CROQUANTES

MARINADE

1 cup tightly packed basil leaves, chopped

1 garlic clove, peeled and smashed

1 tablespoon chopped thyme

1 piquillo pepper (see Sources, page 330) (optional)

1 cup extra virgin olive oil

8 pairs (about 3 ounces per pair) frogs' legs (see Sources, page 330)

Peanut oil for deep-frying

SAUCE GRIBICHE MAKES ABOUT 1 CUP

1 tablespoon red wine vinegar

1 teaspoon Dijon mustard

2 teaspoons each chopped hard-cooked egg white and egg yolk (see page 326)

1 tablespoon minced nonpareil capers

2 tablespoons minced shallots

2 teaspoons each minced tarragon, chives, chervil, and parsley

1 tablespoon minced cornichons

¼ teaspoon kosher salt

¼ teaspoon freshly ground black pepper

½ cup mayonnaise

COATING

½ cup all-purpose flour

½ cup cornstarch

Kosher salt and freshly ground black pepper

2 large eggs

¼ cup milk

1 ounce mâche

Kosher salt and freshly ground black pepper

Extra virgin olive oil

Sherry vinegar

Fleur de sel

These frogs' legs are marinated, then deep-fried until crisp and served with a dipping sauce.

FOR THE MARINADE: Puree all the ingredients.

FOR THE FROGS' LEGS: If the backbones or belly flaps are still attached, cut them off and discard. If the feet are still on, pinch each foot to extend the toes, then cut them off and discard.

Choose a square or rectangular baking dish that will hold the frogs' legs in a single layer. Cut a piece of cheesecloth long enough to line the dish twice, wet the cheesecloth, and wring it dry. Coat the bottom of the dish with half the marinade. Cover the marinade with a single layer of cheesecloth, letting what remains hang over one end of the dish, and arrange the frogs' legs on the cheesecloth. Fold the remaining cheesecloth over the legs and pour the remaining marinade over the cheesecloth. Press a piece of plastic wrap against the cheesecloth. Refrigerate for at least 3 hours, or up to 6 hours.

FOR THE SAUCE: Toss all the ingredients except the mayonnaise together in a bowl. Gently stir in the mayonnaise. Let the sauce sit for at least 30 minutes, or refrigerate for up to a day.

TO COMPLETE: Heat 3 to 4 inches of peanut oil to 375°F in a deep fryer or large deep saucepan.

Meanwhile, mix the flour, cornstarch, and a pinch each of salt and pepper in a shallow bowl. In another shallow bowl, whisk together the eggs, milk, and a pinch each of salt and pepper.

Remove the frogs' legs from the marinade (if legs are joined in pairs, see page 122 to keep them that way) and dry well with paper towels (discard the marinade and cloth). Season with salt and pepper. Dip half the legs in the egg mixture to coat, then lift out, letting excess liquid fall from the legs. Toss with the flour mixture and pat off any excess flour. Place the legs in the hot oil and cook for about 5 minutes, or until crispy and cooked throughout. Drain on paper towels and repeat with the others.

Place the mâche in a small bowl and toss with salt and pepper and sprinklings of olive oil and sherry vinegar. Fill four small ramekins with sauce and place one on each plate with a mound of mâche and 2 pairs of frogs' legs. Sprinkle with fleur de sel.

PHOTOGRAPH ON PAGE 123   **MAKES 4 SERVINGS**

MELTED RACLETTE CHEESE
WITH BOILED POTATOES AND BAYONNE HAM
RACLETTE AUX POMMES DE TERRE VAPEUR ET JAMBON DE BAYONNE

About 8 ounces (12 small) fingerling potatoes (no larger than 2 inches long and 1 inch wide)

Generous 1 tablespoon kosher salt, or to taste

1/4 teaspoon black peppercorns

2 thyme sprigs

5 bay leaves

2 garlic cloves, skin left on, smashed

One 8-ounce wedge raclette cheese, top and bottom rind left on, outside rind cut away

4 slices Bayonne ham (about 2 ounces total; see Sources, page 330)

Dijon mustard

About 16 cornichons

1 tablespoon minced chives

Fleur de sel

Crusty bread

The traditional way of serving raclette, a Swiss-style cow's milk cheese made in the Alps, is melted and served with potatoes. We add dry-cured ham, cornichons, and mustard to the plate for a very satisfying winter dish. In the end, it's not all that different from a really good grilled ham-and-cheese sandwich.

Put the potatoes, salt, peppercorns, thyme, 1 bay leaf, and garlic in a large saucepan and add cold water to cover by 1 inch; the water should be seasoned aggressively. Bring to a boil, reduce the heat, and simmer for about 15 minutes, or until the potatoes are tender. Drain the potatoes, reserving the cooking liquid; return the cooking liquid to the pan and set the potatoes aside separately (discard the garlic and flavorings). (The potatoes can be cooked up to a few hours ahead and kept at room temperature.)

Cut 4 equal portions of cheese, about 1/2 inch thick—the thickness will enable you to move the cheese easily once it has been heated. Arrange the cheese in one layer in four small nonstick skillets, which will keep the cheese from spreading too much, or in one large one.

Put the rack as close as possible to the broiler and preheat the broiler. Place a slice of ham, a dollop of mustard, 4 cornichons, and a bay leaf on each serving plate, leaving space for the potatoes.

Bring the potato cooking liquid to a boil. Add the potatoes and reheat for a minute, then drain and remove the potatoes briefly to paper towels. Arrange 3 potatoes in a stack on each plate.

Meanwhile, place the skillet(s) of cheese on the broiler rack and broil for 1 to 2 minutes, just to melt the cheese. Place a portion of cheese over each stack of potatoes. Sprinkle the cheese with the chives and a little fleur de sel. Serve with crusty bread.

MAKES 4 SERVINGS

RESTAU
A
LA CA

STUFFED QUAIL ON DANDELION GREENS
CAILLE FARCIE ET SALADE AUX PISSENLITS

STUFFING

5 ounces garlic sausage
    (see Sources, page 330)
2 tablespoons unsalted butter
3 tablespoons chopped shallots
2 teaspoons thyme leaves
Kosher salt and freshly ground black pepper
3 ounces morels, chanterelles, or other
    mushrooms (cleaned, page 326,
    if necessary), cut into ¼-inch dice
6 ounces baby spinach leaves,
    washed and dried if necessary
1 large egg, beaten

QUAIL

4 semiboneless quail (see Sources, page 330),
    rinsed and dried
Kosher salt and freshly ground black pepper
Canola oil
1 tablespoon unsalted butter
4 thyme sprigs
4 garlic cloves, peeled

SAUCE

1 cup Chicken Jus (page 321),
    reduced to ¼ cup
1 tablespoon minced shallots

¼ cup red wine vinegar
1 tablespoon minced chives

DANDELION GREENS

12 ounces dandelion greens, preferably baby
    greens, any tough stems removed
2 tablespoons minced shallots
2 tablespoons minced chives
¼ cup Italian parsley leaves
¼ cup tarragon leaves
¼ cup chervil leaves
About ¼ cup House Vinaigrette (page 315)

At Bouchon we serve most birds as a main course, but this salad is a good wintertime starter. Quail are stuffed with sausage meat, pan-roasted, and served with a simple jus, shallots, and flavorful dandelion greens. Look for baby dandelion greens at the farmers' market; they are sweeter and more tender than the larger greens. If you can't find dandelion greens, use frisée or a combination of frisée and mâche.

FOR THE STUFFING: Crumble the sausage and place it in a small bowl.

Melt the butter in a small skillet over medium heat. Add the shallots, thyme, and salt and pepper to taste and sweat for about 2 minutes to soften the shallots. Add the mushrooms and sauté for 1 to 2 minutes to soften them. Add the spinach and a little more seasoning and cook for about 1 minute, just to soften the leaves. Remove from the heat and stir well to mix the ingredients throughout the spinach. Taste and adjust the seasonings if necessary. Place on a cutting board and coarsely chop the spinach.

Add the spinach mixture to the sausage and stir to combine. Let cool slightly, then stir in the egg. Depending on the seasoning of the garlic sausage, you may need to add a little salt and pepper; to check the flavor of the stuffing, sauté a little of the mixture, then taste and correct the seasoning if necessary.

Place the stuffing in a pastry bag without a tip or with a large plain tip.

FOR THE QUAIL: Season the inside of the quail with salt and pepper. Fold the wing tips underneath the birds. Open up the cavities of the birds and fill generously with the stuffing. Reshape the quail, plumping the breasts, then pulling down the neck skin and tucking it under each bird. Push the legs in toward the breast, to plump the breast and re-form the bird, and cross the drumsticks. Cut four 2-foot lengths of kitchen twine. Place the center of one piece under a quail at the neck and bring it up over the wing tips and around the bird. Tie the twine once to tighten it, then bring the ends of the twine up and tie the ends of the drumsticks together.

Preheat the oven to 450°F.

Sprinkle the quail breasts with salt and pepper. Heat a thin film of canola oil in a large ovenproof nonstick skillet over high heat. When the oil is hot, add the birds breast side up and sauté for about 1 minute. Tilt the skillet and baste the breasts of the bird with the hot oil for about a minute, then transfer the skillet to the oven to cook for 5 minutes.

Remove the skillet from the oven and add the butter, thyme sprigs, and garlic cloves. Tilt the skillet and baste the quail for a minute or two. Take out the sprigs and place one on each bird; return to the oven for 5 minutes, or until the breasts are medium. If you would like to brown the quail breasts, turn on the broiler and broil for a minute or two.

FOR THE SAUCE: Combine the chicken jus, shallots, and red wine vinegar in a small saucepan, bring to a simmer, and reduce to $1/4$ cup.

TO SERVE: Just before serving, toss the greens in a bowl with the shallots, herbs, and just enough vinaigrette to coat. Divide the greens among four serving plates.

Remove the twine from the quail. Cut each quail lengthwise in half and arrange the halves stuffing side up on the greens. Swirl the chives into the jus and moisten the quail with it.

MAKES 4 SERVINGS

NOTE: Semiboneless quail, available at many butcher shops and some supermarkets, are partially boned to make stuffing them and eating them easier; the wing tips and leg bones are left intact.

STUFFED DUCK NECK WITH TUSCAN KALE
COU DE CANARD FARCI AU CAVOLO NERO

STUFFING

2 duck legs (see Sources, page 330)

1 duck liver (optional)

Kosher salt and freshly ground black pepper

1½ tablespoons unsalted butter

¼ cup minced shallots

1 teaspoon thyme leaves

6 ounces garlic sausage
(see Sources, page 330)

2 tablespoons Dijon mustard

2 tablespoons Pernod

¼ cup shelled pistachios, toasted, rubbed in
a towel to remove most of the skins, and
coarsely chopped

1 large egg

1 tablespoon chopped Italian parsley

1 tablespoon chopped tarragon

4 duck necks (6 to 8 inches long;
see Sources, page 330)

8 cups Chicken Stock (page 317),
Chicken Jus (page 321), or water

POTATOES

⅓ pound fingerling potatoes (no wider than
a quarter), cut into ½-inch-thick slices

¼ teaspoon black peppercorns

2 thyme sprigs

1 bay leaf

2 garlic cloves, skin left on, smashed

Kosher salt

KALE

1 pound (2 bunches) cavolo nero
(Tuscan kale)

2 large thyme sprigs

2 garlic cloves

4 tablespoons (2 ounces) unsalted butter

2 tablespoons minced shallots

2 teaspoons minced thyme

Kosher salt and freshly ground black pepper

1 cup Chicken Jus (page 321)

16 red pearl onions, cooked according to
the directions on page 326

1 tablespoon minced chives

Duck is not far behind pig in terms of versatility: In addition to its flavorful meat, a duck's fat and skin are both delicious accompaniments and invaluable tools. Duck fat results in tasty, crisp potatoes. The legs can be confited in fat to preserve them. You can make a pâté from the duck meat and roll it in the skin and roast it.

This rustic preparation uses the skin from a duck neck as a casing for a savory *farce,* or "stuffing." Garlic sausage is combined with chopped duck meat and liver, pistachios, egg, herbs, and aromatics, but the stuffing might include virtually any kind of garnish—bacon, onion, potato, anything that goes well with duck. The stuffed duck neck is gently poached and cooled, then it's browned and sliced and paired with potatoes and Tuscan kale; it is delicious with lentils (page 139) as well.

FOR THE STUFFING: Remove the skin and fat from the duck legs and remove the meat from the bones. Cut the meat into 1-inch pieces. (You should have about ¾ cup.) Transfer to a small bowl. Cut the liver, if using, into pieces. Add to the duck meat and season with salt and pepper.

Melt the butter in a small skillet over medium heat. Add the shallots, thyme, and salt and pepper to taste. Sweat for about 2 minutes to soften the shallots. Remove from the heat and cool.

All your equipment and the duck meat must be ice cold in order to create and hold the emulsification as the meat is ground. Chill a meat grinder and the large and small dies, then set up the grinder with the large die. Put a metal bowl in a larger bowl of ice and place under the grinder to catch the ground meats.

Run the duck (and liver) through the grinder (on low speed if using an electric grinder), letting the mixture fall into the chilled bowl. Run the sausage through. Transfer the mixture to another bowl and mix to combine. Replace the first bowl over the ice, replace the large die with the small one, and run the mixture through again. Keeping the bowl over the bowl of ice, stir in the shallot mixture, mustard, and Pernod; do not overwork the mixture.

Stir in the pistachios and egg, then the herbs. Depending on the seasoning of the garlic sausage, you may need to add a little salt and pepper; to check the flavor of the stuffing, bring a small pan of water to a simmer, poach a spoonful of the mixture, and taste it. Refrigerate the stuffing.

FOR THE DUCK NECKS: Turn each neck inside out. Pull away any large chunks of fat. With a paring knife, scrape away any glands or fat remaining on the skin. The top of the neck will be smaller than the bottom; the bottom may be very wide.

Put the stuffing in a pastry bag without a tip or with a large plain tip and pipe it into the necks. You will probably have enough stuffing for the 4 necks, but if you have a little less, it won't matter in the final presentation, since they are served sliced. Squeeze the ends of each neck to compress the mixture into a compact log shape, then tie the ends securely with kitchen twine. Cut 4 single-layer rectangles of cheesecloth and 4 pieces of plastic wrap about 12 by 16 inches. Place a duck neck on a short side of a piece of cheesecloth. (If possible, have a second person hold the other end of the cheesecloth flat against the work surface as you roll.) Roll up the neck in the cloth, squeezing the ends from time to time to make the diameter as uniform as possible. Twist the ends of the cheesecloth and tuck them underneath the roll, then roll the neck up the same way in a piece of plastic wrap. Tie the ends of the plastic wrap securely with twine and tie with additional pieces of twine at 1-inch intervals down the neck. Repeat with the remaining necks. Trim away excess plastic wrap and twine.

Bring the stock to a simmer in a large saucepan and add the necks. Place a plate slightly smaller than the diameter of the pan on the necks to keep them submerged but still allow you to see the liquid. Bring to just below a simmer and poach gently for 35 minutes. Don't boil the liquid or the skins might burst.

Turn off the heat and let the necks cool in the liquid for 30 minutes. Drain the necks, wrap in plastic wrap, and refrigerate for at least 12 hours, or up to 2 days.

FOR THE POTATOES: Put the potatoes, peppercorns, thyme, bay leaf, and garlic in a medium saucepan, add cold water to cover by 1 inch, and season the water assertively with salt. Place over high heat and bring to a boil. Reduce the heat and simmer for about 10 minutes, until the potatoes are tender. Drain the potatoes; discard the garlic and herbs. Set the potatoes aside at room temperature.

FOR THE KALE: Bring a large pot of salted water to a boil. Prepare an ice bath. Meanwhile, fold each kale leaf lengthwise in half and cut out or tear away the stem that runs the length of the leaf. Tear each leaf into 1- to 1 1/2-inch pieces. Blanch the kale in the boiling water for a minute or two, until just tender, with a slight bite left. Remove the leaves and place in the ice bath to chill for a minute. Drain and squeeze out excess moisture. Coarsely chop the kale; set aside. (The kale can be prepared several hours in advance.)

TO COMPLETE: Preheat the oven to 325°F.

Unwrap the duck necks. Heat a small nonstick ovenproof skillet over medium heat. Once it is hot, add the necks, reduce the heat so the necks brown slowly, and cook, rolling the necks from time to time so they brown evenly, for about 18 minutes, until lightly browned. Fat will be released from the skin as the necks brown; drain the excess as it accumulates, but always leave a light coating in the skillet. Add the thyme sprigs and garlic cloves and continue to cook another minute, or until richly browned. Transfer the skillet to the oven to keep warm while you finish the kale.

Melt the butter in a large saucepan over medium heat. Add the shallots, minced thyme, and a pinch each of salt and pepper. After a minute or two, add the kale and a bit more salt and pepper and cook for 2 to 3 minutes, until hot. Add the chicken jus, bring to a simmer, and let the liquid reduce slightly. Add the potatoes and pearl onions and stir gently. Simmer for 2 to 3 minutes to warm the ingredients. Just before serving, stir in the chives.

Meanwhile, transfer the necks to a cutting board; let rest for 5 minutes. Slice the necks into 1/2-inch-thick slices. Place a mound of the kale on each serving plate and top with one-quarter of the duck neck slices.

MAKES 4 SERVINGS

Duck confit My first experience with duck confit was, appropriately, at La Rive, where my love of this style of cooking really began. At the time, in the early 1980s, duck confit was not something you saw on a lot of menus. René liked me to offer duck breast, which was popular, and he loved to make the duck confit so that we could eat it ourselves.

Duck confit's origins go back many generations to a time when the technique was used primarily to preserve the duck. Now we make it because it tastes so good. Duck confit is a versatile preparation that works on its own or as a component in a more complex dish. While preparing it is a three-stage process, it's quite easy to do, and the rewards are great. And it actually improves over time, so you can make this as much as two weeks in advance.

In the first stage, duck legs are rubbed with a dry marinade of salt, herbs, and aromatics to season the meat. At Bouchon, we use a green salt technique: The dry marinade ingredients are all blended together to make a green paste, which ensures an even distribution of seasonings. It is best is to weigh your meat so you can measure two tablespoons of green salt per pound. The duration of the dry marinade, or cure, is important—too long and the legs can become too salty. Thicker duck legs can be marinated for twenty-four hours; rabbit, which we also confit (below), for eighteen hours. The other critical factor in the cooking stage is oven temperature: low, low heat, 190°F, for ten to twelve hours.

The final stage of the confit process is cooling the legs, completely submerged in their cooking fat. To serve, remove them from the fat—it's best to let them out for a few hours to allow the fat to soften so that you avoid tearing the meat and skin. Then start them on top of the stove in a hot pan skin side down and finish them slowly in a moderate oven. Very crispy skin is the benchmark of a great duck confit. Part of the pleasure of eating confit is the crispness of the skin and the contrasting tender succulence of the meat.

FOR RABBIT CONFIT: Follow the recipe for duck confit opposite, using rabbit legs that weigh 6 to 9 ounces each (see Sources, page 330). Cure them for only 18 hours before rinsing away the salt. If you want to confit only 4 legs, you'll need half the green salt and, because you can use a smaller pot, only about 4 cups of duck fat.

DUCK CONFIT—CONFIT DE CANARD

GREEN SALT **MAKES ABOUT ½ CUP**
½ cup kosher salt
2 bay leaves, broken into pieces

2 tablespoons chopped thyme
¼ cup packed Italian parsley leaves
1 teaspoon black peppercorns

Eight 8-ounce whole Pekin (Long Island) duck
legs (see Sources, page 330)
6 to 8 cups rendered duck fat, melted

There are countless ways to flavor duck confit, but to my taste, the simpler the better—some salt, pepper, fresh herbs.

FOR THE GREEN SALT: Place the salt in a coffee or spice mill or small food processor. Add the bay leaves, thyme, parsley, and peppercorns. (If all the herbs do not fit, start grinding the mixture using only part of the parsley, then add more as the leaves break down.) Process until well combined and a vivid green. Set aside.

FOR THE DUCK: Rinse the duck legs under cold running water and pat dry with paper towels. Pull away and discard any excess fat. With scissors, trim excess skin near the bottom of the legs and around the edges, leaving ¼ inch overhang of skin.

The skin and fat can be discarded or rendered. *To render the fat,* place the trimmed fat and skin in a small saucepan with a tablespoon of water. Heat on a heat diffuser over low heat for several hours, allowing the fat to melt and render, then strain the fat. Use in the confit or save for other uses. Cover and refrigerate.

Once the legs are trimmed, weigh them so you won't oversalt them. The correct proportion is 2 tablespoons of green salt to 1 pound duck legs, or about 1 tablespoon per leg. Rub the salt over the legs, rubbing a little extra on the thicker parts and around the joint. Place the legs flesh side up in a single layer in a baking dish that holds them comfortably (use two if necessary). Cover with plastic wrap and refrigerate for 24 hours.

FOR THE CONFIT: Place an oven thermometer in the center of the oven and preheat the oven to 190°F. It is important to check the heat from time to time while the legs cook to be certain that the oven maintains the proper temperature.

Rinse the legs well under cold water and dry thoroughly with paper towels. Layer the duck legs (no more than 2 deep) in a 9- to 10-inch-wide heavy ovenproof pot with a lid. Pour enough melted duck fat to cover the legs. Place over medium heat just until the fat is warm. Cover, place in the oven, and cook for 10 hours.

Check a duck leg by carefully lifting it from the fat and piercing it with a paring knife. The meat should be meltingly tender; if necessary, return the duck to the oven for up to 2 hours longer, checking the legs frequently, but keep in mind that if they are cooked for too long, later they may fall apart as they are sautéed. Remove the legs from the oven and cool them in the fat.

Once they have cooled enough to handle, gently lift the legs from the fat and place in a container. Strain the fat over the legs, submerging them in fat; transfer them to a smaller container if not completely covered with the fat. Cover and refrigerate for up to 2 weeks.

TO USE: When you are ready to use the duck legs, remove the container from the refrigerator and allow it to sit at room temperature for a few hours in order to soften the fat enough to remove the desired quantity of legs without breaking them.

PHOTOGRAPHS ON PAGES 132 AND 133   **MAKES 8 DUCK LEGS**

NOTE: You can keep confit for months rather than weeks if you remove all meat juices from the fat. To do this, separate the confited duck or rabbit from the fat and refrigerate the fat. As the fat solidifies, the meat juices will settle to the bottom of the container, where they'll gel. When the fat is sufficiently firm, carefully spoon it off the top, without disturbing the gel. Discard the gel, melt the fat, and pour it over the duck or rabbit.

DUCK CONFIT WITH BRUSSELS SPROUTS AND MUSTARD SAUCE
CONFIT DE CANARD AUX CHOUX DE BRUXELLES, SAUCE MOUTARDE

4 pieces Duck Confit (page 137)

BRUSSELS SPROUTS
Kosher salt
16 (about 12 ounces) Brussels sprouts

1 tablespoon plus 1 teaspoon minced shallots
1 tablespoon minced thyme
12 cloves Garlic Confit (page 312)
1¼ cups Chicken Stock (page 317)
2 tablespoons plus 2 teaspoons Dijon mustard

¼ cup crème fraîche
2 tablespoons minced chives

Duck confit can be served in countless ways, from salad to pasta filling to this rich combination, set atop Brussels sprouts that have been tossed in a sauce of chicken stock, crème fraîche, sharp mustard, and aromatics.

Remove the duck confit from the refrigerator and let the fat soften until you can remove the legs without damaging them.

FOR THE BRUSSELS SPROUTS: Bring a large pot of salted water to a boil. Prepare an ice bath. Line a baking sheet with a dish towel. Remove and discard the tougher outer leaves from the Brussels sprouts. Trim the bottom of the root ends and cut a small slit in the center of each root end. Place in the ice bath for 5 minutes to chill.

Remove half of the sprouts from the ice bath and add to the boiling water, a few at a time, to keep the water at a boil. Boil the sprouts for 5 to 6 minutes, or until they are tender when pierced with the tip of a paring knife. Just before they are done, remove the remaining sprouts from the ice bath; reserve the ice bath.

Dip a strainer into the pot, remove the cooked Brussels sprouts, and plunge in the ice bath to chill while you cook the remaining batch. Once the sprouts are cold, remove and drain on the dish towel. (The Brussels sprouts can be held for a couple of hours at room temperature or refrigerated for up to a day.)

TO COMPLETE: Remove the duck legs from the fat and let them come to room temperature. Gently scrape away any fat still clinging to the legs.

Preheat the oven to 375°F.

Cut the Brussels sprouts lengthwise in half; set aside.

Heat a nonstick skillet that will hold the duck legs in a single layer over medium-high heat. Reduce the heat to medium and carefully add the duck pieces skin side down—stand back, the moisture in the fat in the skin will pop. Sauté the legs for 5 to 6 minutes, or until the skin is a rich golden brown. Remove the skillet from the heat, tilt it, and use a large spoon to transfer enough fat to coat the bottom of a baking dish large enough to hold the legs in a single layer. Place the duck legs skin side up in the baking dish. Transfer to the oven and cook for 8 minutes to thoroughly heat them.

Meanwhile, discard all but about 2 teaspoons of the fat remaining in the skillet. Return the skillet to medium-high heat and add the shallots, thyme, and garlic confit. Sweat the shallots for a minute, then add the chicken stock, bring to a simmer, and simmer for 2 minutes. Whisk in the mustard and crème fraîche. Add the Brussels sprouts and simmer until the sprouts are warmed through and the sauce is reduced enough to coat the sprouts. Remove from the heat and stir in the chives.

Drain the duck legs on paper towels. Divide the Brussels sprouts and sauce among four serving plates and top each with a duck leg.

MAKES 4 SERVINGS

GARLIC SAUSAGE WITH FRENCH GREEN LENTILS
SAUCISSON À L'AIL AUX LENTILLES

BOUQUET GARNI

Two 6- to 7-inch pieces outer leek leaves,
    washed

2 or 3 large thyme sprigs

3 cloves

3 bay leaves

12 black peppercorns

SAUSAGE AND LENTILS

2 leeks

1 onion

1 head garlic, halved horizontally

2 large carrots, peeled

1½ pounds garlic sausage
    (2 inches in diameter and 11 inches long;
    see Sources, page 330)

4 ounces slab bacon

8 ounces Le Puy lentils (see Sources, page 330),
    picked over for stones and rinsed

½ teaspoon kosher salt

½ teaspoon red wine vinegar

1 cup Chicken Jus (page 321) or Lamb Jus
    (page 322)

2 tablespoons unsalted butter

8 cloves Garlic Confit (page 312)

12 Glazed Red Pearl Onions (page 244)

12 Glazed White Pearl Onions (page 244)

Kosher salt and freshly ground black pepper

1 teaspoon red wine vinegar

1 tablespoon minced chives

1 tablespoon chopped Italian parsley,
    plus a few leaves for garnish

This big garlic sausage, sliced and presented on a bed of lentils, is a very appealing meal to serve, family style, in fall or winter. As a chef, I love the simple mechanics of this dish. Fully cooked and cooled a day ahead, a substantial sausage can then be kept warm all day at 140°F in a bouillon ready to serve. When the order comes up, the lentils, also cooked a day ahead, are simply reheated with a little of the bouillon. We use a large French-style sausage from Salumeria Biellese (see Sources, page 330); it is only partially cured and so requires some gentle cooking.

FOR THE BOUQUET GARNI: Lay out 1 leek leaf and place the thyme and spices on top. Wrap in the second leaf to form a circular bundle and encase the ingredients; tie the bouquet garni securely with twine in three or four spots.

FOR THE SAUSAGE: Trim the roots from the leeks, leaving the root ends intact, and remove the tough dark green outer leaves. Split them lengthwise and wash well under cold running water. Tie the green tips together with kitchen twine. Peel the onion and cut lengthwise in half. Put one onion half in a large pot at least 12 inches in diameter and add the bouquet garni, garlic, 1 carrot, and 1 leek. Put the sausage in the pot and add enough water to cover it by 2 inches, then remove the sausage and set aside. Place the pot over high heat and bring to a boil, then reduce the heat and simmer for a minute or two.

Remove the pot from the heat and add the sausage (you don't want the sausage to boil or it might split). Set the pot over very low heat (there should not be any bubbles breaking the surface) and let the sausage poach gently for 45 to 60 minutes, or until the internal temperature is 155°F. Remove the sausage from the cooking liquid and set aside to cool. Strain the cooking liquid and reserve it to cook the lentils.

When the sausage has cooled for about 30 minutes, wrap it in plastic wrap and refrigerate for at least 2 hours, or preferably overnight.

FOR THE LENTILS: Score the fatty side of the slab bacon about $1/8$ inch deep in a crosshatch pattern with the cuts about $1/4$ inch apart.

Heat a large saucepan over medium heat. Add the bacon fat side down and let the fat render for 2 to 3 minutes, turning the bacon to brown lightly on all sides. Add the remaining onion half cut side down, carrot, and leek and cook for a minute. Add 4 cups of the reserved sausage cooking liquid (discard the remainder) and the lentils. Turn up the heat to medium-high and bring to a simmer. Adjust the heat as necessary to keep the lentils at a low simmer (cooking them too quickly will cause them to break apart) and cook for 25 to 35 minutes, or until the lentils are tender.

Pour the lentils, vegetables, and liquid into a large shallow baking pan or other container. Add the salt and vinegar. (The lentils can be refrigerated for up to a day in the liquid.)

TO COMPLETE: Cut off the ends of the sausage. Peel off and discard the casing. Cut the sausage into 12 slices.

Drain the lentils and discard the bacon and vegetables. Transfer the lentils to a wide saucepan or sauté pan large enough to hold the sausage slices in a single layer. Add the jus, butter, garlic confit, and pearl onions and set over medium heat to warm through. Season to taste with salt and pepper. When the lentils are beginning to simmer, arrange the sliced sausage over the top in a single layer. Spoon some of the lentils over the sausage, cover the pan, and heat for about 4 minutes, or until the sausage is warmed through. Transfer the sausage to a plate and keep warm. Add the vinegar, chives, and parsley to the lentils and season with salt and pepper to taste.

Spoon the lentils, vegetables, and jus into serving bowls. Top each bowl with 3 slices of sausage. Garnish with parsley leaves.

PHOTOGRAPH ON PAGE 141   **MAKES 4 SERVINGS**

GARLIC SAUSAGE IN BRIOCHE—SAUCISSON À L'AIL EN BRIOCHE

Butter

Brioche dough (page 324), prepared through refrigeration

2 eggs, lightly beaten

All-purpose flour

1 garlic sausage (14 inches long and about 2 inches wide; see Sources, page 330)

Mixed greens

House Vinaigrette (page 315)

Sausage baked in a rich dough is a dish that can be traditional bistro fare or a Michelin three-star *amuse bouche,* as it was when I had it at Restaurant Paul Bocuse outside Lyon. I appreciate the craftsmanship involved in this dish, and its visual appeal.

Generously butter a Pullman loaf pan (see Note).

Place the chilled dough on a lightly floured board. Roll out or pat the dough into a rectangle approximately 20 inches long and 8 inches wide. Brush the length of the dough down the center with a 3-inch-wide band of beaten egg and dust with a sprinkling of flour. Lay the sausage lengthwise on the dough. Brush the sausage with egg and dust the top with a light sprinkling of flour. Fold over the two short ends of the dough and brush the top of the dough with egg. Fold one long side of the dough over the sausage, brush it with egg, and roll over to completely encase the sausage in dough.

Place in the loaf pan and set, uncovered, in a warm place to rise for about 3 hours, or until the dough rises about $\frac{1}{2}$ inch over the top of the pan.

Put a rack in the center of the oven and preheat the oven to 350°F.

Bake the brioche for about 40 minutes, or until well browned on top. Remove from the oven and immediately turn out onto a wire rack to cool.

TO SERVE: Slice the brioche into 1-inch pieces. Serve with a handful of mixed greens tossed with a little mustard vinaigrette.

MAKES 16 SERVINGS

NOTE: A Pullman loaf pan, or *pain de mie* pan, is a long straight-sided loaf pan with a lid (see Sources, page 330).

THE IMPORTANCE OF
{ THE PIG }

The array of flavors and textures and recipes that comes from the pig is astonishing. My favorites are specialty preparations—the head and trotters, or pigs' feet, for instance—which work as well in an upscale restaurant as they do in a bistro. The other more readily available cuts have their own pleasures. Pork chops, for example, are one of America's staple dishes. And big cuts such as racks and loins are excellent for brining. The shanks and shoulders work beautifully in slow-cooked dishes. The back legs become hams. Fresh sausages made from shoulder and trimmings can be exceptional. The belly and the hocks can be cured and smoked for extraordinary flavor. And, of course, the specialty charcuterie items, such as fermented sausages (for example, saucisson sec and rosette de Lyon) and hams, represent a historically important use of the pig in terms of food preservation that is fundamental to all societies before refrigeration and remains a great culinary craft today.

In the bistro, the pig lends itself to efficient and easy service. Dried sausages and hams can be hung from the ceiling, ready to be sliced and served anytime. Pork rillettes are a staple. Pâtés almost always rely in some way on pork or its fat. Slow-cooked roasts made from the tougher parts of the pig only get better as the week progresses. Hot sausages, such as the garlic sausage, can be kept warm all day in stock or water and sliced to order.

And then there's the fat. Fat is perhaps the pig's most distinguishing feature. Not only is it abundant but it is unlike that of any other animal in terms of neutrality of flavor and creaminess of texture. Beef fat is hard, even crystalline, far more saturated than the soft, silky lard of the pig. It's what gives lardons and bacon their succulence. Pig fat can be cured and eaten raw, an Italian preparation called *lardo*. Its fat is fundamental in preparations of the pig as well—so try to find pork grown by small farmers (see Sources, page 330) who encourage fatty pigs. The big growers, the mass producers of pork, have tried to eliminate as much fat as possible from their breeds, and they've been so effective at breeding out the fat that it's almost impossible to find pork of any quality in most supermarkets. It may seem ironic that as the quality of pork in this country has gone down, the dining public should begin to embrace it. But maybe it makes perfect sense—people are craving the kind of pork they once knew, pork that truly is flavorful. I find this a hopeful time for the pig.

CORNICHONS: Some fat-rich dishes go well with more fat—buttery, creamy potatoes go great with more butter and cream. At other times we want fat's opposite, acid—the vinegar with the oil, the lemon with fried food. The cornichon not only adds an acidic counterpoint to many charcuterie dishes on a bistro menu, but it also adds crunch to a soft, fatty pâté or to soft dry-cured ham. It's an elegant item with the elegant flavor of tarragon that I enjoy. The cucumbers for cornichons are easily grown in the garden; picked fresh and pickled, they can be kept on hand all year long (see Gloria's Cornichons, page 30). DeBourbonnes and Vert de Massy cucumbers make the best cornichons, but you can use any cucumber labeled for pickling. Grow them yourself, or look for them at farmers' markets.

ENTRÉE
PORTE À COTÉ

Trotters is a classic bistro dish: It uses an inexpensive cut of meat, must be prepared well in advance, is easily stored, and is served in a snap. A lowly cut of meat is transformed into a rich, succulent, flavorful dish. When it's done well, it's one of my favorite things to eat. It's so rich, though, you don't want to eat it in large portions.

Often pigs' feet, called trotters, were braised, then split in half, sometimes stuffed, and reheated. The actual foot doesn't have a lot of meat, but it does have a lot of little bones. Our recipe is a very refined preparation of the classic dish that uses the more meaty section of the leg, the fresh hock, rather than the less meaty foot.

The cooking method is much like a classic rillette. The hock is braised until the meat is falling off the bone and the tough pigskin is as delicate as tissue paper. The meat is then removed from the bone and mixed with shallots, mustard, salt, and pepper. The skin is scraped of fat and finely chopped, then added to the meat with a little of the cooking liquid, which will have a lot of gelatin in it. (You must work with the skin while it's warm or it will become too stiff to mix and shape.) The mixture is simply rolled in aluminum foil to shape (or packed in a terrine mold) and cooled. Finally, the trotters are sliced, then coated with panko bread crumbs, which give the meat a very crisp coating, and then sautéed. It's a very elegant preparation, more fun to cook and serve and more satisfying to eat than the traditional rustic preparation.

The sauce is another classic, one that goes well with just about any kind of pork. It's chunky—what we'd now think of as salsa consistency—studded with chopped egg, cornichons, capers, and shallots.

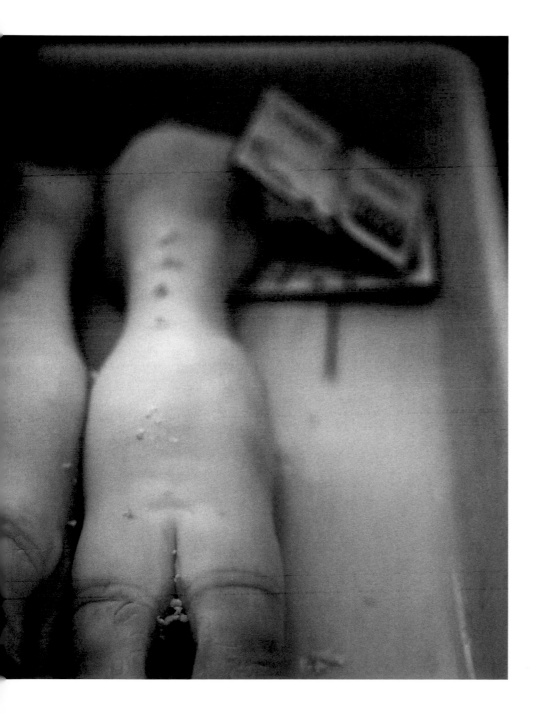

This dish, with the greens and gribiche, is perfectly satisfying without overdoing it. However, you could vary the presentation by serving it with a poached egg and a simple vinaigrette.

You should be able to order fresh whole hocks from the meat department of your grocery store. Because the quantity of meat on hocks varies considerably, it's helpful to use a scale to weigh the amount of cooked meat you get to ensure that you have enough.

No animal is better suited to the bistro tradition than the pig. From both an emotional standpoint (connotations of hearty, homey fare) and a practical one (the extraordinary variety of preparations it lends itself to), the pig is unequaled. Indeed, we may even be on the verge of the pig's rise to prominence, as pork and charcuterie dishes work themselves onto more and more elegant menus. Caviar and lobster were once denigrated fare; I wouldn't be surprised if future diners look back and wonder how we managed to be so unappreciative of the pig.

HAM HOCKS

5 pounds (2 large) fresh (not smoked)
    ham hocks
1 large leek
1 large onion, peeled
8 ounces (2 large) carrots, peeled
Kosher salt
2 bay leaves
1 teaspoon black peppercorns
¼ ounce (a small handful) thyme sprigs,
    tied together with kitchen twine,
    plus 1 teaspoon minced thyme
1 head garlic, split horizontally in half
2 tablespoons unsalted butter
1 cup minced shallots
¼ cup Dijon mustard

Freshly ground black pepper
1 tablespoon plus 1 teaspoon chopped
    Italian parsley

SAUCE GRIBICHE   MAKES ABOUT 1 CUP

1 tablespoon red wine vinegar
½ cup extra virgin olive oil
1 teaspoon Dijon mustard
2 teaspoons each chopped hard-cooked egg
    white and egg yolk (see page 326)
1 tablespoon minced nonpareil capers,
    preferably Spanish
2 tablespoons minced shallots
2 teaspoons minced tarragon
2 teaspoons minced chives
2 teaspoons minced chervil

1 tablespoon minced cornichons
2 teaspoons minced Italian parsley
¼ teaspoon kosher salt
¼ teaspoon freshly ground black pepper

Kosher salt and freshly ground black pepper
All-purpose flour
About 1 tablespoon Dijon mustard
½ cup panko (Japanese bread crumbs) or
    fine dried bread crumbs
2 tablespoons canola oil
1½ ounces (2 to 3 cups) mâche
Red wine vinegar
Extra virgin olive oil

This dish is so rich that you don't want to eat it in large portions. But when you make it, it's better to err on the side of having more of the trotter mixture than you need because it can be packed into a terrine mold, chilled, sliced, and heated through, or thinly sliced and served cold on a charcuterie plate. The meat should be prepared at least a day and up to five days before serving. Leftovers are fantastic served with toasted slices of baguette and Dijon mustard or butter, but they also freeze well.

FOR THE HAM HOCKS: Place the ham hocks in a large stockpot and add water to cover by about 2 inches. Place the pot over medium-high heat and bring to a boil, skimming away the foam that rises to the top. Reduce the heat and simmer the hocks for 3 to 5 minutes, or until you have skimmed away all the impurities.

Meanwhile, remove the root end from the leek and any tough outer leaves. Cut away the top few inches of very dark green leaves. Cut the leek lengthwise in half, stopping about 2 inches from the root end. Hold the leek open under cold running water to wash away any dirt embedded in the layers.

Cut an X three-quarters of the way through the onion, starting at the top and leaving the root end intact.

Remove the ham hocks from the pot, discard the liquid, and rinse out the pot. Return the hocks to the pot (note that the skin feels tough at this point, like a football; when it has cooked thoroughly, you will be able to poke your finger through it quite easily). Cover with cold water again, place the pot over high heat, and bring to a simmer.

Add the leek, onion, carrots, 1 tablespoon salt, bay leaves, peppercorns, thyme sprigs, and garlic and return the water to a simmer. Cook gently, skimming often, for 2 to 3 hours, or until the fat on the hocks is completely softened and the meat is tender and pulling away from the bone. (Prepare the remaining ingredients while the hocks cook.) Turn off the heat and leave the hocks in the liquid.

Melt the butter in a large sauté pan over medium heat. Add the shallots and cook for about 2 minutes to soften them. Stir in 1 teaspoon salt and remove from the heat.

Lift the hocks from the pot and place on a baking sheet; reserve the cooking liquid. It is important to work with ham hocks while they are hot; once they cool, they will be rubbery and impossible to deal with. Use a fork to help separate the meat from the skin and fat, reserving the skin. Pull the meat apart, and remove and discard the tendons and any small pieces of bone.

Weigh the meat: You need 1 pound for this recipe (if you have less, adjust the ingredients accordingly). Place the meat in a large bowl and keep in a warm spot. Scrape the fat from the skin and discard the fat.

Finely chop the skin and weigh it. Stir 8 ounces of the chopped skin (or half the weight of the meat) into the meat. (If you have less than 8 ounces of skin, that's fine.)

Add 2 tablespoons of the mustard, 1 teaspoon of salt, and ¹/₂ teaspoon pepper, or to taste, to the meat and use a large rubber spatula to combine. Stir in the shallots. As you stir, the meat will break apart and shred; pull apart any large pieces that don't break up on their own. Add 1 tablespoon of the braising liquid to moisten the mixture slightly; don't be tempted to add additional liquid or the meat may fall apart when it is heated. Stir in the minced thyme and parsley.

Cut two 22-by-18-inch sheets of heavy-duty aluminum foil (if you don't have heavy-duty foil, use four pieces, stacking and overlapping them to make a 22-by-18-inch rectangle). Stack the pieces together and arrange so that a short end is closest to you. Spoon the pork mixture in a log across the bottom of the foil, about 3 inches up from the bottom edge and about 4 inches from each side. The log should be approximately 10 inches long, 2 inches wide, and 1 ¹/₂ inches high. Shape the meat into a rough log, then bring the bottom edge of the foil up and over the meat,

extending the foil flap about 2 inches past the meat, and press and flatten the foil flap against the surface to enclose the meat. Carefully roll the log up in the foil.

Squeeze and twist the ends to compress the meat into a log 8 to 10 inches long and 2 to 2¹/₂ inches in diameter. Trim off the excess foil. Refrigerate the log overnight, or for as long as 5 days.

FOR THE SAUCE: Combine all the ingredients in a bowl, adding them in the order given. Let the sauce sit for at least 30 minutes, or refrigerate for up to a day. (You will have about 1 cup. The sauce will still be good after a day, but it may lose some of its fresh taste; the extra sauce is great with steamed mussels or cold meats.)

TO COMPLETE: Preheat the oven to 400°F.

Unwrap the pork log and trim the ends to even them. Cut the log into 6 thick slices. Season both sides of each slice with salt and pepper and dip in flour; the flour should come slightly up the sides of each slice. Spread a very thin layer (about ¹/₄ teaspoon) of Dijon mustard over the flour on both sides of each slice, then dip into the panko to coat. (The trotters can be refrigerated for up to 30 minutes at this point, or sautéed immediately.)

Heat the canola oil in an 8-inch ovenproof nonstick skillet over medium-high heat. When the oil is hot, carefully add the trotters and brown for about 30 seconds on one side (because they splatter a lot as they cook, they are finished in the oven).

Place the skillet in the oven for about 4 minutes. Turn the trotters and brown the second side in the oven, about 4 minutes. The trotters should be heated through, but if they are cooked for too long, they may break apart. Remove the skillet from the oven and drain the trotters briefly on paper towels.

TO SERVE: Toss the mâche with a splash of vinegar and a touch of olive oil. Place about 2 tablespoons of the sauce on each serving plate. Top with a trotter and garnish each plate with a mound of mâche.

MAKES 4 TO 6 SERVINGS

4

{ PLATS DE RÉSISTANCE }

MAIN COURSES

These are the big dishes, the emblematic bistro meals: roast chicken, mussels steamed with wine and aromatic herbs, sautéed trout, sole with brown butter sauce, steak frites, sausage and potatoes, and the stews—beef bourguignon, lamb navarin, blanquette de veau. Dishes as satisfying to cook as they are to eat.

We have the capacity, today, to make the best food ever because of improved equipment and higher-quality ingredients. I've liked stew since I was a boy—even when it was Dinty Moore out of a can, which it often was in a household of five kids and a working mother. If my mother made a stew from scratch, the quality of the stew was usually determined by how much time she had. Almost always the stew was opaque, with a thick sauce (often flour-thickened) and vegetables the color of the sauce. Put some butter on it, and to my mind it was great.

As I learned to cook, as I discovered tools of refinement, I wanted to put those tools to work on the things I loved, such as a beef stew richly flavored with wine. I strove for intensity of flavor, the right viscosity of the sauce, vegetables the color they're supposed to be. Some butter to finish it off, maybe even some mustard on the side. This chapter is a guide to working with those tools of refinement.

speed, add 3 eggs, one a
incorporated before ad
medium and add anoth
each one. Turn off the
spatula, then turn the sp
the spatula very slowly;
falls off in a clump, beat

Place the dough in a
tip and let it rest for ab
have only a small pastry

Bring a large pot of
baking sheet with pape
parchment paper.

Because this recipe
arm may get tired: An
large inverted pot, cani
than the pot on the rig
handed) and set the fill
over the side and the c
Twist the end of the pa
(From time to time, as

1½ cups water
12 tablespoons (6 ounces)
1 tablespoon plus 1 teaspo
2 cups all-purpose flour, s

Parisienne gnocc
versatile dough
together until the flou
in. It can then be pip
profiteroles (page 300
preparations such as
as gnocchi.

Parisienne gnocchi
Italian gnocchi or an
ingredients and trans
excellent simply saut
flavored with fines he
we don't serve much
an interesting base f
They're not a classic
French one, dating b

This recipe will ma
you'll need for the fo
poached, gnocchi ca

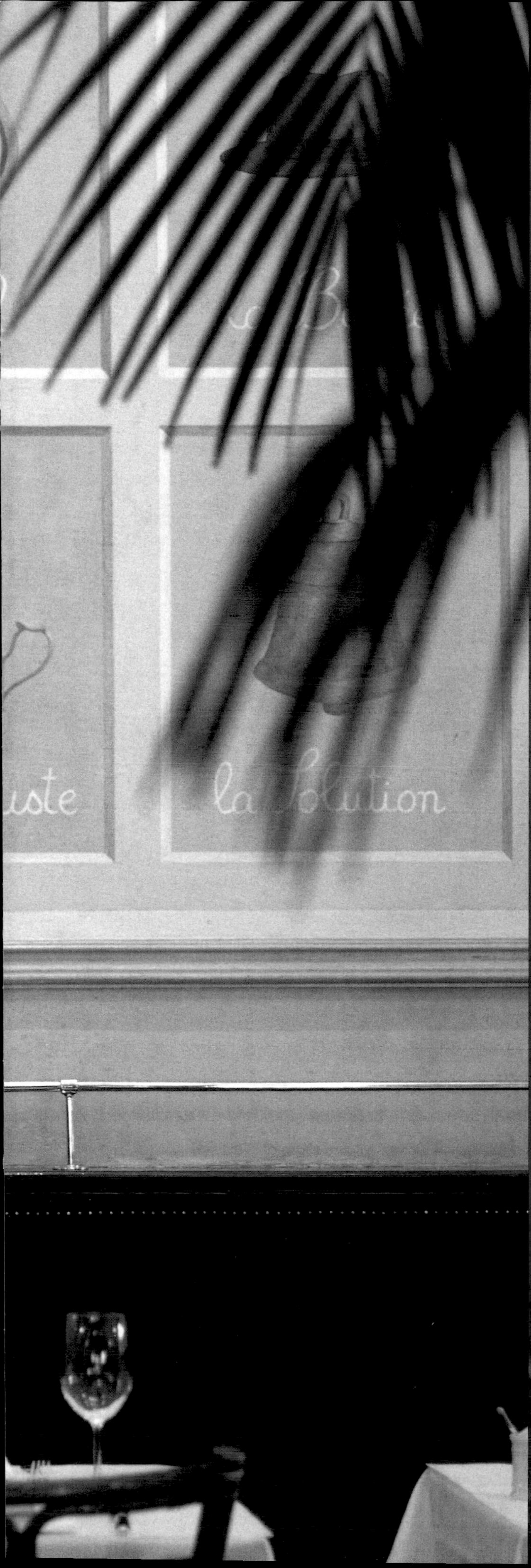

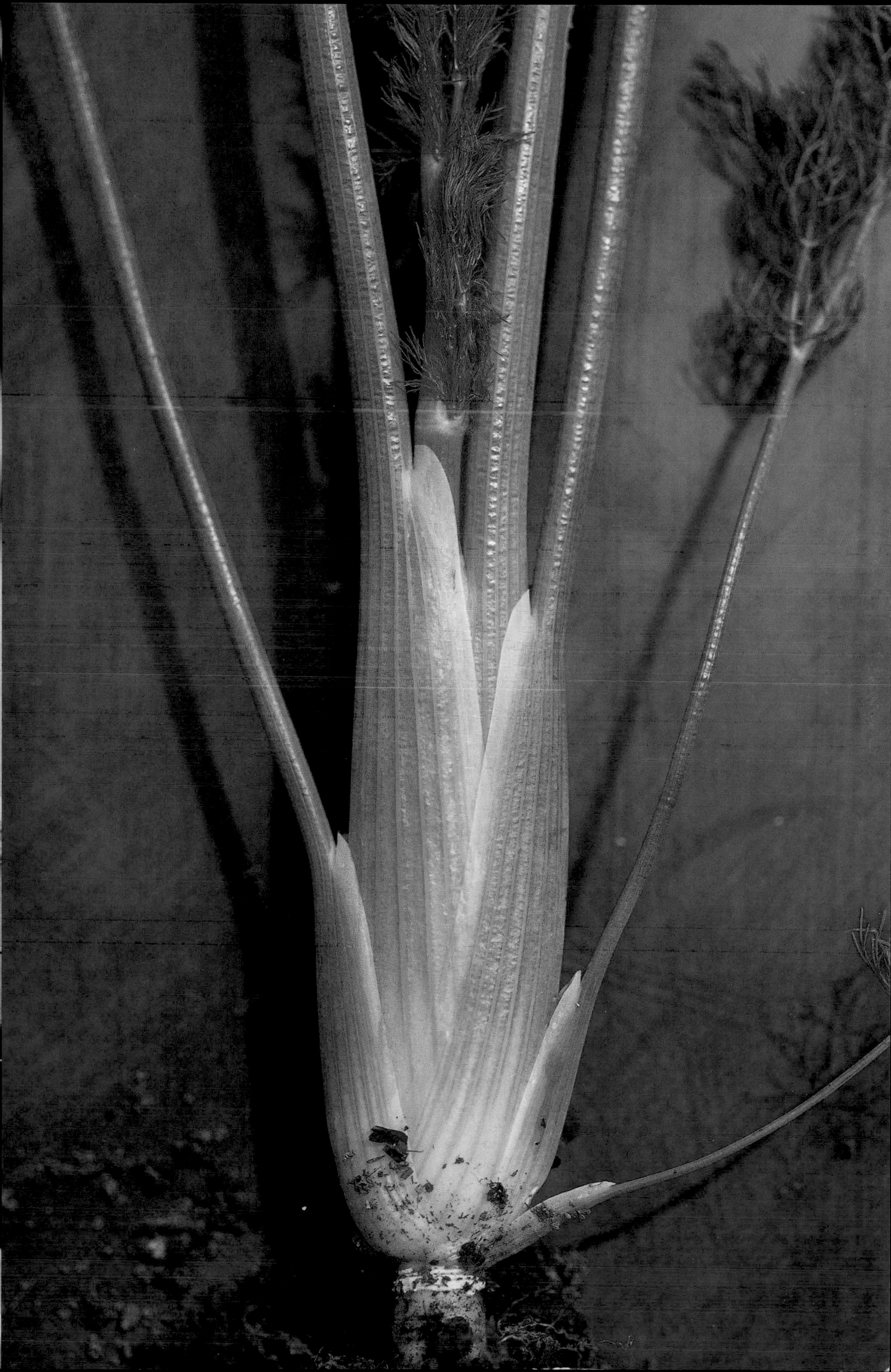

Mussels There's a young customer at the restaurant, six or seven

years old now, who likes our mussels so much that his mother drives

him an hour to the restaurant on his birthday just so that he can

have them. He's a mussel eater now; he's hooked. He'll order mussels

throughout his life, and the ones he ate when he was young are

going to be the standard for the rest of his life. Steamed mussels,

if you like them, are like onion soup, a dish you encounter again

and again throughout your life.

Certainly one pleasure of mussels is how easy they are to cook

(though they're good raw, too). If you find a source you like, if your

mussels are excellent, you hardly need to do anything to them—

just steam them open in a little white wine with garlic and thyme,

maybe some butter. If you're making them for a group, you can

make the broth ahead, then, a few minutes before you want to

serve them, bring the liquid to a boil, add your mussels, cover,

and cook. By the time you've set out your bowls, the mussels

are done. It's that easy.

. Mussels are the perfect bistro food because they're abundant,

inexpensive, festive, casual, satisfying on so many levels, and can

be prepared in a snap in a busy kitchen.

SCALLOPS WITH CITRUS-BRAISED ENDIVE
COQUILLES ST. JACQUES AUX ENDIVES BRAISÉES

ENDIVE

1 1/2 pounds (about 7) Belgian endive

Kosher salt

3 thyme sprigs and 3 lavender sprigs
 (optional)

2 cups fresh orange juice

2 tablespoons honey

2 bay leaves

2 garlic cloves, skin left on, smashed

Freshly ground white pepper

1/2 cup Fish Fumet (page 320) or
 Chicken Stock (page 317)

2 tablespoons cold unsalted butter,
 cut into chunks

2 tablespoons chopped tarragon

1 tablespoon chopped Italian parsley

SCALLOPS

Twelve 2-ounce diver scallops
 (see Sources, page 330)

Kosher salt and freshly ground white pepper

About 1/4 cup Clarified Butter (page 316)

About 16 chervil sprigs

Scallop season begins around the first of November in Maine and lasts until mid-April, so our scallop dishes are truly seasonal. The unconventional preparation here is very clean compared with traditional scallop dishes that rely on creamy sauces. It's an interesting dish in its pairing of endive, which has pleasing bitter notes, with the sweetness of scallops served in a brothy citrus sauce.

FOR THE ENDIVE: Pull off and discard any brown exterior leaves. Cut off the bottom of each endive—you'll see the rings of the core. Use a paring knife to cut a cone shape from the bottom of each endive to remove as much of the core as possible.

Salting the endive will pull out any bitter taste. Put about 1/2 inch salt in a container large enough to hold all the endive upright. Stand the endive upright in the salt. The salt should reach about one-quarter of the way up the endive; if not, add more salt as necessary. Cover the endive with a dampened towel and refrigerate for at least 12 hours, or up to a day.

Rinse the endive under cold running water. Cut off about 1/2 inch from the bottom of each endive and cut lengthwise in half. Cut a V shape from the bottom of each half to remove any remaining core or discolored portion. Remove leaves a few at a time, lay them on a cutting board, and cut lengthwise into 1/4-inch-wide julienne strips.

Tie together the thyme sprigs and lavender sprigs, if using, with kitchen twine. Bring the orange juice and honey to a boil in a large deep skillet over medium-high heat. Reduce the heat to a simmer and add the herb bundle, bay leaves, garlic, 1 teaspoon salt, and a few grinds of white pepper. Add the endive (the liquid should cover most of the endive). Cover with a parchment lid (see page 326) and simmer for 15 to 20 minutes, or until the endive is translucent but still has a slight bite. Remove from the heat. (The endive can be made ahead to this point, cooled, and refrigerated in its liquid for up to a day.)

Drain the endive, reserving the liquid. Discard the herb bundle and bay leaves and strain the liquid into a saucepan. Add the fumet or stock and bring to a simmer over medium-high heat. Lower the heat and simmer to reduce to 1 1/2 cups.

FOR THE SCALLOPS: Season the scallops with salt and white pepper. Melt the clarified butter (about 1/8 inch) in a large skillet over medium-high heat. When the butter is hot, add the scallops and cook for 2 to 3 minutes, or until the bottoms are richly browned. Turn the scallops and cook briefly, just to "kiss" the other side.

TO SERVE: Add the endive to the reduced fumet. When the liquid is simmering, stir in the chunked butter. Stir in the tarragon and parsley.

Place a bed of endives and sauce on each serving plate, top with 3 scallops, and surround with the sprigs of chervil.

MAKES 4 SERVINGS

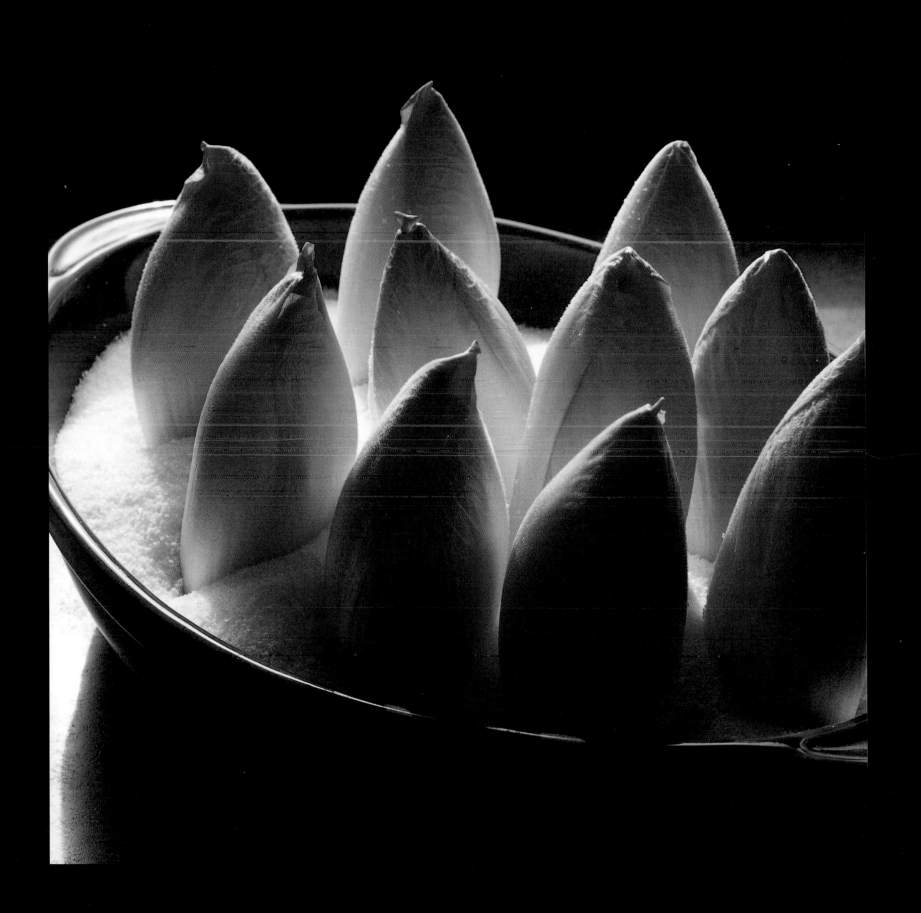

Beurre de Bresse

le kilo EUROS  8€38 FRANCS 55fr

THE IMPORTANCE OF
{ BROWN BUTTER }

My favorite quotation from any chef is from Fernand Point: "Butter, butter, butter! Give me more butter!" I love butter emulsified into pureed potatoes and sauces, spread on crusty bread or on radishes, and melted for lobster, but what makes it such an exciting substance to work with is its unique ratios of fat, water, and milk solids, which allow it to do its broad range of culinary work. Often overlooked, though, is the fact that butter is a ready-made sauce base. When you melt it and leave it over enough heat so that the solids brown, you have one of its most amazing transformations: brown butter, or *beurre noisette*, an all but instant finishing sauce. The aroma of it, its nutty smell (*noisette* means "hazelnut"), is exquisite, and its versatility and economy in the kitchen are indispensable.

When butter takes on that nutty flavor, it can be used in both sweet and savory preparations. It goes beautifully with sugar; we make financiers (almond-flavored cakes) using brown butter; we make a filling for sweet pastry with it; we add it to frangipane. Some chefs today are even making brown butter ice cream. Brown butter is so rich and aromatic that it becomes almost like an extract.

Brown butter goes equally well with acid (see page 177) and is the perfect sauce for bistro cooking because it can be done in a snap, *à la minute,* in the same pan the fish or meat has been sautéed in. There's no waste, no bain-marie of *beurre blanc* left over at the end of the night as there is in the classic kitchen.

The key to perfect brown butter sauce is simply not to burn it. This takes some care, some sense of sight and smell. You have to stop the cooking when the solids hit the right aromatic pitch. The fat clarifies and gets really hot, so the solids will burn quickly. You must be aware when to add the other ingredients. First, you add the acid, the element that will cool down the butter and stop the solids from turning black and bitter. You've got to be careful with the amount of acid: It's easy to add too much and overwhelm the nutty flavor of the butter. When that's right, you season it appropriately, then at the last minute, you add the delicate garnish—parsley or some other herb—so that it will stay bright green in the acidic environment.

FLAT-LEAF PARSLEY is often overlooked or used as an afterthought, but I think it is making a comeback in America. Remember that curly foliage on the side of your plate that your mother told you to eat last because it would freshen your breath? That was the problem: Parsley eaten by itself isn't great. But parsley as a flavor component is. On a steamed potato with butter, chopped parsley is beautiful. It's integral to *à la meunière* dishes, sautés finished with lemon juice, parsley, and brown butter. I don't know a stew that isn't improved by the addition of chopped parsley. Parsley is excellent in salads, on pommes frites, and on coq au vin, beef bourguignon, and blanquette de veau, where it adds a bright color component as well as flavor. I prefer flat Italian parsley to curly; it has a truer flavor, almost sweet, without the bitterness curly parsley often has.

2 medium fennel bulbs

POTATOES
24 marble-sized potatoes
    (about 8 ounces total)
1/4 teaspoon black peppercorns
2 thyme sprigs
1 bay leaf

2 garlic cloves, skin left on, smashed
1 tablespoon kosher salt

FISH AND SHELLFISH
12 small squid (about 12 ounces total)
One 1 1/4-pound monkfish fillet
32 small mussels, preferably bouchot
    (see page 166)

24 Manila clams
Kosher salt and freshly ground white pepper

About 4 cups Shellfish Broth (page 321),
    warmed
16 cloves Garlic Confit (page 312)
2 tablespoons Aïoli (page 315)
1 tablespoon plus 1 teaspoon chopped
    Italian parsley

In a bistro kitchen, this fisherman's stew would be made with whatever fish were available. We use monkfish, shellfish, and squid, along with fennel, garlic, and potatoes, in our shellfish broth. Monkfish is a perfect fish for soup or stew because, while you *can* overcook it, it's more tolerant of long cooking than are most other fish. Squid is the opposite and must be cooked at the last minute. But the actual cooking time is brief, and all the ingredients can be prepared ahead.

FOR THE FENNEL: Trim the bottoms of the bulbs and cut the bulbs lengthwise in half. Place the fennel halves cut side down and cut crosswise into 1/2-inch-thick slices. Separate the slices and set the large crescent pieces aside. (Reserve the cores and center sections for fish fumet or another use, if desired.)

Bring a large saucepan of salted water to a boil. Prepare an ice bath. Add the fennel to the boiling water and blanch for about a minute. Drain the fennel in a strainer and plunge the strainer into the ice bath for 1 minute to cool. Drain the fennel, dry on paper towels, and set aside.

The traditional brown butter sauce is really a warm vinaigrette, though less sharp, with perhaps a five-to-one fat-to-acid ratio, versus the three-to-one for a standard vinaigrette. You can vary the acid and garnish to make a sauce go in any direction you choose. Lemon and parsley are among the most common acid-garnish pairs, creating a sauce that's perfect for fish, chicken, and veal. Add almonds and you have *sauce amandine* for trout or green beans, or both. Change the pair to sherry vinegar and capers and you have a classic sauce for calves' brains. Add lemon, capers, and croutons to that, and you have another classic sauce from Grenoble. If you add sage instead of the acid, you have a classic pasta sauce.

Opposite: Trout with Haricots Vert and Almonds (page 178). *Above:* Skate with Fennel-Onion Confit and Tapenade Sauce (page 180).

TROUT WITH HARICOTS VERTS AND ALMONDS
TRUITE AUX HARICOTS VERTS ET AMANDES

Four 10-ounce boned whole rainbow trout
8 ounces haricots verts, stem ends removed
Kosher salt and freshly ground white pepper
Canola oil

10 tablespoons (5 ounces) unsalted butter
$^3/_4$ cup sliced blanched (skinned) almonds,
  lightly toasted

2 teaspoons minced Italian parsley
2 teaspoons fresh lemon juice

Fresh sweet trout with lemony brown butter and crunchy almonds has become one of my favorite Bouchon dishes. We cook and serve trout with the skin and head on, though the head can be removed after cooking. When I see trout on menus, it brings to mind mountain rivers and fresh air; indeed, in inland France trout was traditionally served only in bistros that had access to freshwater fish, in rivers coming down off the Alps. Most of the trout you find, and the trout we use, is farm raised.

TO PAN-DRESS THE TROUT: With scissors, cut away the dorsal fin along the back of each fish. Hold each pectoral fin (the one closest to the head) and cut away and discard the gill plate and pectoral fin. Turn the fish on its back and open it up. Starting at the head, cut away the belly flap on each side, along with the pelvic fin. Remove the tail by cutting across the fish about an inch from the bottom of the tail. Set aside.

FOR THE HARICOTS VERTS: Bring a large pot of generously salted water to a boil. Prepare an ice bath. Blanch the haricots verts in the boiling water for 2 to 6 minutes, or until they are barely tender, with a slight bite still left to them. Drain the beans and transfer to the ice bath to chill quickly, then drain again and dry on paper towels.

TO COMPLETE: Lightly sprinkle both sides of each trout with salt and pepper. If you have them, heat two 12-inch nonstick pans (special oval pans work best for fish) over medium-high heat. If you have only one pan, cook two trout first, cover, and keep them in a warm place while you cook the final two. Coat each pan with a light film of canola oil. Add the trout skin side down and sauté for about 4 minutes on one side only. The fish may still look undercooked at the top of the flesh, but the hot ingredients that will top them will complete the cooking.

Meanwhile, put the beans in a sauté pan, add 2 tablespoons of the butter and $^1/_3$ cup water, and place over medium heat. Heat, stirring occasionally, until the water has evaporated and the beans are hot and glazed with butter. Season to taste with salt and pepper. Remove the pan from the heat and keep warm.

When the fish are done, cut off the heads and discard, if desired, and place the fish on serving plates. Drain the oil from one of the pans and return the pan to the heat. Add the remaining 8 tablespoons butter and a pinch of salt to the hot pan. When the butter begins to brown, add the almonds, shaking the pan to brown them evenly. When they are a rich golden brown, add the parsley and lemon juice.

Meanwhile, cover each trout with one-quarter of the beans.

Spoon the foaming butter and almonds over the haricots verts and around the edges of the plates.

PHOTOGRAPH ON PAGE 176   **MAKES 4 SERVINGS**

TROUT WITH HARICOTS VERTS, CAPERS, AND LEMON
TRUITE À LA GRENOBLOISE

2 large lemons

Four 10-ounce boned whole rainbow trout

8 ounces haricots verts, stem ends trimmed

Kosher salt and freshly ground white pepper

Canola oil

8 tablespoons (4 ounces) unsalted butter

¼ cup nonpareil capers, preferably Spanish, drained

½ cup ¼-inch cubes bread, preferably day-old Brioche (page 324), baked in a 350°F oven until dry

2 teaspoons chopped Italian parsley

Because it's mild, trout lends itself nicely to the salty savory effects of capers, lemons, and croutons in this classic *grenobloise* garnish. Most people use too many capers, piling them on as if they were a vegetable garnish—think of capers as a seasoning, like vinegar, and use them that way.

Cut off the top and bottom of the lemons. Stand a lemon up on a cutting board and use a paring knife to cut away the peel and pith in wide strips from top to bottom. Cut between the membranes to release the "suprêmes," or lemon sections. Repeat with the remaining lemon. Set aside.

TO PAN-DRESS THE TROUT: With scissors, cut away the dorsal fin along the back of each fish. Hold each pectoral fin (the one closest to the head) and cut away and discard the gill plate and pectoral fin. Turn the fish on its back and open it up. Starting at the head, cut away the belly flap on each side, along with the pelvic fin. Remove the tail by cutting across the fish about an inch from the bottom of the tail. Set aside.

FOR THE HARICOTS VERTS: Bring a large pot of salted water to a boil. Prepare an ice bath. Blanch the haricots verts in the boiling water for 2 to 6 minutes, or until they are barely tender, with a slight bite still left to them. Drain the beans and transfer to the ice bath to chill quickly, then drain again and dry on paper towels.

TO COMPLETE: Lightly sprinkle both sides of each trout with salt and pepper. If you have them, heat two 12-inch nonstick pans (special oval pans work best for fish) over medium-high heat. If you have only one pan, cook two trout first, cover, and keep them in a warm spot while you cook the other two. Coat each pan with a light film of canola oil. Add the trout skin side down and sauté for about 4 minutes on one side only. The fish may still look undercooked at the top of the flesh, but the hot ingredients that will top them will complete the cooking.

Meanwhile, put the beans in a sauté pan, add 2 tablespoons of the butter and ⅓ cup water, and place over medium heat. Heat, stirring occasionally, until the water has evaporated and the beans are hot and glazed with butter. Season to taste with salt and pepper. Remove the pan from the heat and keep warm.

When the fish are done, cut off the heads and discard, if desired, and place the fish on serving plates. Drain the oil from one of the pans and return the pan to the heat. Add the remaining 6 tablespoons butter and a pinch of salt to the hot pan. When the butter begins to brown, add the capers and croutons and fry for a minute. Add the parsley and lemon suprêmes.

Meanwhile, cover each trout with one-quarter of the beans.

Spoon the foaming butter, capers, croutons, and lemon sections over the haricots verts and around the edges of the plates.

MAKES 4 SERVINGS

SKATE WITH FENNEL-ONION CONFIT AND TAPENADE SAUCE
AILE DE RAIE AU CONFIT DE FENOUIL ET OIGNONS, SAUCE TAPENADE

¼ cup Tapenade (page 16)

½ cup extra virgin olive oil

Four 8-ounce pieces skate wing, skinned but
    not filleted

Kosher salt and freshly ground white pepper

Canola oil

All-purpose flour

4 tablespoons (2 ounces) unsalted butter

4 thyme sprigs

4 garlic cloves, peeled and smashed

4 lemon slices

Fennel-Onion Confit (page 313), warmed

Skate cooks very well on the bone, or actually cartilage, which helps the meat maintain its shape and its juiciness. It needs a little more aggressive cooking and can stand higher heat than leaner, more delicate fish. In this dish, which we serve in the spring, it pairs perfectly with the Provençal flavors of onion, olives, and fennel, also, happily, staples in our part of California.

Preheat the oven to 375°F.

Mix the tapenade and olive oil together in a small bowl and set aside.

Season the skate on both sides with salt and pepper. Heat two large ovenproof skillets over medium-high heat, then add ⅛ inch of canola oil to each one. Have two smaller pans ready to weight the fish.

The cartilage runs more or less through the center of the skate, but the flesh will be thicker on one side than on the other: Dredge the thick side of each piece of skate in flour and place 2 pieces floured side down in each hot skillet. To keep the fish from curling, place the smaller pans over the skate to weight it down for the first minute of cooking. Then remove the smaller pans and add 1 tablespoon of the butter to each pan. Continue cooking for 3 minutes, or until the fish is golden brown on the first side.

Turn the skate over and add another tablespoon of butter to each skillet, along with 2 thyme sprigs, 2 garlic cloves, and 2 lemon slices. Tilt each skillet slightly and use a large spoon to baste the fish with the butter and oil for another 2 minutes.

Transfer the skillets to the oven. After a minute, open the oven door and baste the fish again. Cook for an additional 3 to 4 minutes, or until the cartilage pulls away easily from the fish. Remove from the oven.

TO SERVE: Place a mound of fennel confit on each plate. Top with the fish, then top each piece with a lemon slice, garlic clove, and thyme sprig taken from the skillets. Drizzle the tapenade sauce around the dish.

To eat the skate, eat the thicker top half of the fish fillet first, then lift off and remove the cartilage in one piece and eat the remaining skate.

PHOTOGRAPH ON PAGE 177 **MAKES 4 SERVINGS**

SKATE WITH LYONNAISE POTATOES AND RED WINE JUS

AILE DE RAIE POMMES LYONNAISE, SAUCE AU VIN ROUGE

2 cups Lyonnaise potatoes (page 251), hot

1 cup Red Wine Jus (page 323), warm

Four 8-ounce pieces skate wing, skinned but not filleted

Kosher salt and freshly ground white pepper

Canola oil

All-purpose flour

4 tablespoons (2 ounces) unsalted butter

4 thyme sprigs

4 garlic cloves, peeled and smashed

In the winter, we serve skate with a red wine jus and hearty Lyonnaise potatoes.

Omit the tapenade, olive oil, and lemon slices called for in the recipe on page 180. Instead of the fennel-onion confit, prepare the Lyonnaise potatoes and red wine jus; keep the potatoes hot, and rewarm the jus. Prepare the fish as directed there.

TO SERVE: Place a mound of potatoes on each of four plates. Pour about ¼ cup of the jus around each portion of potatoes. Top each mound of potatoes with a piece of fish, a sprig of thyme, and a clove of garlic.

TIP: To eat the skate, eat the thicker top half of the fillet first, then lift off and remove the cartilage in one piece and eat the remaining skate.

MAKES 4 SERVINGS

ROUGET WITH COUSCOUS AND TOMATO CONFIT BROTH

ROUGET À LA MAROCAINE

Sixteen 1¼-ounce rouget fillets, skin on

Kosher salt and freshly ground white pepper

Canola oil

2½ cups Shellfish Broth (page, 321)

10 pieces Tomato Confit (page 313), finely minced

1 tablespoon minced Italian parsley, plus 4 parsley sprigs

Moroccan Couscous (page 256), warmed

Extra virgin olive oil

Rouget is a fish from the Mediterranean that has lots of character—excellent bite and delicate texture. It's oily, like a sardine, so it won't take on the characteristics of its garnish the way a lot of fish do. Here it's served with rustic couscous and a shellfish broth seasoned with tomato confit. If you like larger fillets, the dish can be made with red snapper.

FOR THE FISH: Season both sides of the fish with salt and sprinkle the flesh side with pepper. Heat ⅛ inch of canola oil in one very large or two medium skillets over medium-high heat. Add the fish skin side down, reduce the heat to medium-low, and sauté for about 3 minutes, or until the skin is a rich golden brown. Turn over and cook for 1 to 2 minutes longer, or until the fish is just cooked through.

Meanwhile, combine 1½ cups of the shellfish broth and the tomato confit in a small saucepan and heat until warm. Heat the remaining 1 cup broth in another small pan and keep warm. Just before serving, stir the minced parsley into the tomato confit broth.

TO SERVE: Spoon the broth and tomato confit into four rimmed soup plates. Top each serving with a mound of couscous and arrange 4 fish fillets on the couscous. Garnish with the parsley sprigs and drizzle with a little olive oil. Serve extra broth on the side.

MAKES 4 SERVINGS

ARTICHOKES BARIGOULE

4 lemons, halved

4 large artichokes

2 large onions, peeled

1 large carrot (1 to 1½ inches in diameter),
    peeled

½ cup extra virgin olive oil

Kosher salt and freshly ground black pepper

2 tablespoons minced garlic

2 cups dry white wine, such as
    sauvignon blanc

About 2 cups Chicken Stock (page 317)

Bouquet Garni (page 325)

1 boquerones anchovy (see Sources,
    page 330), drained and minced, or
    1 regular anchovy, rinsed and minced

2 tablespoons minced Italian parsley

A squeeze of lemon juice

PIKE

Four 6-ounce pieces walleyed pike fillet,
    any pinbones removed

Kosher salt and freshly ground white pepper

Canola oil

Extra virgin olive oil

A versatile freshwater fish, pike lends itself nicely to a variety of preparations from sautés to stews. Here it's simply sautéed with the skin on and served with artichokes barigoule, a kind of artichoke stew, which complements its sweet notes. The very flavorful broth becomes part of the sauce for the fish.

FOR THE ARTICHOKES: Place enough water in a container to submerge the 4 trimmed artichoke hearts. Add the juice of 3 lemons and the lemon shells to the water. (The acidulated water will keep the artichoke hearts from discoloring.)

To trim the artichokes, hold an artichoke with the stem end toward you and pull off the very small bottom leaves. Working your way around the artichoke, bend the lower leaves back until they snap and break naturally, then pull them off. Continue removing the tougher outer leaves until you reach the cone of tender, predominantly yellow inner leaves. Set the artichoke aside and repeat with the remaining artichokes.

Cut off the stems flush with the meaty artichoke bottoms. As you work, rub the cut surfaces with a lemon half to keep the flesh from discoloring. Turn each artichoke on its side and cut off the top two-thirds of the artichoke, from its tip to where the meaty heart begins; discard the trimmings. The remaining artichoke hearts should be 1 to 1½ inches high.

Hold an artichoke heart in your hand stem end down and, using a sharp paring knife, trim the sides of the heart all around to remove the tough dark green exterior—this is easiest if you turn the artichoke while keeping the knife held in place. Then turn the artichoke stem side up and, working around the artichoke, trim the bottom of the heart at a 45-degree angle to remove all the dark green, exposing the light flesh. Rub all cut portions with lemon. With a melon baller or a sharp spoon, scrape out the fuzzy choke, beginning at the outside and working toward the center of the heart. Give the heart a final check and trim away any remaining rough spots. Drop the heart into the lemon water and repeat with the remaining artichokes.

Cut the onions lengthwise in half. Pull out the solid flat center pieces of onion running up from the core and reserve for another use. Place the onions cut side down on a cutting board and cut crosswise into ⅛-inch-thick slices. Separate the slices into half rings. (You should have 4 cups of sliced onions.)

Score ridges down the length of the carrot using the waffle blade of a mandoline, then cut the carrot into ⅛-inch-thick rounds. Or, if you don't have a mandoline, slice the carrots, then use a small fluted cutter to cut out rounds. (You should have 2 cups of carrot rounds.)

Pour the oil into a heavy pot that will hold the artichoke bottoms snugly in a single layer (if the pot is too big, too much liquid will be needed to keep the artichokes submerged) and place the pot over medium heat. When the oil is hot, add the onions, 1 teaspoon salt, and a pinch of pepper and cook gently to sweat for 2 to 2½ minutes. Add the garlic and stir to combine, then add the carrots and season with an additional 1 teaspoon of salt and another pinch of pepper. Cover and cook over low heat for 2 minutes.

Drain the artichoke hearts, place them stem side up on the vegetables, and heat for about 30 seconds. Turn over and cook for another 30 seconds. (This initial heating will prevent any discoloration of the hearts.) Add the white wine, bring to a simmer, and cook for 1 minute. Add enough chicken stock to cover the artichokes by ¼ to ½ inch. Add the bouquet garni and season to taste with salt and pepper; the liquid should be well seasoned. Bring to a simmer. Lay a clean dish towel or piece of cheesecloth against the hearts to keep them submerged in the liquid and cook for 35 to 40 minutes, or until the hearts are tender when pierced with a paring knife.

Stir in the anchovy and remove the pot from the heat. Let the artichokes cool in the liquid. (Once cooled, the artichokes can be stored in their liquid in the refrigerator for 1 to 2 days.)

TO COMPLETE: Remove the artichoke hearts from the liquid and place them upside down on a cutting board. Remove and discard the bouquet garni and transfer the liquid and remaining vegetables to a saucepan.

Cut each artichoke heart in half, then cut each half into 4 wedges. Return the artichoke wedges to the liquid in the pan and bring to a simmer over medium heat. Just before serving, stir in the parsley and a squeeze of lemon juice.

Meanwhile, season the skin side of the fish fillets with salt and the flesh side with salt and white pepper. Heat a thin film of canola oil in a large skillet over medium-high heat. Have a smaller skillet ready to weight the fish. When the oil is hot, add the pike fillets skin side down and immediately place the smaller skillet on top for 15 to 20 seconds, to prevent the fillets from curling. Remove the top skillet and cook the fillets for about 3 minutes, or until the bottoms are golden brown and the flesh is cooked halfway through. Flip the fish over to "kiss" the flesh side for about 10 seconds. Remove the fillets and drain them on paper towels.

Divide the barigoule among four serving plates and top with the fillets, skin side up. Drizzle a little additional olive oil over the barigoule.

MAKES 4 SERVINGS

COD WITH A STEW OF SWEET PEPPERS—CABILLAUD ET PIPÉRADE

Four 6-ounce pieces cod fillet (1 1/2 inches thick), skin and any bones removed
3 to 4 cups extra virgin olive oil
Kosher salt and freshly ground white pepper
4 thyme sprigs

1 small head garlic, cut horizontally in half
Piperade (page 314)
1/2 to 3/4 cup Chicken Stock (page 317), Fish Fumet (page 320), or Vegetable Stock (page 320)

1 tablespoon plus 1 teaspoon minced Italian parsley
Fleur de sel

A neutral fish with excellent body, cod goes well with all kinds of assertive garnishes, such as piperade, a sweet, garlicky, brothy roasted sweet pepper stew from the Basque region of northern Spain and southern France. This is an interesting dish to me because of its techniques. The cod is poached in just-warm olive oil for twelve minutes or so. The result is sensational, especially if you use a good fruity olive oil and a flavorful, moist fish. You can use this method with many fish, particularly, but not limited to, lean, delicate fish such as hake, any snapper, or halibut.

Piperade is a versatile preparation that's also great with chicken, eggs (a classic), clams, sausage, even spread on a baguette. And it gets even better after a couple of days in the fridge.

Pat the pieces of fish dry with paper towels. To calculate the amount of oil you will need, place the pieces of cod in a single layer in a saucepan that just holds them. Add enough olive oil to cover the fish by 1/2 inch. Remove the fish from the oil, pat off the excess, and season generously on both sides with salt and pepper. Set aside on a plate.

Add the thyme and garlic to the oil. Place the saucepan over low heat and warm the oil until it registers 140°F on a deep-fat

(or instant-read) thermometer. Remove the pan from the heat and let the garlic and thyme infuse the oil for about 30 minutes.

Return the oil to the heat and bring it to between 120° and 125°F. (The oil should feel warm to the touch, but you should be able to submerge your finger in it for a count of ten.) Place the fillets in the oil skinned side up and poach gently, adjusting the heat as necessary to keep the oil between 115° and 125°F. At an average of 120°F, the fish will be cooked in 12 to 14 minutes. (The cooked fillets will be opaque throughout; they can be kept warm in the oil for several minutes while you complete the dish.)

Meanwhile, combine the piperade and 1/2 cup stock in a medium saucepan, bring to a simmer, and simmer for 8 to 10 minutes. If the piperade becomes too thick, add some or all of the remaining stock as necessary so that it is still brothy. Just before serving, stir in the parsley.

Divide the piperade among four serving plates. Carefully lift up each piece of fish on a narrow spatula, place on a paper towel to drain, and carefully invert the fish onto the piperade. Sprinkle each fillet with fleur de sel and pepper, and drizzle each plate with a little olive oil.

PHOTOGRAPHS OPPOSITE AND ON PAGE 153   **MAKES 4 SERVINGS**

PAN-SEARED SOLE WITH POTATOES AND
PARSLEY-LEMON BROWN BUTTER—SOLE MEUNIÈRE POMMES CHÂTEAU

POTATOES

6 red-skin potatoes, long and narrow (about
　　3 ¹/₂ to 4 inches long) rather than round

¹/₄ teaspoon black peppercorns

2 thyme sprigs

1 bay leaf

2 garlic cloves, skin left on, smashed

1 tablespoon kosher salt

FISH

One 3-pound black sole, Dover sole, or
　　flounder, cleaned, head and skin
　　removed

Canola oil

Kosher salt and freshly ground white pepper

All-purpose flour

5 tablespoons plus 1 teaspoon unsalted butter

1 tablespoon plus 1 teaspoon chopped
　　Italian parsley

1 tablespoon plus 1 teaspoon fresh
　　lemon juice

After this mild fish is sautéed, a brown butter sauce with lemon and parsley is made in the same pan, then spooned over the fish and the potatoes that accompany it. Very simple, very satisfying, very bistro. Because it's so simple, the quality of the fish makes a big difference—yellowtail sole, Dover sole, flounder, or other flatfish all work well.

FOR THE POTATOES: The potatoes should be "turned," or trimmed to oval shapes about 2 ¹/₂ inches long and 1 inch in diameter at the thickest part. Trim each potato into a rectangular shape that is larger than the finished size, then trim off the ends. Holding the potato by the cut ends, use a paring knife to cut around the potato, trimming away the sides from top to bottom to form a rough football shape, then continue to trim and shave the sides to make a uniform oval (see the photograph on page 242).

Place the potatoes, peppercorns, thyme, bay leaf, garlic, and salt in a large saucepan and add cold water to cover the potatoes by 1 inch. Bring to a boil over high heat, then reduce the heat and simmer for about 15 minutes, or until the potatoes are tender. Keep the potatoes warm in the water while you cook the fish. (The potatoes can also be cooked a few hours ahead. Drain, reserving the water to reheat the potatoes, and set aside.)

FOR THE FISH: Preheat the oven to 375°F.

Pat the sole dry with paper towels. Heat ¹/₈ inch of canola oil in a large ovenproof nonstick skillet over high heat. Season the sole on both sides with salt and pepper. Coat the fish with flour and pat off any excess. Place the fish in the hot oil, reduce the heat to medium to medium-high, and add the 1 teaspoon of butter. Cook for about 5 minutes, or until cooked halfway through. Turn the fish over and place in the oven for another 5 minutes, or until just cooked through.

Meanwhile, if the potatoes have cooled, rewarm them in the cooking liquid; drain well.

Remove the fish from the oven. Use two large spatulas to transfer the fish to a warm serving platter and place in a warm spot. Drain the oil from the skillet and return the skillet to medium-high heat. When the oil is hot, add the 5 tablespoons butter and a pinch of salt. Swirl the skillet and let the butter brown. Add the potatoes and roll them in the butter for a minute to coat. Turn off the heat, add the parsley, and let it crackle; add the lemon juice. Keep warm.

TO SERVE: Cut down the center line of the fish to the bone to separate the top 2 fillets. With a long spatula, carefully transfer the fillets to a plate. Cut out and remove the backbone, then return the top fillets to their original place. Arrange the potatoes around the fish and spoon the brown butter over the top. Present the whole fish at the table, then serve.

MAKES 2 SERVINGS

MEDITERRANEAN BASS WITH SQUID, FENNEL, AND TOMATOES
LOUP DE MER À LA PROVENÇALE

8 small squid (about 8 ounces total)

About 1 cup milk

12 baby fennel bulbs, stalks trimmed to 1 inch, root ends trimmed

2 cups Shellfish Broth (page 321)

Kosher salt and freshly ground white pepper

Extra virgin olive oil

4 garlic cloves, skin left on, smashed

4 thyme sprigs

8 pieces Tomato Confit (page 313), halved lengthwise

Canola oil

4 large or 8 small pieces loup de mer fillet (1½ pounds total), any pinbones removed

1 tablespoon minced Italian parsley

Loup de mer, literally "sea wolf," is a bass from the Mediterranean with characteristics similar to those of our striped bass: It's fleshy and flavorful and carries garnishes well. Here it's paired with squid, from the same waters, which add great visual and textural elements, and also fennel (a classic combination with bass), garlic, and thyme—all Mediterranean ingredients. It's an especially good dish to make when baby fennel is available. If you can't find loup de mer, it's fine to substitute black or striped bass, or even snapper.

FOR THE SQUID: *To clean the squid,* one at a time, holding each squid under cold running water, pull off the head and reserve. Pull away and discard the outer skin from the body. Pull out and discard the piece of cartilage from the body cavity and use your fingers to clean the inside of the cavity. Lay the bodies on a cutting board. Hold each body down on the board and use the blade of a knife to scrape from the tapered end toward the other end, forcing out anything that may be left in the body.

Cut away the tentacles below the eyes and discard the heads. Drain the tentacles on paper towels. Cut off and discard the bottom tip of each squid body. Cut the bodies lengthwise in half. Place the bodies and tentacles in a small bowl and add enough milk to cover. [ ] soak, refrigerated, for at least 2 hours, or up to a day. [ ] salted water in a large pot. Prepare an ice bath. Add the [ ] and simmer for 5 to 6 minutes, or until tender. Remove and [ ]ickly in the ice bath, then drain and dry on paper towels.

TO COMPLETE: Preheat the oven to 325°F. Bring the shellfish broth to a simmer and reduce to 1 cup. Keep warm.

Meanwhile, drain the squid on paper towels and season with salt and pepper. Heat ⅛ inch of olive oil over medium heat in an ovenproof sauté pan that will hold the fennel in one layer. Add the fennel, garlic, and thyme. When the oil is hot and beginning to sizzle, place the pan in the oven. After about 2 minutes, add the tomato confit and let it warm while you sauté the fish.

Heat a thin film of canola oil in one large skillet or two smaller skillets over medium-high heat. Have another large skillet or two smaller ones ready to weight the fish. Season both sides of the fish with salt and the flesh side with pepper. Add the fish skin side down, reduce the heat to medium-low, and weight the fillets briefly with the skillet(s) to keep them from curling, then remove the skillet(s). Cook for 4 to 5 minutes, or until the skin is golden and crisp. Cook for just a minute on the other side. Drain on paper towels.

Bring the shellfish broth back to a simmer, add the squid, and simmer gently for about a minute: The bodies will curl up when they are done. Add the parsley and remove from the heat.

Remove the pan from the oven and drain the fennel and tomatoes on paper towels.

TO SERVE: Arrange the fish fillets skin side up in the center of four serving plates. Arrange the fennel, tomatoes, and squid around the fish. Pour one-quarter of the broth around each serving.

MAKES 4 SERVINGS

THE IMPORTANCE OF
{ SLOW COOKING }

The transformation that happens to a tough, unappealing cut of meat as it cooks long and gently is to me a fundamental pleasure of cooking—it lies at the core of why cooking is such a soul-satisfying act. It's a physical and sensory thrill to turn barely edible food—whether tripe or a well-worked muscle such as the shoulder, or even dried beans—into something that's great to eat, flavorful, and nourishing. Also, it reflects the craft, knowledge, and care of the cook.

From the standpoint of culinary fundamentals, the braise is a combination of two cooking methods—using first dry heat (for searing the meat), then moist heat (cooking it gently in liquid)—for tough cuts such as the shank or shoulder. By definition, braising means searing the meat first, so a distinction between a braised dish and any slow-cooked dish should be noted. Braising is a *form* of slow cooking, not another word for it. Lamb navarin, coq au vin, and oxtails are seared before being covered in liquid to cook. Blanquette de veau, a white veal stew, is not a braise, as the veal is poached briefly to remove impurities before being cooked slowly in stock. What is important is that all of these slow-cooked proteins undergo a precooking stage; this eliminates a substantial amount of blood and albumin, which would affect the finished dish.

The ultimate difference between a braised stew and a nonbraised stew is that one has a complex roasted flavor from Maillard browning, the browning of proteins (that of sugars is called *caramelization*), and a deeper color. The other is lighter in color and can have subtle distinctions in the resulting stock or sauce that can be almost veloutélike, and is often finished with cream. One isn't more refined or cleaner than the other. Both ought to be refined, both clean—but that's up to the cook, not the technique.

It's easy to understand why the slow-cooked dish is so important in the bistro kitchen. A chef can cook a big batch of oxtails or veal shoulder on Monday morning and serve it all week long. All that needs to be done before getting it to the customer is reheating. It doesn't require making a sauce, because it makes its own. Garnishes—onions, potatoes, and carrots—are inexpensive, always on hand, the perfect accompaniments, and are cooked in the same pot. And the flavors gather more depth and nuance as the week wears on.

Veal Stew (page 226)

SACHETS: A common restaurant technique that should be more widely used at home is something we call a *sachet d'épices*. It's simply spices and aromatics, used for flavoring, that you don't want in the finished dish—whole peppercorns, for instance, or cloves, bay leaves, or whole fresh herbs—enclosed in cheesecloth. It is submerged like a tea bag in stocks and slow-cooked dishes to infuse them with flavor, then removed. At Bouchon, we create what is in effect a giant sachet by placing a layer of cheesecloth over the pan of aromatic vegetables, then resting the meat on top and covering it with stock. This way, the meat can be lifted straight out of the pot, eliminating the need to pick it out of clumps of disintegrating vegetables.

Two 2¼- to 2½-pound chickens

Brine (page 325)

Kosher salt and freshly ground black pepper

2 tablespoons canola oil

2 teaspoons chopped thyme leaves

1 cup Chicken Jus (page 321), warmed

Fleur de sel

When I roast a chicken, one of my favorite things to cook at home, I usually just salt it thoroughly and put it in a hot oven, but at the restaurant we like to brine our chickens, which results in very juicy, uniformly seasoned birds, with deep brown, crispy skin. The brine does dehydrate the skin, though, because the salt pulls moisture from it as it adds flavor. If you see that the skin is beginning to brown too quickly, lay a sheet of foil over the bird to deflect the heat without trapping steam and moisture.

TO BRINE THE CHICKENS: Rinse each chicken under cold running water. Put the chickens in the pot of brine, weighting them with a plate if necessary to keep them submerged. Refrigerate for 6 hours.

TO ROAST THE CHICKENS: Preheat the oven to 475°F.

Remove the chickens from the brine (discard the brine), rinse them, and pat dry with paper towels. Season the inside of each one with a light sprinkling of salt and pepper.

To truss the chickens, place one chicken on a tray with the legs toward you. Tuck the wing tips under the bird. Cut a piece of kitchen twine about 3 feet long and center it on top of the neck end of the breast. Lift the neck end of the bird and pull the twine down around the wings and under the chicken, then bring the ends up over the breast, toward you, and knot the twine, pulling it tight to plump the breast. Bring the ends of the twine around the ends of the drumsticks and straight up. Tie as before to pull the drumsticks together and form a compact bird; tie again to secure the knot. Repeat with the second chicken. Let the chickens sit at room temperature for 20 to 30 minutes before roasting.

(The trussed chickens can be refrigerated for a few hours, but remove them from the refrigerator about 30 minutes before cooking.)

Season the outside of the chickens with a light sprinkling of salt and pepper. Place two heavy ovenproof skillets about 10 inches in diameter over high heat. (Heating the skillets will help keep the skin of the birds from sticking to them.) When they are hot, add half the oil to each and heat until hot. Put the birds breast side up in the skillets, and then into the oven with the legs facing the back of the oven.

Roast for 40 minutes, checking the birds every 15 minutes and rotating the skillets if the chickens are browning unevenly. After 40 minutes, check the temperature of the birds by inserting an instant-read thermometer between the leg and the thigh: The temperature should read approximately 155°F. (The chicken will continue to cook as it sits, reaching a temperature of about 165°F.) When the birds are done, remove from the oven, add the thyme leaves to the skillets, and baste the birds several times with the juices and thyme leaves. Let sit in a warm spot for about 10 minutes.

TO CARVE: Cut the twine between the legs of each chicken and pull on one end; the entire piece will pull away easily. Cut each bird into 4 serving pieces. Remove each leg by cutting through the joint where the thigh joins the body. Slice off each side of the breast, leaving the wings attached to the breast meat; cut off and discard the wing tips.

TO SERVE: Arrange one piece of breast and a leg on each serving plate and top with about ¼ cup chicken jus. Sprinkle with fleur de sel.

MAKES 4 SERVINGS

Roast Chicken with a Ragout of Wild Mushrooms (page 194)

CRÊPES WITH CHICKEN AND MORELS
CRÊPES AU POULET ET AUX MORILLES

1 pound fava beans in the pod
Kosher salt and freshly ground black pepper
5 ounces (about 3 cups) morels or other
    wild mushrooms
4 tablespoons (2 ounces) unsalted butter
$\frac{1}{4}$ cup brandy

1 cup Mornay Sauce (page 316)
Heavy cream, if necessary for thinning
    the sauce
2 cups shredded cooked chicken
2 tablespoons minced tarragon,
    plus 2 tablespoons whole tarragon leaves

2 tablespoons minced chives
4 Savory Crêpes (page 199)
1$\frac{1}{3}$ cups shredded Comté or Emmentaler
    cheese (about 4 ounces)

This French version of pot pie—a rich, creamy one-pot meal, with loads of chicken, fresh bright favas, and spring mushrooms within a savory pastry—is an excellent way to use leftover chicken, or freshly poached or roasted chicken (a two-and-a-half-pound bird will yield enough meat). We serve this in the spring; in winter, vegetables such as butternut squash or Swiss chard can be substituted for the fava beans.

FOR THE FAVAS: Shell the fava beans and peel their skins (peeling the beans before cooking them prevents gases from being trapped between the beans and their skins that could cause discoloring). Remove the small germ at the side of each bean. (You should have about 1 cup of beans.)

Bring a large pot of water to a boil and add enough salt so the water tastes like the sea. Meanwhile, prepare an ice bath and place a colander in the bowl. (This will make it easier to remove the chilled cooked beans from the ice water.) Blanch the beans for about 5 minutes, or until tender. Using a skimmer, immediately transfer them to the ice bath to chill. When the favas are cold, lift the colander from the ice bath and drain them well. Spread on paper towels to dry thoroughly.

FOR THE MUSHROOMS: Trim the stems from the mushrooms and cut any large ones lengthwise in half. If necessary, swish the mushrooms around briefly in warm water to remove any embedded dirt. Dry the mushrooms well with paper towels.

Melt the butter in a large sauté pan over medium-high heat. Add the morels, reduce the heat slightly, add a pinch each of salt and pepper, and cook gently for about 2 minutes, taking care not to brown the mushrooms. Add the brandy, increase the heat to high, and continue to cook for a minute or two to allow the alcohol to evaporate. Add the fava beans and heat through. Keep warm.

Meanwhile, heat the Mornay sauce in a medium saucepan over low heat. If it is too thick, thin with a bit of heavy cream. Add the chicken and warm over low heat. Season to taste with salt and pepper, then stir in the minced tarragon and 1 tablespoon chives; keep warm. Stir the remaining chives into the morels and fava beans.

Preheat a crêpe machine (see Sources, page 330) or heat a crêpe pan or nonstick skillet over medium heat. Place a crêpe on the preheated machine or in the hot pan, sprinkle with one-quarter of the cheese, and heat for a few seconds to melt the cheese. Transfer the crêpe to a serving plate. Place a second crêpe on the pan, sprinkle with another quarter of the cheese, and let it melt while you finish the first crêpe. Spoon one-quarter of the chicken mixture onto the center of the crêpe and spread out slightly, leaving a 2- to 3-inch border all around. Top the chicken with one-quarter of the fava mixture. Fold the four sides of the crêpe over toward the center leaving the center exposed. Repeat with the second crêpe, heating the third one as you do so, and then the fourth crêpe. Serve immediately.

PHOTOGRAPH ON PAGE 197

MAKES 4 SERVINGS

SAVORY CRÊPES

The crêpe is a lost art in America. Though it may not be an art on the high order of puff pastry, it's a great vehicle for all kinds of ingredients nevertheless, and it is an excellent way to make leftovers elegant. We seem to have completely abandoned it, or perhaps have never really understood it, which to me is a culinary sin. I think we lost the taste for crêpes because we've been able to buy them frozen for so long. These crêpes can be made and refrigerated for up to two days before you serve them.

1 cup all-purpose flour
¼ teaspoon kosher salt
⅛ teaspoon freshly ground black pepper
4 large eggs
¾ cup milk
¾ cup heavy cream
3 tablespoons unsalted butter, melted and kept warm
2 tablespoons minced chives
Canola oil (optional)

Combine the flour, salt, and pepper in a large bowl.

Whisk together the eggs, milk, and cream in a medium bowl. Vigorously whisk half of the wet mixture into the dry ingredients until smooth, then whisk in the remaining liquid. Let the batter rest in the refrigerator for at least 30 minutes, or up to a day.

TO COOK THE CRÊPES: Strain the batter through a chinois or fine-mesh strainer into a bowl. Whisk in the melted butter and chives.

Preheat a 12-inch crêpe machine (see Sources, page 330) or a large crêpe pan or nonstick skillet over low heat. (Working over low heat makes spreading the batter before it sets easier; if you are experienced, you can work over higher heat.) If the pan is new or you think the crêpes may stick, put some canola oil on a paper towel and rub a light coating of oil over the pan before heating.

Ladle about ½ cup of the batter into the center of the pan and quickly spread it evenly to form an 11-inch crêpe (see the photograph on page 196). The crêpe machine and many crêpe pans come with a special wooden spreader; if you don't have one, use an offset spatula or swirl the pan to spread the batter. If there are any thin spots or holes, add a bit more batter to fill them in and prevent the crêpe from burning. (If you find this method difficult, you can pour a larger amount of batter into the pan instead, lift the pan off the burner and quickly rotate it to coat the bottom, then pour the excess batter back into the bowl.) Turn up the heat to medium and cook the crêpe for about a minute, or until the bottom is lightly browned. Use a rubber spatula to lift up an edge of the crêpe, then gently lift and invert the crêpe. Lightly brown it on the second side; the crêpe will be heated again, so do not overcook it—it should remain pliable and not become brittle. Transfer the crêpe to a plate and cook the remaining crêpes, stacking them between sheets of wax paper. (The crêpes can be used immediately or stacked between layers of wax paper and stored in the refrigerator for a day or two. Bring to room temperature before filling.)

MAKES 3 CUPS BATTER, OR ABOUT SIX 11-INCH CRÊPES

STUFFING

2 tablespoons unsalted butter

1 cup diced (about ¼ inch) cèpes, morels, chanterelles, or other wild or cultivated mushrooms

Kosher salt and freshly ground black pepper

3 tablespoons minced shallots

1 tablespoon minced thyme

4 ounces spinach, large stems removed

8 ounces garlic sausage (see Sources, page 330), casing removed, crumbled

2 tablespoons chopped Italian parsley

1 tablespoon Dijon mustard

1 large egg, lightly beaten

CHICKEN

One 3- to 4-pound stewing hen

Kosher salt and freshly ground black pepper

3½ to 4 quarts Chicken Stock (page 317), heated until hot

Bouquet Garni (page 325)

1 head garlic, halved horizontally

4 medium parsnips

2 large turnips

8 small new potatoes, scrubbed

2 large leeks, washed, roots and dark green leaves removed

2 large carrots, peeled

1 tablespoon chopped Italian parsley (if serving the chicken on a platter)

4 thyme sprigs (if serving the chicken on individual plates)

FOR SERVING

Dijon mustard

Cornichons

Fleur de sel

Crusty bread

Poule au pot falls into the category of a light stew. A whole chicken is poached in stock with a variety of root vegetables and aromatics, resulting in a cross between a stew and a soup. Traditionally, such dishes were one-pot meals served in courses—first the broth, followed by the vegetables and meat—but at the restaurant we serve it as we do a stew, ladling the hot broth over the main ingredients. We enhance the broth with turnips, parsnips, potatoes, carrots, and leeks, and we pack the chicken with a sausage stuffing. Serve it sprinkled with fleur de sel, along with mustard, cornichons, and good bread.

It's important that the bird be completely covered with liquid as it cooks. Use an appropriate-size stockpot, one that just holds the bird comfortably. If the pot is too large, you'll need to add too much liquid, and the broth will be bland. The best kind of bird for this preparation, if you can get one, is a large hen that can stand up to a long cooking time.

FOR THE STUFFING: Line a baking sheet with paper towels.

Melt the butter in a large skillet over high heat. Add the mushrooms, season with salt and pepper to taste, and reduce the heat to medium-high. Cook, stirring for about 2 minutes, or until browned. Add the shallots and thyme and cook for another 2 minutes, or until softened. Add the spinach, season with a pinch each of salt and pepper, and sauté briefly to wilt the spinach. Transfer the spinach mixture to the paper towel–lined baking sheet to drain and cool.

Place the spinach mixture on a cutting board and finely chop until it is about the consistency of the sausage.

Place the crumbled sausage in a medium bowl, add the parsley, and stir to combine. Stir in the mustard and the spinach mixture until combined. Season with a bit of salt and pepper. If you aren't sure of the seasoning of the sausage you're using, sauté a small spoonful of the mixture to check and adjust the seasonings if necessary. Stir in the egg.

FOR THE CHICKEN: Season the cavity of the bird with salt and pepper. Stuff the hen, packing in the stuffing. Use a trussing needle and kitchen twine to sew up the cavity and keep the stuffing inside. To keep the shape of the bird compact, tuck the wings under the bird and tie the ends of the drumsticks together.

Place the bird breast side up in a stockpot and add enough hot stock to just cover the drumsticks. Cover the pot and bring to a simmer over medium heat. Add the bouquet garni and garlic, turn down the heat, and simmer gently for 45 minutes. Do not let the liquid boil or the skin could split.

Meanwhile, peel the parsnips. Cut off and discard the tops of the parsnips and cut a 2- to 2½-inch-long piece from the upper part of each one. (Reserve the remaining parsnips for another use.) Peel the turnips and cut them into quarters. The chunks should be about the same size as the pieces of parsnips.

After 45 minutes, check the seasoning of the broth and add additional salt to taste if necessary. Turn the heat up and add the potatoes, leeks, and carrots to the pot. Once the liquid returns to a simmer, reduce the heat and simmer for 15 minutes.

Add the parsnips and turnips and simmer for 30 minutes longer, or until all the vegetables are tender.

TO SERVE: Remove the chicken from the pot and remove the twine and trussing. *To present the chicken whole,* arrange the chicken and vegetables on a deep platter. Sprinkle with the parsley and ladle a little of the hot chicken stock over the chicken and vegetables.

Or, for individual plates, cut off the thigh and drumstick from each side of the bird, then cut them into 2 pieces. Cut away the breast from the carcass. Cut each breast into 2 pieces. Cut each potato in half, cut each leek in half, and cut each carrot on the diagonal into 4 pieces. Cut each piece of parsnip lengthwise in half, and cut each piece of turnip crosswise in half. Arrange 1 piece of breast meat, 1 piece of dark meat, 4 potato halves, 1 leek half, 2 carrot halves, 4 turnip pieces, 2 parsnip pieces, and one-quarter of the stuffing in each serving bowl. Garnish each bowl with a sprig of thyme and ladle some of the hot stock through a strainer over each portion.

Serve the chicken with the mustard, cornichons, fleur de sel, and some crusty bread.

MAKES 4 SERVINGS

BRAISED RABBIT LEGS
WITH BUTTERED EGG NOODLES AND MUSHROOMS
CUISSES DE LAPIN À LA MOUTARDE AUX NOUILLES ET CHAMPIGNONS

Four 8-ounce whole rabbit legs
    (see Sources, page 330)
Kosher salt and freshly ground black pepper
About ¼ cup canola oil
Flour for dusting
1¾ cups sliced (½ inch thick) leeks,
    white and light green parts only
1 cup diced (½ inch) onions
¾ cup sliced (½ inch thick) peeled carrots
3 garlic cloves, peeled and smashed
6 thyme sprigs
2 bay leaves
1 teaspoon black peppercorns
1 cup dry red wine
¾ ounce (1 large bunch) tarragon
3 to 4 cups Chicken Jus (page 321)

CARROTS

24 baby carrots, preferably 12 orange and
    12 yellow (no longer than 4 inches long)
1 teaspoon black peppercorns
4 thyme sprigs
4 tarragon sprigs
2 bay leaves
2 garlic cloves, skin left on, smashed
Kosher salt

MUSHROOMS

12 ounces black trumpet mushrooms or
    golden chanterelles
2 tablespoons unsalted butter
Kosher salt and freshly ground black pepper

PEARL ONIONS

12 red pearl onions, cooked according to the
    instructions on page 326
12 white pearl onions, cooked according to
    the instructions page 326
⅓ cup Chicken Stock (page 317)
1 tablespoon unsalted butter
Kosher salt and freshly ground black pepper

EGG NOODLES

4 ounces egg noodles
¾ cup Chicken Stock (page 317)
¼ cup Dijon mustard
2 tablespoons whole-grain mustard
1 tablespoon unsalted butter
Kosher salt and freshly ground black pepper
¼ cup roughly chopped tarragon

Tarragon leaves for garnish
Fleur de sel

This excellent braise should be prepared at least one day and up to three days ahead to allow the flavors to mature. Rabbit, which has a sweetness to its flavor and is richer and stronger-tasting than other lean meat such as chicken, poses unique challenges for a cook. Rabbit tends to be sold whole, but you wouldn't cook it whole. You'd cook the forequarters, back legs, and saddle separately. You might roast the saddle on the bone or sauté it off the bone. The tougher legs are perfect for braising, but since they have very little fat, it's important not to overcook them. It's also important to allow the braised meat to cool submerged in the liquid in order to reabsorb juices that it lost during cooking. (A favorite way to cook rabbit legs is to confit them, which aggressively addresses the fat issue.)

When buying rabbit, look for healthy pink color with some streaks of white in it. The flesh should be firm. And the best test for any small animal—and what inspectors usually look for—are the heart, kidneys, liver, and other organs, which should look good and smell clean.

FOR THE RABBIT: Pull away and discard any excess fat that remains on the legs (the skin will already have been removed). Season the legs generously with salt and pepper.

Preheat the oven to 350°F.

Place a rack over a baking sheet and line the rack with paper towels. Heat ⅛ inch of oil in a large sauté pan over high heat. Dust 2 legs on both sides with flour, patting off any excess. Add to the hot oil flesh side up, turn down the heat to medium-high, and sauté for a minute, or until golden brown. The lean legs will not give off much fat, so if the flour begins to burn, lower the heat. Turn the legs and brown the second side. Transfer to the rack. Add more oil to the pan as necessary and repeat with the remaining 2 legs.

For braising the rabbit, use a heavy lidded ovenproof pot (about 9 1/2 inches in diameter) that will hold the legs in a single layer. Cut a piece of cheesecloth about 3 inches longer than the diameter of the pot. Cut a parchment lid (see page 326) to fit the pot.

Heat 2 tablespoons oil in the pot over medium-high heat. When the oil is hot, reduce the heat to medium and add the leeks, carrots, onions, and a pinch of salt. Cook for 2 to 3 minutes, until softened. Add the garlic, thyme, bay leaves, and peppercorns and cook for 2 minutes, or until aromatic. Add the red wine and bring to a boil. Reduce the heat and simmer for 2 to 3 minutes to reduce by half. Add the tarragon. Wet the cheesecloth with cold water and wring out, then place the cheesecloth over the mixture. (This prevents the vegetables and herbs from clinging to the rabbit legs.) Lay the legs flesh side down on the cheesecloth. Add enough chicken jus to barely reach the top of the legs and bring to a simmer.

Cover with the parchment lid, cover the pot with its lid, and place in the oven; reduce to 300°F. Braise for 45 minutes.

Remove the pot from the oven and carefully turn the rabbit legs over. Cover again and return to the oven for an additional 20 minutes or so. Check the legs: The meat around the knuckle joint should be completely tender and falling from the bone. If it is not, return it to the oven and check often—it may take up to 1 1/2 hours.

Transfer the rabbit legs to an ovenproof container. Remove and discard the cheesecloth, then strain the braising liquid through a fine strainer or a regular strainer lined with a clean dampened tea towel or cheesecloth into a saucepan. Press lightly on the solids while straining in order to extract all the juices, then discard the vegetables. Bring the liquid to a simmer, spooning off the fat that rises to the top. Strain the liquid over the rabbit legs. Let cool to room temperature, then cover and refrigerate overnight, or for up to 3 days.

FOR THE VEGETABLES: Trim any greens of the baby carrots to 1/4 inch and peel the carrots. Scrape the tops of the carrots with a paring knife to remove any skin that remains. Place the carrots in a saucepan, add the peppercorns, thyme, tarragon, bay leaves, garlic, and salt to taste, and cover generously with water. The water should be well seasoned. Bring to a boil, reduce the heat, and simmer the carrots for 2 to 3 minutes, or until tender. Transfer to a plate and let cool. If the carrots are thick enough, cut lengthwise in half.

Wash or soak the mushrooms briefly in warm water. Trim the tough stems and drain on paper towels. Melt the butter in a large skillet over high heat. Add the mushrooms, reduce the heat to medium, and season with salt and pepper. Cook gently, tossing often for about 5 minutes, or until they are completely tender. Set aside.

TO COMPLETE: Preheat the oven to 250°F.

Place the container of rabbit in the oven just to warm the liquid. Remove from the oven and turn up the heat to 400°F.

Carefully transfer the rabbit legs to an ovenproof sauté pan. Strain enough of the liquid into the pan to come halfway up the legs. Place the pan in the oven and warm for about 15 minutes, basting with the stock from time to time.

Meanwhile, drain the onions, place in a small skillet with the carrots, chicken stock, butter, and salt and pepper to taste, and reheat over very low heat. Just before serving, turn up the heat to reduce the liquid and glaze the onions and carrots. Keep warm.

Add the noodles to a pot of salted boiling water. Meanwhile, combine the stock and mustards in a large sauté pan and whisk together over low heat. When the noodles are cooked, drain and add to the large sauté pan. Increase the heat, toss in the mushrooms and butter, and glaze the noodles with the sauce. Season to taste. At the last second, toss in the chopped tarragon.

TO SERVE: Place the noodles in the center of large serving bowls. Arrange the carrots over the noodles and the onions around them. Top with a rabbit leg and strain the sauce over and around. Sprinkle with a few tarragon leaves and a pinch of fleur de sel.

PHOTOGRAPH ON PAGE 202   **MAKES 4 SERVINGS**

SKIRT STEAK WITH CARAMELIZED SHALLOTS AND RED WINE JUS
BAVETTE À LA BORDELAISE

Four 10-ounce pieces trimmed outside
    skirt steak (see below)
Kosher salt and freshly ground black pepper
¼ cup canola oil
4 tablespoons (2 ounces) unsalted butter
4 cups thinly sliced shallots
4 teaspoons minced thyme

SALAD

2 to 3 ounces watercress, large stems
    removed
2 teaspoons minced shallots
1 teaspoon minced Italian parsley
1 teaspoon minced tarragon

1 teaspoon minced chives
1 teaspoon minced chervil
Extra virgin olive oil
Kosher salt and freshly ground black pepper

½ cup Red Wine Jus (page 323), warmed

The *bavette* is a variation of the classic steak frites, and every bit as satisfying. The skirt steak is quickly sautéed and served medium-rare with shallots, heaps of them: About a cup per portion, a mat of them, richly caramelized, is spread atop the beef. A red wine jus takes the place of the herb butter, echoing the deep, rich flavors of the meat.

Skirt steak, cut from along the ribs of the animal, is fibrous. When you order it from your butcher, keep in mind that there is an inside skirt steak as well as an outside steak. At Bouchon, we use the outside cut; thicker and more uniform in size, it can stand up to longer cooking, giving you time to baste the meat and flavor it with shallots and thyme.

Preheat the oven to 375°F.

Season both sides of the steaks generously with salt and pepper, keeping in mind that the salt and pepper will also season the shallots as they cook.

Heat two large skillets over medium-high heat until hot. Add 2 tablespoons canola oil to each skillet. When the oil is hot, add 1 tablespoon butter to each skillet, swirling them to brown the butter. Add the steaks and sear the first side for about 1½ minutes, or until nicely browned. Turn the steaks to brown the second side, tilt the skillets, and use a spoon to baste the meat with the oil and butter. After about 3 minutes, total cooking, remove the skillets from the heat and transfer the meat to a baking pan. Set aside while you cook the shallots.

Set the skillets, with the butter and oil, over medium heat. Add half the sliced shallots to each skillet, toss them in the oil and butter, and cook for about 2 minutes, until they have started to soften. Combine all the shallots in one skillet, add the remaining 2 tablespoons butter and the thyme, reduce the heat, and cook gently until the shallots are completely softened and golden brown. Season to taste with salt and pepper and cook for an additional 2 to 3 minutes to caramelize.

Stir any juices that have accumulated around the steaks into the shallots, then spread the shallots over the steaks. Place in the oven to cook for about 5 minutes, or until the steaks are medium-rare.

FOR THE SALAD: Place the watercress in a bowl and toss with the minced shallots, herbs, and a drizzle of olive oil. Season to taste with salt and pepper.

Place the steaks on serving plates and spoon about 2 tablespoons jus alongside each one.

Divide the watercress salad among the plates.

MAKES 4 SERVINGS

At Bouchon, I don't think we braise or slow-cook food any differently from the

way cooks have been doing it for centuries—another facet of the pleasure of this

kind of cooking—but we do serve it differently. At Bouchon, as at the French

Laundry, we strive for an elegant presentation. Vegetables that have been cooked

for a long time in a stew are often pale and mushy, and have usually contributed

all their flavor and nutrients to the sauce. We keep the meat and vegetables

separate in the cooking pot so we can readily discard the spent vegetables.

And then we cook more of the same vegetables—the traditional stew vegetables—

to perfection and use the freshly cooked vegetables as garnish. It's an excellent

way to turn a rustic stew into an elegant dish.

Preparing Braised Beef with Red Wine (page 212): Brown the meat *(opposite)*; refine the sauce by straining *(above left)*; separate the meat from the aromatics with cheesecloth *(above right)*.

BRAISED BEEF WITH RED WINE—BŒUF BOURGUIGNON

RED WINE REDUCTION

1 bottle red wine, such as cabernet sauvignon

1 cup diced (¹/₂ inch) onions

1 cup sliced (¹/₂ inch) peeled carrots

1 cup sliced (¹/₂ inch) leeks, white and light
    green parts only

1 cup sliced (¹/₄ inch) shallots

1 cup sliced (¹/₄ inch) button mushrooms
    and/or mushroom stems

3 thyme sprigs

6 Italian parsley sprigs

2 bay leaves

¹/₂ teaspoon black peppercorns

3 large garlic cloves, skin left on, smashed

2 ³/₄ pounds boneless short ribs (about 1 inch
    thick; see Sources, page 330)

Kosher salt and freshly ground black pepper

Canola oil

1 cup diced (¹/₂ inch) yellow onions

²/₃ cup sliced (¹/₂ inch) peeled carrots

1 ¹/₂ cups sliced (¹/₂ inch) leeks, white and
    light green parts only

2 garlic cloves, skin left on, smashed

3 thyme sprigs

3 Italian parsley sprigs

2 bay leaves

About 4 cups Veal Stock (page 318) or
    Beef Stock (page 319)

POTATOES

8 ounces fingerling potatoes, preferably small

1 tablespoon kosher salt

¹/₄ teaspoon black peppercorns

2 thyme sprigs

1 bay leaf

2 garlic cloves, skin left on, smashed

CARROTS

16 round French baby carrots or other
    baby carrots

1 tablespoon kosher salt

1 teaspoon black peppercorns

4 thyme sprigs

2 bay leaves

2 garlic cloves, skin left on, smashed

BACON AND MUSHROOMS

4 ounces slab bacon, cut into 24 lardons
    about 1 ¹/₂ inches long and ³/₈ inch thick

32 small button mushrooms, cleaned
    (see page 326)

2 tablespoons unsalted butter

Kosher salt and freshly ground black pepper

PEARL ONIONS

12 red pearl onions, cooked according to the
    instructions on page 326

12 white pearl onions, cooked according to
    the instructions on page 326

2 tablespoons chopped Italian parsley

Fleur de sel

Dijon mustard

The primary techniques for Bouchon's beef bourguignon are those of refinement—removing the impurities at every opportunity. That means skimming the stock thoroughly, removing all the fat and particles, straining it well, and then removing the fat and vegetable particles from the sauce. There will be fat from the searing of the meat, and this fat collects on the surface. It's these particles and fat that muddle flavor and dull the color and sheen of a stew. Moreover, because you've removed those fat and fat-sodden impurities,

this is a very healthful technique as well. (Unless you, like me, insist on adding some butter to the finished stew.)

One of our practical rules of refinement is to separate all the ingredients. Make a bed of the vegetables in the braising vessel, lay down a sheet of cheesecloth, put the stew meat on top of this, then cover the ingredients with stock. When the meat is done, you can lift out the meat and strain the sauce, discarding the vegetables, which have given all their flavor to the sauce and meat. You can further refine the

Leg of Lamb with Flageolets in a Thyme Jus (page 220)

Of the classic stews—beef bourguignon, blanquette de veau, coq au vin—lamb stew may be my

favorite because I find that the meat has the most character. And it's one of those dishes I remember

making as staff meal cook in 1977 at a big club in Rhode Island. Tough cuts of meat and other

products and trimmings not appropriate for the dining room were reserved for staff meals, so

learning to turn these into something a hundred of my older colleagues might not only find edible

but actually enjoy was a challenge. It's one of the best memories I have of when I was on my own

and learning not only the basics of cooking, but also what it meant to cook for and serve people.

LAMB STEW WITH SPRING VEGETABLES
NAVARIN D'AGNEAU AUX LÉGUMES PRINTANIERS

LAMB CHEEKS

5 pounds lamb cheeks

Kosher salt and freshly ground black pepper

Canola oil

1 cup diced (½ inch) onions

1 cup sliced (½ inch) peeled carrots

1½ cups sliced (½ inch) leeks,
     white and light green parts only

1 head garlic, cut horizontally in half and
     broken up

3 thyme sprigs

3 Italian parsley sprigs

12 black peppercorns

2 bay leaves

About 3 cups Veal Stock (page 318)

About 3 cups Chicken Stock (page 317)

CARROTS AND TURNIPS

16 round French baby carrots or
     other baby carrots

16 baby turnips (about 1 inch in diameter)

2 tablespoons kosher salt

4 bay leaves

24 black peppercorns

4 thyme sprigs

POTATOES

4 fingerling potatoes (about 3 inches long
     and no wider than 1 inch in diameter)

1 tablespoon kosher salt

¼ teaspoon black peppercorns

2 thyme sprigs

1 bay leaf

2 garlic cloves, skin left on, smashed

RAMPS

Kosher salt

12 ramps, baby leeks, spring onions,
     or scallions

FAVAS

Kosher salt

8 ounces fava beans in the pod

PEAS

½ cup English peas

1 tablespoon granulated sugar

Kosher salt

2 teaspoons chopped Italian parsley

Fleur de sel

We use lamb cheeks for this stew because they're very juicy, tender, and rich when braised. They don't keep well, so if you won't be using them the day you buy them, freeze them. If you can't find them, substitute shoulder. We associate lamb with spring, and so we use spring vegetables, which add great color and a bright, fresh flavor to the stew.

FOR THE LAMB CHEEKS: Place the cheeks fat side down on a cutting board. You'll see the meat of the cheeks and at one end of each, a small salivary gland, which you want to remove. Using a sharp knife, make a vertical cut between the gland and the meat, then run the knife underneath the meat to cut away the fat and silver skin; discard. The sinews in the meat can remain.

Place a rack over a baking sheet. Generously season all sides of the meat with salt and pepper. Heat ⅛ inch of oil in a large sauté pan over high heat. When the oil is hot, add only as many cheeks as will fit comfortably in a single layer; do not crowd the pan or the meat will steam rather than brown. Brown the meat, turning occasionally, on all sides, 3 to 4 minutes total. Transfer the pieces to the rack and brown the remaining meat in batches, adding more oil to the pan as necessary; set aside.

Preheat the oven to 350°F.

Combine the onions, carrots, leeks, garlic, thyme, parsley, peppercorns, and bay leaves in a pot that can hold the lamb in a single layer. Cut a piece of cheesecloth that is about 4 inches bigger than the diameter of the pot; wet it with cold water and wring it out. Place over the vegetables and fold over the edges to form a nest for the meat. (The cheesecloth allows the liquid to flavor and cook the meat but prevents vegetables and herbs from clinging to it.) Place the cheeks on the cheesecloth and add the veal and chicken stocks; it should just cover the meat.

It is important that the liquid not evaporate too quickly. If the pot does not have a tight-fitting lid, cut a parchment lid (see page 326). Bring the liquid to a simmer over medium-high heat. Cover the meat with the parchment lid, if using, then cover the pot with the lid. Place in the oven and reduce the heat to 325°F. Braise the meat for 1 to 1½ hours, or until very tender.

Transfer the meat to an ovenproof pot or storage container. Remove and discard the cheesecloth. Strain the braising liquid twice through a fine strainer or a medium strainer lined with a clean dampened tea towel or cheesecloth, straining it the second time into a saucepan. Discard the vegetables. Bring the liquid to a simmer, spooning off the fat as it rises to the top. Strain the liquid over the lamb and let cool, then cover and refrigerate for at least 1 day, or up to 3 days.

FOR THE VEGETABLES: Cut off the carrot tops and peel the carrots. Cut off the tops of the turnips and peel the turnips. Place the carrots and turnips in separate small saucepans and add cold water just to cover. Add 1 tablespoon salt, 2 bay leaves, 12 peppercorns, and 2 thyme sprigs to each pan. Bring to a simmer and cook until the vegetables are just tender, 4 to 5 minutes. Drain them and spread on a plate to cool. Discard the seasonings.

Wash the potatoes and cut into slices about ½ inch thick. Place them in a medium saucepan, along with the salt, peppercorns, thyme, bay leaf, and garlic, and add cold water to cover the potatoes by 1 inch. Bring to a boil over high heat, reduce the heat, and simmer for about 15 minutes, or until the potatoes are tender. Drain the potatoes and transfer to a plate to cool. Discard the seasonings.

Bring a large pot of water to a boil and salt assertively; the water should taste like the sea. Prepare an ice bath. Meanwhile, rub the outside of each ramp with a damp paper towel, working from the leaves toward the root end, to clean and remove the outer layer. Trim off the root end and the tough tops of the dark green leaves or trim the spring onions or scallions. Cook in the boiling water until tender. Remove and chill in the ice bath, then remove and drain on paper towels. Reserve the ice bath.

Bring another large pot of water to a boil and add enough salt so it tastes like the sea. Meanwhile, shell the fava beans and peel the skins from the beans (peeling the beans before cooking them prevents gases from being trapped between the beans and their skins that could cause discoloring). Remove the small germ at the side of each bean. (You should have about ½ cup beans.)

Replenish the ice bath if necessary and place a colander in the bowl. (This will make it easier to remove the chilled cooked beans from the ice.) Blanch the fava beans for about 5 minutes, or until tender, then immediately transfer to the ice bath to chill. Lift the colander from the ice bath and drain the favas well, then spread on paper towels to dry thoroughly.

Place the peas in a bowl, cover with ice, and toss to chill the peas (this step will help restore their bright color). Fill a large pot with water, add the sugar and enough salt so the water tastes like the sea, and bring to a boil. Add the peas and cook until tender, about 7 minutes.

Meanwhile, replenish the ice bath as necessary and set the colander in the bowl. When the peas are tender, transfer them to the colander to chill quickly, then drain and spread on paper towels.

TO COMPLETE: Preheat the oven to 250°F.

Place the container with the lamb in the oven for a few minutes just to liquefy the stock. Remove from the oven and turn the oven up to 400°F. Carefully transfer the lamb to an ovenproof sauté pan. Strain enough of the liquid over the lamb to come about three-quarters of the way up the meat.

Place the sauté pan in the oven and warm the lamb for about 5 minutes, basting occasionally with the cooking liquid. Add the carrots, turnips, and potatoes and toss gently. Return to the oven for 5 to 10 minutes, or until the vegetables and meat are hot.

Toss in the ramps, fava beans, and peas and heat for another minute. Remove from the oven and gently toss in the parsley.

With a slotted spoon, divide the meat and vegetables among serving plates or bowls. Spoon some of the sauce over each serving and sprinkle with fleur de sel.

MAKES 4 SERVINGS

LEG OF LAMB WITH FLAGEOLETS IN A THYME JUS
GIGOT D'AGNEAU AUX FLAGEOLETS, JUS INFUSÉ AU THYM

One 5 1/2- to 6-pound "short leg" of lamb, separated into top round, bottom round, and knuckle (see below)

MARINADE

2 tablespoons thyme leaves

8 cloves Garlic Confit (page 312)

1/2 cup oil from the garlic confit

Kosher salt and freshly ground black pepper

Canola oil

1 tablespoon unsalted butter

8 thyme sprigs

12 garlic cloves, peeled

Flageolets (page 257; finish the flageolets while the lamb rests)

1 cup Lamb Jus (page 322), warmed

Fleur de sel

Although traditional bistros served a whole leg of lamb, at Bouchon we approach the dish in a more modern way, separating the muscles of a lamb leg and removing all connective tissue by hand, so that each piece can be cooked to an exact temperature (typically heat breaks down the connective tissue, but that requires cooking the meat a little longer than we like). By separating the muscles before cooking the leg, we transform the dish from a rustic preparation into a very elegant one that's both easier to cook and finer to eat. The muscles of the leg become almost like a loin.

We use what is called the long leg, which breaks down into four pieces—the sirloin, top and bottom rounds, and knuckle. The leg of lamb available in most supermarkets, the short leg, normally doesn't include the sirloin. Ask the butcher to break down a short leg for you into the top round, the bottom round, and the knuckle. Or, if you want to try all four cuts of lamb, order a long leg and include the piece of sirloin. At Bouchon, we rely on the meat from Keith Martin at Elysian Fields Farm in Pennsylvania (see Sources, page 330).

In this recipe, we marinate the lamb with garlic and herbs, pan-roast it, and serve it with beans and a lamb jus. The cooking time can vary greatly depending on the weight of the trimmed muscle, the temperature of the meat when it goes into the oven, and the length of time the meat is sautéed. The best way to know if it's done is to use an instant-read thermometer.

In terms of traditional bistro cooking, a leg of lamb was a delicious bit of efficiency—one large piece of meat to slice and serve all night as it was ordered. A leg of lamb could be set out before the fire to keep warm, ready to go. With some beans reheated in a casserole, it made a complete and satisfying meal. Leftovers could be served as a sandwich (see page 99), and the bone could be used in a *garbure,* a hearty vegetable stew, or in a stock. A rack of pork, with a small change in accompanying dishes, could serve the same functions.

Remove any fat, silver skin, and connective tissue from the lamb. There is a gland imbedded in fat on the underside of the top round: Cut it away and discard. Lightly score the top of each individual cut so the seasonings will permeate the meat.

FOR THE MARINADE: Combine the thyme, garlic confit, and garlic oil in a blender and pulse several times; leave some texture— it should not be a puree. Season both sides of each piece of lamb with pepper and a tablespoon or so of the marinade. Cover and marinate in the refrigerator for at least 6 hours, or up to a day.

TO COOK THE LAMB: Preheat the oven to 325°F.

Use kitchen twine to tie each piece of lamb into a compact roll. First tie a piece of twine around the center or widest area of the meat, then continue to tie pieces at 1-inch intervals along the roast. The twine should be tied securely enough to make a compact, uniform roast, but not so tightly that it cuts into the meat. Generously season each roast with salt and pepper.

Pour ⅛ inch of canola oil into a large ovenproof skillet and heat until hot. (If your skillet won't hold all the pieces comfortably, sauté them in two batches, then return all the meat to the skillet before adding the butter.) Add the lamb to the skillet and sauté gently, rolling the meat around to brown evenly on all sides, 3 to 4 minutes. Add the butter, thyme sprigs, and garlic and sauté for another 2 to 3 minutes, basting the lamb with the oil and butter.

Transfer the skillet to the oven. Each piece will cook in a different amount of time, so carefully check the lamb with an instant-read thermometer. The bottom round and knuckle will take 20 to 25 minutes, and the top round about 30 minutes. (If you are using the sirloin, it will cook the most quickly; begin checking after about 7 minutes.) Remove each piece of lamb when it has reached an internal temperature of approximately 125° to 130°F, for medium-rare. Allow the lamb to rest for about 15 minutes in a warm place.

TO SERVE: Remove and discard the twine from each roast and slice the lamb. Place a bed of flageolets in the center of each serving plate. Arrange about 4 overlapping slices of lamb over the beans, giving each plate a sampling of cuts, and ladle about ¼ cup of jus over the lamb and around each plate. Garnish with a sprinkling of fleur de sel and a sprig of the cooked thyme.

PHOTOGRAPH ON PAGE 216   **MAKES 6 SERVINGS**

BRINED ROASTED RACK OF PORK—CÔTE DE PORC RÔTIE

One 4½-pound (8 ribs) whole rack of pork
Brine (page 325)

Kosher salt and freshly ground black pepper
Canola oil
3 tablespoons unsalted butter

8 garlic cloves, skin left on, smashed
½ ounce (1 bunch) thyme sprigs

This rack of pork, a straightforward roast, can be a winter or summer dish. In winter, treat it like the *boudin blanc* (page 228) and serve it with potatoes and prunes or a potato gratin; in summer, accompany it with a simple jus and fresh tomatoes or a salad. Larger cuts of pork, such as racks, really benefit from brining, a process that seasons the interior of the meat and results in a juicier finished roast.

Submerge the pork in a pot of brine and refrigerate for 24 hours.

Remove the pork from the brine, rinse under cold water, and pat dry with paper towels. Score the fat slightly, making shallow cuts about 1 inch apart in a crosshatch pattern.

Tying the roast helps it cook more evenly, and here it makes for an especially fine presentation by keeping the roast in a compact shape. To tie the roast, cut 7 pieces of twine 15 to 16 inches long. Stand the roast on a baking sheet meat side down and facing you. Thread a trussing needle with a piece of the twine. Run the needle just over the "eye" of the meat, between the first two bones, exiting at the back of the rack. Remove the needle and leave the twine hanging on both sides of the bones. Repeat, running a length of twine between each set of bones just above the meat. Lay the rack meat side down on the baking sheet. Bring up both ends of each piece of twine and tie at the back of the rack to form a compact eye. Trim any excess twine. Generously season the entire surface of the pork with salt and pepper.

Let the meat sit at room temperature for about an hour before searing.

TO ROAST THE PORK: Preheat the oven to 350°F.

Heat a roasting pan over medium-high heat until hot. Add ⅛ inch of canola oil to the pan, and when the oil is hot, add 1 tablespoon of the butter. Add the pork and sear for about 5 minutes, turning the rack to brown on all sides. Turn off the heat and carefully (the oil may spit) add the garlic and thyme, tossing them in the oil to crackle and brown for a couple of minutes. If the pan seems dry, add a little more oil.

Turn the rack meat side up and arrange the garlic and thyme over it. Place the roasting pan in the oven and turn down the heat to 325°F. Cook for 15 minutes. Remove the pan from the oven, add the remaining 2 tablespoons butter, and baste the meat. Return to the oven for another 15 minutes.

Baste the meat again and check the temperature with an instant-read thermometer; it should register about 135°F for medium to medium-rare. Return the meat to the oven, if necessary, to cook a bit longer.

Remove the roast from the oven and let it rest in a warm place for 10 to 15 minutes. Place the pork on a cutting board; cut and remove the twine. Slice between the ribs and serve on the bone.

PHOTOGRAPH ON PAGE 222   **MAKES 6 SERVINGS**

VEAL ROAST—RÔTI DE VEAU

One 4 1/2-pound veal top round roast

Kosher salt and freshly ground black pepper

2 ounces (1 large bunch) basil

2 heads garlic, separated into cloves but skin left on, smashed

3 ounces (1 1/2 large bunches) thyme sprigs

Canola oil

2 tablespoons unsalted butter

We use a top round of veal, which is called the *noix,* or "nut." It's a big solid muscle that's easy to cook, feeds a lot of people, and is delicious.

Trim away any sinew, silver skin, or glands from the meat. Season lightly on all sides with salt and pepper. Remove the basil leaves from the stems. Lay a large piece of plastic wrap on the counter. Distribute half of the basil leaves, one-quarter of the garlic cloves, and one-third of the thyme over the plastic. Place the roast on top and distribute the remaining basil, another quarter of the garlic cloves, and half of the remaining thyme over the top of the meat. Tightly wrap the plastic around the meat and refrigerate for 24 hours.

TO ROAST THE MEAT: Preheat the oven to 350°F.

Unwrap the roast and place it on a cutting board. Remove and discard any herbs or garlic clinging to the meat. Tie a piece of kitchen twine around the center of the roast, then, moving outward from the center to each end, tie the roast at about 1-inch intervals.

Season the roast generously with salt and pepper, pressing the salt and pepper into the meat, and let rest at room temperature for 30 minutes.

Heat a thin film of canola oil in a large heavy ovenproof skillet over high heat. Add the butter, then add the roast and lightly brown on all sides. Baste the meat from time to time with the oil and butter by tilting the skillet and using a large spoon. When the roast is evenly browned, after about 5 minutes, add the remaining thyme and garlic to the skillet. Baste the meat with the butter and arrange the thyme over it.

Transfer the skillet to the oven and roast for 50 to 60 minutes, or until an instant-read thermometer inserted in the center of the meat registers 140°F. Remove the skillet from the oven and let the roast rest in the skillet for about 10 minutes.

Remove the twine before carving into 1/2-inch-thick slices.

MAKES 6 TO 8 SERVINGS

WHITE SAUSAGE WITH PRUNES AND POTATO PUREE
BOUDIN BLANC ET PURÉE DE POMMES DE TERRE, PRUNEAUX AUX ÉPICES

PRUNES

1 bay leaf

1 star anise

4 whole cloves

1 thyme sprig

½ teaspoon black peppercorns

½ cup dry red wine, such as cabernet
    sauvignon

1 stick cinammon

20 prunes, pitted

4 boudin blanc (see Sources, page 330),
    patted dry

Kosher salt and freshly ground black pepper

4 tablespoons (2 ounces) unsalted butter

4 garlic cloves, peeled and smashed

4 thyme sprigs

Potato Puree (page 250), kept warm

6 tablespoons (3 ounces) unsalted butter

Kosher salt and freshly ground black pepper

1 tablespoon plus 1 teaspoon fresh lemon
    juice

1 tablespoon plus 1 teaspoon chopped
    Italian parsley

As is customary for a bistro, at Bouchon we buy our *boudin* from a charcuterie. Since the sausages are fully cooked, all the chef needs to do at service is reheat them, usually in some delicious fat, such as duck or butter, to crisp up the skin and give them a nice caramelized color. The boudin blanc is accompanied by spiced prunes (quince would work well too), the noir (page 229) with apples sautéed in the same pan used to reheat the sausage. We serve both with the whipped potatoes.

FOR THE PRUNES: Place the bay leaf, star anise, cloves, thyme, and black peppercorns on a piece of cheesecloth and tie into a sachet with kitchen twine. Place in a small saucepan just big enough to hold the prunes in a single layer, add the red wine and cinnamon stick, and bring to a boil over medium-high heat. Add the prunes, return to a simmer, and cook for 2 minutes.

Remove the pan from the heat, partially cover, and let the prunes sit in the liquid for 30 minutes. (The prunes can be refrigerated for up to 2 weeks. Transfer the prunes, sachet, cinnamon stick, and liquid to a covered container and refrigerate.)

TO COMPLETE: Preheat the oven to 350°F.

Season the sausages generously with salt and pepper. Heat a large ovenproof sauté pan over medium-high heat. When the pan is hot, add the 4 tablespoons butter and swirl it until it has browned. Add the sausages, reduce the heat to medium, and add the garlic and thyme. (Don't cook the sausages over high heat or the casings may split.) Cook for about 2 minutes, or until the sausages are browned on the first side. Turn the sausages and brown the second side for about 2 minutes.

Meanwhile, drain the prunes and discard the spices. Add the prunes to the sauté pan and place in the oven to cook for 6 to 10 minutes, until hot throughout.

Just before the sausages are done, place a small skillet over medium-high heat.

Spoon a mound of potato puree on each serving plate. Place a sausage to the side of the potatoes and arrange the prunes between the sausages and the potatoes.

Add the 6 tablespoons butter to the hot skillet, along with a pinch each of salt and pepper. When the butter has browned, remove the skillet from the heat and add the lemon juice and parsley. Swirl for a few seconds and drizzle over the sausages, prunes, and potatoes.

MAKES 4 SERVINGS

BLOOD SAUSAGE WITH POTATO PUREE AND CARAMELIZED APPLES

BOUDIN NOIR, PURÉE DE POMMES DE TERRE, POMMES CARAMÉLISÉES

4 boudin noir (see Sources, page 330),
    patted dry
Kosher salt and freshly ground black pepper

3 apples, such as Granny Smith, Galas, or Fuji
Canola oil
Potato Puree (page 250), kept warm
6 tablespoons (3 ounces) unsalted butter

Kosher salt and freshly ground black pepper
4 teaspoons fresh lemon juice
4 teaspoons chopped Italian parsley

A boudin blanc is a white sausage traditionally made with cream as part of its fat. Boudin noir is a blood sausage, classically made of pig's blood and aromatic vegetables. The word *boudin* means "pudding," which describes the very light, airy, almost moussellinelike texture of these sausages. The blanc is light in flavor as well, whereas the noir has a coarser consistency and a pronounced pork flavor.

Preheat the oven to 250°F.

Season the sausages generously with salt and pepper.

Peel the apples, cut in half, and use a melon baller to scoop out the core and seeds. Trim any remaining peel with a paring knife. Cut each half lengthwise, then cut in half again to make 12 wedges. Season with salt and pepper.

Pour 1/8 inch of canola oil into each of two large skillets and heat over medium-high heat. When the oil is hot, reduce the heat to medium and add half the sausages and half the apples rounded side down to each skillet. Brown the sausages for 3 to 4 minutes

on the first side, then turn them over to brown on the second side. Turn the apples as they brown. When the sausages are browned, reduce the heat (if they cook too quickly, the casings may burst) and cook until heated throughout, another 1 to 2 minutes.

Transfer the sausages to a baking pan and place in the oven to keep warm. Transfer the apples in one skillet to the other, leaving the oil in the skillet. Continue to brown and cook the apples until they are soft but not falling apart. Drain the apples and keep warm.

Just before serving, place a small skillet to heat over medium-high heat.

Spoon a mound of potato puree on each serving plate. Place a sausage to the side of the potatoes, and arrange 3 pieces of apple between each sausage and the potatoes.

Add the butter to the hot skillet, along with a pinch each of salt and pepper. When the butter has browned, remove the skillet from the heat and add the lemon juice and parsley. Swirl for a few seconds and drizzle over the sausages, apples, and potatoes.

MAKES 4 SERVINGS

LIVER AND ONIONS WITH FIGS
FOIE POÊLÉ AUX OIGNONS ET FIGUES AUX ÉPICES

SACHET

1 bay leaf

1 star anise

4 whole cloves

1 thyme sprig

½ teaspoon black peppercorns

FIGS

12 black mission, brown turkey, or other
    fresh figs

½ to ¾ cup dry red wine, such as cabernet
    sauvignon

1 cinnamon stick

GARNISHES

8 thin slices bacon

One 4-ounce piece slab bacon

20 small cipollini onions, peeled

Canola oil

1 tablespoon unsalted butter

Kosher salt and freshly ground black pepper

2 large thyme sprigs

2 garlic cloves, skin left on, smashed

½ cup Chicken Stock (page 317)

LIVER

Four 6- to 8-ounce pieces calves' liver
    (¾ to 1 inch thick)

Kosher salt and freshly ground black pepper

All-purpose flour

Canola oil

4 tablespoons (2 ounces) unsalted butter

12 thyme sprigs

4 garlic cloves, skin left on

1 tablespoon minced chives

1 tablespoon minced Italian parsley

4 chervil sprigs

1 cup Red Wine Jus (page 323), warmed

I like liver cooked *à point,* or "medium-rare," so that it's
creamy and rich. Here the sautéed liver is garnished
with bacon, cipollini onions, and figs stewed in spiced wine.
The sweetness of the onions, of course, goes perfectly with
the earthy flavor of the organ meat, and the figs raise the
sweetness to dramatic proportions.

   Try to use thick pieces of liver, which allow for a deeply
caramelized crust and give you time to baste and add
aromatics to the cooking fat to develop more flavor.

FOR THE SACHET: Place the bay leaf, star anise, cloves, thyme,
and black peppercorns on a piece of cheesecloth and tie into a
sachet with kitchen twine.

FOR THE FIGS: Place the sachet and stand the figs in a saucepan
that holds the figs snugly in one layer, add enough red wine to
come one-third of the way up the figs, and add the cinnamon
stick. Bring to a simmer, then reduce the heat and cook over low
heat for 10 to 15 minutes, or until the figs are soft. Transfer the
figs, wine, sachet, and cinnamon to a bowl or another container.
(The figs can be refrigerated for up to 2 days. Bring to room
temperature before using.)

FOR THE BACON: Preheat the oven to 375°F. Line a baking sheet with foil and place a rack over the pan.

Place the strips of bacon on the rack and bake for 15 to 20 minutes, or until crisp. Remove from the oven and allow the bacon to sit on the rack for about 15 minutes to drain.

Meanwhile, trim away and discard the rind from the slab of bacon. Cut into lardons 1 ½ inches long and ⅜ inches thick. Spread the lardons in a single layer in an ovenproof nonstick pan and place in the oven for about 10 minutes. Stir the lardons and return to the oven for another 10 to 20 minutes, or until just cooked. Drain on paper towels.

FOR THE CIPOLLINI: Use a paring knife to score an X in the root end of each onion. Heat an ovenproof skillet that will hold the onions in a single layer over medium-high heat, then add a thin film of oil and the butter. When the butter has browned, add the onions, season to taste with salt and pepper, and add the thyme and garlic. Cook, tossing the onions with the seasonings, for 2 to 3 minutes, or until a rich, golden brown.

Add the stock to the skillet and place in the oven to cook for about 15 minutes. Turn the onions and return to the oven for another 15 minutes, or until tender when poked with a paring knife. Remove from the oven and leave the oven on.

TO COMPLETE: Pat the pieces of liver dry with paper towels. Season both sides with salt and pepper and dredge lightly in flour. Pat to remove any excess flour.

Heat a thin film of canola oil in a large skillet over medium-high heat. (It is important that the skillet be large enough to hold the liver without crowding or it may steam rather than sauté.) When the oil is hot, add the butter and let it brown, then turn the heat down to medium, add the liver, and sauté for about 2 minutes, or until the underside is a rich, golden brown. Turn the liver and sauté for another minute, using a spoon to baste the liver with the oil and butter. Place the sprigs of thyme over the pieces of liver, baste again, and transfer the liver to a baking pan; set the skillet aside. Remove the figs from the liquid and place alongside the liver and top each piece of liver with a garlic clove.

Transfer the baking pan to the oven to cook for 3 to 4 minutes, or until the liver is medium-rare.

Meanwhile, drain the fat from the skillet and add the cipollini. Sauté over medium heat just to add a little color and rewarm the onions. Reduce the heat and add the lardons to the skillet to heat through.

Return the sliced bacon to the oven to rewarm as necessary.

At the last minute, toss the chives and parsley into the onions.

TO SERVE: Arrange the onions, figs, and lardons on serving plates. Discard the thyme and garlic on top of the liver, arrange a piece of liver on each plate, and crisscross 2 pieces of bacon over each piece. Garnish each with a sprig of chervil and spoon the red wine jus around the plates.

MAKES 4 SERVINGS

HARICOTS VERTS
WITH SHALLOTS
HARICOTS VERTS AUX ÉCHALOTES

1 pound haricots verts

4 tablespoons (2 ounces) unsalted butter

2 tablespoons minced shallots

¼ cup Chicken Stock (page 317) or water

Kosher salt and freshly ground black pepper

1 tablespoon chopped Italian parsley

Cooking fresh beans properly—that is, all the way through so that they're just tender to the bite—is the secret to their excellence. We blanch them first in plenty of rapidly boiling, heavily salted water (one cup kosher salt per gallon) and cool them in an ice bath, then finish them in chicken stock and butter, seasoned with shallots, parsley, and pepper.

Bring a large saucepan of generoulsy salted water to a boil. Prepare an ice bath. Trim the stem ends of the beans and wash under cold running water. Blanch the beans until just tender; the cooking time can vary greatly depending on how fresh the beans are, so begin to taste them after about 2 minutes.

Drain the beans and place them in the ice bath just until cold, then drain them and dry well on paper towels. (The blanched beans can be wrapped in paper towels and stored in the refrigerator for a couple of hours.)

Heat a large skillet over medium heat. Melt half the butter in the skillet, then add the shallots and cook gently for a minute, or until softened. Add the chicken stock or water, the remaining butter, and the beans. Season to taste with salt and pepper. Heat, swirling the skillet, for about 2 minutes, to heat the beans and glaze with the butter mixture. At the last minute, toss in the parsley.

Transfer the beans to serving plates or a platter and spoon the butter sauce over the top.

MAKES 4 SERVINGS

SAUTÉED SPINACH
WITH GARLIC CONFIT
ÉPINARDS SAUTÉS À L'AIL CONFIT

About 1 pound spinach, preferably baby spinach,
    or two 10-ounce bags

3 tablespoons unsalted butter

¼ cup minced shallots

8 cloves Garlic Confit (page 312)

Kosher salt and freshly ground black pepper

The spinach in this rich, nutritious side dish should be perfectly cooked—not just wilted, but not overcooked either—sautéed over gentle heat until the leaves are tender and bright. Be sure to season it with salt as soon as it goes into the pan, while it's raw, so that the seasoning is evenly distributed. This is a very easy and quick dish to make.

If using large-leaf spinach, remove the thick stems and wash the leaves. If necessary, wash the baby spinach.

Melt the butter in the largest skillet you have over medium-low heat. Add the shallots and sauté gently for a minute. Add the garlic confit and only as much spinach as will fit in the skillet, sprinkle with salt and pepper, and use tongs to turn the spinach in the butter. As the spinach wilts, continue to add handfuls of spinach until it has all been used. Taste the spinach from time to time and season additionally as needed. Do not overcook: The spinach is done when it is wilted and tender but still bright green. Serve immediately.

MAKES 4 SERVINGS

MORELS AND PEAS WITH ONION CONFIT
MORILLES ET PETITS POIS AU CONFIT D'OIGNONS

10 to 12 ounces (4 cups) morel mushrooms

1 cup shelled English peas (about 1 pound in the pod)

1 tablespoon sugar

Kosher salt

4 tablespoons (2 ounces) unsalted butter

Freshly ground black pepper

1/2 cup Onion Confit (page 312)

1 teaspoon minced thyme

1/4 cup Chicken Stock (page 317) or Vegetable Stock (page 320)

2 teaspoons minced Italian parsley

This all-purpose side dish is all about spring—the premier season of the year for a cook. It announces spring the same way asparagus does. Two components of this dish, once unavailable to Americans, are increasingly common today. Even some grocery stores now carry morel mushrooms when they can get them, as well as fresh English peas. If you haven't shelled and eaten fresh peas, ever or for a while, maybe since you were a kid, now's the time to try them.

Trim the bottoms of the mushrooms; cut smaller mushrooms in half and larger mushrooms in quarters, keeping the pieces about the same size. Place the mushrooms in a large bowl and cover generously with warm water. Swish the mushrooms gently to remove any embedded soil. Lift them from the water and dry on paper towels.

Place the peas in a bowl, cover them with ice, and toss together to chill. (This step will help them retain their bright color when they are blanched.) Bring a large pot of water to a boil and add the sugar and enough salt so the water tastes like the sea. Lift about half the peas with a strainer, letting the ice fall back into the bowl, and add them to the water. (It is important that the water return to a boil almost immediately to keep the peas a vivid green color—it may not if you add too many peas.) Cook the peas until they are fully tender, 5 to 10 minutes, depending on their freshness.

While the peas cook, prepare an ice bath and place a strainer in the bowl. (This will make it easier to remove the chilled cooked peas from the ice bath.) When the peas are tender, remove them with the strainer and plunge into the ice to chill as quickly as possible, then lift the strainer from the ice and drain the peas well on paper towels. Repeat with the remaining peas.

Melt 2 tablespoons of the butter in a large skillet over high heat. Add the mushrooms and season with salt and pepper to taste. Sauté for 2 to 3 minutes, until the mushrooms are tender but not colored. Drain the mushrooms on paper towels.

Combine the remaining 2 tablespoons butter and 2 tablespoons water in a large skillet and bring to a simmer, swirling the skillet until the butter is melted. Add the onion confit and thyme and cook for a minute. Add the mushrooms and stir for another minute. Add the peas and stir gently to combine. Add the stock and simmer to reduce slightly. Season to taste with salt and pepper. Stir in the parsley and serve.

PHOTOGRAPH ON PAGE 239   **MAKES 4 SERVINGS**

SPACE: Space at a bistro is limited, but proprietors have to get as many people as possible into it if they're going to break even every month, which means that a bistro is crowded. The crowdedness is actually a big part of a bistro's appeal, however. There's an energy in confining so much activity in so little space. It might even have an element of danger, with a busy wait staff carrying full trays overhead along an obstacle-filled path. Of course, the kitchen is usually tiny, sometimes amazingly so, given the quantity of food it puts out.

BANQUETTE: Having to work with very little space, the bistro owner needs a seating plan both practical and social; hence the banquette. A banquette can accommodate three couples arriving at the same time as easily as it can a party of six. And banquettes create a situation in which half the people look out at the other half—that important people-watching dynamic—as opposed to the more insular circular interaction you'll find at a fine restaurant.

Glazing root vegetables is a great technique when it's done right because it results in tender, sweet-savory vegetables—in fact, it may be the perfect way to cook root vegetables. And yet it's underused in the home kitchen and misunderstood in the professional kitchen. I've seen cooks throw a handful of sugar into the pot of water, cook the vegetables, and then strain them, dumping out the water. Or they sauté the vegetables in butter and sugar.

The first thing to realize is that glazing does not mean sugary or sweet. There is sweetness from the small amount of added sugar along with the natural sugars in the vegetable, but we're not talking candied yams. Second, glazing is a specific technique that takes some experience and attention.

Because the shape of the vegetable affects how it cooks, I turn vegetables so that they're about an inch and a half long and about a half inch wide. It's an elegant shape, but one that allows them to roll in the pan, aiding the glazing process. If you're glazing very small pieces, you may need to only add water to cover; for larger pieces, you may need to cover them by an inch of water. Cooking times and amounts will depend on the size and shape of a vegetable.

To glaze, cover the peeled and turned vegetables with about an inch of water, add a teaspoon of sugar and a pat of butter, and simmer gently. The aim is to have your vegetables three-quarters cooked by the time the water level is reduced to about half their height. They'll actually create a kind of stock that will reduce down with the sugar and butter to a glaze. (If they're not cooked enough at this point, add a little water; if you feel they're overcooking, remove them from the pan and reduce the liquid to a glazing level, then return the vegetables to the pan.)

When the vegetables are nearly done and the water is low, turn up the heat to boil down the remaining water quickly, taking care to "jump" your vegetables in the pan—to swirl and move them around in the sauce as it reduces and coats them. When the liquid is gone, the vegetables are done. They should be beautiful to look at. Season with salt and—very important—keep them warm if not serving right away. I find that root vegetables will keep warm for hours without any compromise in flavor or texture, but if they're refrigerated and reheated, they lose their freshness, their bright color, and their flavor.

Almost all root vegetables can be glazed. Turnips are excellent, as are rutabaga, celeriac, and

carrots. Pearl onions are everywhere in these recipes. Even baby leeks and scallions are excellent

candidates. Glazing vegetables is worth the time and effort. Only time and attention will result in

success. Remember, a perfectly glazed vegetable is cooked with the right amount of water, butter,

and sugar and, when it's done, has no resistance to the bite and a beautiful sheen.

2 cups peeled and trimmed root vegetables
(see below), up to 1¹/₂ inches long and
¹/₂ inch in diameter

FOR EACH ¹/₂ CUP VEGETABLES
1 teaspoon unsalted butter
¹/₂ teaspoon sugar

OPTIONAL SEASONINGS
1 thyme sprig
A few black peppercorns
1 bay leaf
1 rosemary sprig
1 savory sprig

Kosher salt
Minced chives and chive bâtons
(about 1¹/₂ inches long)
Minced Italian parsley
Fleur de sel

Glazed vegetables—carrots, turnips, parsnips, rutabaga, celeriac, pearl onions, even scallions and baby leeks— are wonderful as a side dish or garnish, either singly or in combination. You can cut them into balls or give them a beautiful finish by "turning" them *(tourner)* into an oval shape: Cut chunks of the vegetables slightly larger than the size needed, then trim the sides with a paring knife to achieve the classic seven-sided shape (see the photograph opposite). Each vegetable should be cooked separately, since cooking times will vary. The goal is for the vegetables to become tender just as the water evaporates, leaving the butter and sugar to glaze them. The vegetables should have plenty of room in the pan so that they will be able to roll around in the final steps of glazing. Choose one or more of the optional seasonings listed above that will enhance the main dish, such as rosemary if the vegetables will be served with lamb. Prepare about a half cup of trimmed vegetables per person. (See "The Importance of Glazing," page 340.)

Place each type of vegetable in a loose single layer in a separate saucepan. Add cold water to just cover the vegetables. Then add the butter, sugar, optional seasonings, and a pinch of salt. Bring the water to a boil, then adjust the heat and simmer gently for 10 to 15 minutes. Ideally, the vegetables will finish cooking while the liquid reduces to a glaze. If the vegetables are tender before the liquid has reduced to a glaze, remove them and reduce the liquid to about 2 tablespoons, then return the vegetables to the pan.

Season the vegetables with salt and roll them around in the glaze to coat them thoroughly. (The vegetables can be prepared a couple of hours in advance and held at room temperature.)
TO SERVE: Combine all the vegetables in one pan and toss them together. Reheat if necessary and add more salt if needed. Transfer the vegetables to a platter or individual plates, discarding the seasonings, and sprinkle with chives, parsley, and fleur de sel.

PHOTOGRAPHS ON PAGES 241 AND 242   **MAKES 4 SERVINGS**

GLAZED PEARL ONIONS—OIGNONS GRELOTS GLACÉS

2 cups red, yellow, or white pearl onions
or a combination

FOR EACH ¹/₂ CUP ONIONS
1 teaspoon unsalted butter
¹/₂ teaspoon sugar
1 bay leaf
12 black peppercorns

1 thyme sprig
Kosher salt
2 teaspoons red wine vinegar (for red pearl
onions), or champagne vinegar
(for yellow or white pearl onions)

Making these glazed pearl onions varies from the standard glazing technique in that vinegar is added at the end, which intensifies their flavor by balancing the onions' abundant sweetness. These onions can be served on their own or used as a garnish with many vegetables and stews. It's hard to think of a dish in which they wouldn't be appropriate.

Remember, if you are using more than one color of onion, cook red onions separately and divide the additional ingredients accordingly.

To peel the onions, cut an X in the root end of each onion and place in a bowl. Meanwhile, bring to a boil enough water to cover the onions. Pour the boiling water over the onions and let stand for a few minutes. When the onion skins have softened enough to be easily peeled, drain the onions. Peel them once they are cool enough to handle.

Place the onions in the smallest saucepan that will hold them in a single layer. Add cold water to just cover them, then add the butter, sugar, bay leaf, peppercorns, thyme, and a pinch of salt. Bring to a boil, then adjust the heat and simmer gently for 10 to 15 minutes. Ideally, the onions will finish cooking while the liquid reduces to a glaze. If the onions are tender when pierced with a paring knife but the liquid has not reduced to a glaze, remove them and reduce the liquid to about 2 tablespoons.

Add the vinegar and continue to reduce until the liquid is a glaze. Return the onions to the pan if you removed them and roll them around in the glaze to coat them.

Transfer the onions to plates, discarding the seasonings, or transfer to a container and set aside until ready to use.

MAKES 4 SERVINGS

PROVENÇAL VEGETABLES—BYALDI

¼ cup canola oil

1 cup sliced onions (onions halved lengthwise and cut into 1- to 1½-inch-long slices about ¹⁄₁₆ inch thick)

1 red bell pepper, cored, seeded, and cut into ¼-inch-wide julienne

1 yellow bell pepper, cored, seeded, and cut into ¼-inch-wide julienne

1 green bell pepper, cored, seeded, and cut into ¼-inch-wide julienne

Sachet (page 325)

Kosher salt and freshly ground black pepper

1 to 1½ cups thinly sliced zucchini

1 to 1½ cups thinly sliced Japanese eggplant

1 to 1½ cups thinly sliced yellow squash

12 ounces tomatoes (6 small), peeled and thinly sliced

1 teaspoon chopped garlic

2 teaspoons extra virgin olive oil

¼ teaspoon minced thyme

This is a refined interpretation of ratatouille. The vegetables normally diced for a ratatouille—eggplant, zucchini, yellow squash, tomato—are sliced and layered over a stew of onions and peppers, brushed with olive oil, seasoned with salt, pepper, and thyme, and baked. It's best cooked the day before serving to allow the flavors to develop. Use a mandoline to slice the vegetables. *Byaldi* goes well with most meats and seafood.

Preheat the oven to 275°F.

Heat the oil in a large skillet over medium heat. Add the onions, peppers, and sachet, season with salt and pepper, and cook for 15 minutes, or until the vegetables are softened but not browned. Remove the sachet and spread the mixture in an even layer in a 12-inch ovenproof skillet or round baking dish.

Arrange the sliced vegetables over the onions and peppers, beginning at the outside of the skillet and working toward the center, alternating and overlapping the slices. Mix the garlic, oil, thyme, and salt and pepper to taste and sprinkle over the vegetables.

Cover the skillet with aluminum foil, crimping the edges to seal, or with a tight-fitting lid and bake for 2½ hours.

Remove the lid and check the vegetables (the eggplant will take the longest to cook). They should have softened and be almost cooked through. Return to the oven, uncovered, and cook for an additional 30 minutes, or until very tender.

The vegetables can be served immediately or cooled to room temperature and then refrigerated for a day or two. Reheat in a 350°F oven until warmed through.

MAKES 4 SERVINGS

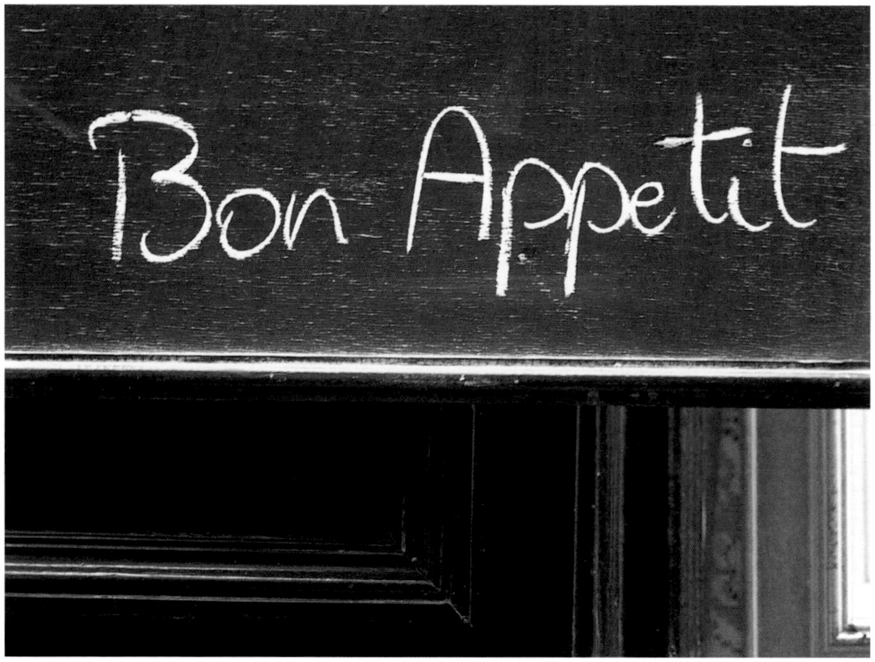
Bon Appetit